3

Liberty, Community, and Justice

Liberty, Community, and Justice

R. E. EWIN

The University of Western Australia

Rowman & Littlefield
PUBLISHERS

ROWMAN & LITTLEFIELD

Published in the United States of America in 1987
by Rowman & Littlefield, Publishers
(a division of Littlefield, Adams & Company)
81 Adams Drive, Totowa, New Jersey 07512

Copyright © 1987 by Rowman & Littlefield

All rights reserved. No part of this publication may
be reproduced, stored in a retrieval system, or transmitted
in any form or by any means, electronic, mechanical,
photocopying, recording, or otherwise, without the prior
permission of the publisher.

Library of Congress Cataloging-in-Publication Data

Ewin, R. E.
  Liberty, community, and justice.

  (Rowman & Littlefield texts in philosophy)
  Includes bibliographies.
  1. Liberty. 2. Community. 3. Justice.
I. Title. II. Series.
JC585.E85   1987   323.44   87–4345
ISBN 0-8476-7538-6
ISBN 0-8476-7539-4 (pbk.)

90 89 88 87
7 6 5 4 3 2 1

Printed in the United States of America

Contents

Acknowledgments

I RECEIVED BENEFIT from discussing this material with many people, and I want to thank all of them. I especially want to thank Stephen Davies, Ted Watt, and Carl Wellman, each of whom read a complete draft and made many helpful comments. I have not always followed their advice, and there is no reason to believe that they approve of the result; I am responsible for all errors.

I also want to thank Lee Carter and Carol Freele for their excellent work in typing my somewhat untidy handwriting. The cheerfulness with which they did the job was beyond the call of duty.

Most of the work for this book was done during twelve months' study leave from the University of Western Australia, and could not have been done otherwise. I want to thank the University for granting me that leave.

I am indebted to the editor of *Mind* for permission to use material that first appeared in that journal.

Liberty, Community, and Justice

1

Introduction

Iᴛ ɪs ʙᴇᴄᴏᴍɪɴɢ more and more common to assume that, if somebody wants to do something, then he should be allowed to do it, and should even be protected from interference unless there is very good reason for stopping him. It is thought that there is at least a presupposition that people ought to be allowed to do what they want to do simply because they want to do it, and this idea of liberty guides a lot of political activity in the world today. It is an idea associated not just with individualistic liberalism in general, but with an invidiously individualistic liberalism that ignores the significance of community. It is a very crude idea of liberty: the idea that having liberty is simply being able to act without interference and that one has more liberty the more one is able to do without interference from others. If one wants to use the words "liberty" and "freedom" in that way, well and good, but tacked on is the idea that liberty is a good thing, and that the more of this liberty anybody has, the better. The only problem in the Hobbesian natural condition, as far as this account of liberty is concerned, is that people, as a matter of fact, keep on getting in each other's way.

But there must be more to it than this, and there is. The problems with this idea of liberty are so obvious that they are often simply set aside and then overlooked: intelligent people could not possibly mean *that*. But then no significant steps are taken to explain precisely what they do mean and what differences that makes to the rest of the argument. There will be a problem about liberty only if there is conflict. If nobody ever wanted to interfere with anybody else's activities, then the concept of liberty, on this account, would be useless because there would be no interference to reject as infringing liberty. It would have no function to serve and would never be called on. Suppose, on the other hand, such conflicts did arise, so that, for example, one person wanted to do something and somebody else wanted to do something incompatible with that (perhaps the second person simply wanted to prevent any activity of that sort). In that case, simply saying that it is a good thing that people be able to do

1

whatever they want would be no help at all in determining which of the two people trying to do what he wants to do should be given precedence. On this account of liberty, the concept is useless one way or the other.

The same sort of point arises with more sophisticated accounts of liberty, according to which the *ideal* is that each person be able to do whatever he wants to do but the best that can really be achieved is some sort of compromise between people's ideal liberties.

How much of what he wants to do he is able to do may be of some importance to a particular person thinking in self-interested terms. If that is what his freedom is, then it is an invidiously individualistic freedom that will clash with the freedoms of others and, insofar as that is all there is to the story, there will be no way of picking out one person's freedom as taking precedence over others', or of arguing that it must be wrong for one person to invade another's freedom. That is a very asocial notion of liberty, though it may sometimes be useful. It could not, as such, be a property of a social system, and reference to it will not usually help in moral or political arguments. Nor, as I shall show, does the point depend on the wants' being self-interested. It depends on a sort of individualism that stresses, and claims moral supremacy for, private judgment. Private judgments differ; for them to have moral supremacy is the core of the Hobbesian state of nature. A peaceful means of resolving the differences is crucial for community life and anybody's liberty.

Some may want to stick with the "commonsense" approach, saying that liberty is simply the ability to do what one wants and is not always a good thing. Such people usually manage to continue working on the assumption that liberty is *quite* a good thing, that it is at least one value among others even if it can be overruled, without arguing out why such untrammeled liberty should be regarded as a value at all, but I bypass this *ad hominem* point. If that line is taken, then nothing substantial has been said until some explanation is given of when and why liberty is a good thing and when and why it is not, or when and why it gives way to other values and when and why it does not. These distinctions, rather than an espousal of liberty, would have to be the core of the political position. No satisfactory account of these distinctions can be given, I think, without accounting for rights and the sorts of problems I shall raise. If one assumes, politely, that all parties to the debate are civilized people and that the claim is to be understood as the claim that people ought to be allowed to do whatever they want within reason, or within the limits of civilized behavior, then the same point applies: nothing has really been said until the limits of reason or civilized behavior are argued out.[1] I shall argue for an account of liberty that does not leave us wondering why anybody could ever have thought liberty important, and which does not require us to think of willfulness and caprice as virtues.

The account of liberty for which I shall argue is one in which liberty consists not of people's doing what they want to do, but of the rights that people have. This account avoids at least the obvious problems in the common idea that liberty consists of being able to do what one wants to do, and it has a number of interesting implications for the proper conduct of moral and political arguments about liberty. Notably, it has interesting consequences about the possibility of guarantees of liberty and about the relationship between liberty and responsibility. I shall argue that there can be no institutional guarantees of liberty in the way of bills of rights or constitutions; the fight for liberty is one that must persist and one that always has a philosophical dimension. And I shall argue that liberty and responsibility go together, not simply in that exercise of liberty involves freewill so that we must take responsibility for our actions, which might well be true even if liberty were no more than doing what one wanted to do, but in a sense that might be made clearer by the use of plurals: one gains liberties only at the expense of taking on concomitant responsibilities that set limits to one's liberty. It has sometimes been thought that liberty and justice are independent of each other in such a way that they can come into conflict and make us choose between them: is there to be a just distribution of wealth, for example, or is each person to be free to make as much money as possible from others? Is educational opportunity to be distributed justly, or are parents to be free to provide their children with the best education they can afford? The appearance of such clashes, I shall argue, depends on a misconstruction of the relationship between liberty and justice, or between rights and responsibilities, and a misunderstanding of the way in which those concepts are related through the idea of a community.

What I am concerned with is individual liberty, and part of the point that I want to make is that the notion of an individual person is often misconstrued. It is often taken that the concept of an individual person is the concept of somebody set over and against other people and the community, the concept of somebody who is related to others only *externally*. The point should be made bluntly that people are social beings, and this is not merely a remark about common tendencies. We are internally related to others. We do not understand ourselves as anything like Cartesian mental substances. We identify and understand ourselves in terms of our families, friends, associations, jobs, hobbies, roles played, and so on. Our relationship to our community is, in this way, *internal*.

The relationship between having a particular liberty and wanting to do what one has a liberty to do is not, of course, one of exclusion, and it is not that there is no conceptual link of any sort between liberty and what people want to do. If nobody ever wanted to do anything at all, there would be no point at all to the concept of a right. This comes out in the idea that if I have a right to do X, then I may do X or not, *as I want*. That idea brings out the point, but it might also be misleading; it would be less misleading to say that if I have a right to do X, I may do X or not, *as I see fit*, and that I shall sometimes see fit to do as I want. A lot of different sorts of considerations might be brought to bear in determining what I see fit to do. A magistrate who has the right to judge a case that comes before him, in a sense in which I have no right to judge it, may reach the decision he judges proper, but he may not simply reach the decision that he wants to reach. The rights he has as a magistrate exist within a framework in which he is required to be impartial; his personal wants are not germane to the deciding of the case. Wants are one of the items giving a point to the concept of a right or to the concept of liberty, but they are not the only item. Opinions and judgments, for a start, are in the game, too. I may want to go fishing, but might exercise my liberty more in terms of my judgment that it would be better for my health to stay out of the rain.

Even where it *is* wants that lie behind the concept, it is not *simply* wants that provide a point to the concept. We need the concept of a right, or the concept of liberty, because wants clash and we often need to resolve the clashes peacefully. The point of reference to rights or liberty in such cases is to locate the want that takes precedence or is protected. What peacefully imposes order on the conflicting wants cannot itself simply be one or more of the wants. What orders the wants is something else, and it is that something else that I want to investigate.

One liberty that I have in Australia is that of voting for any Communist candidate who chooses to stand for parliament in my electorate. This, it seems to me, is an important right,[2] even though it is one that I feel no special inclination to exercise. I have other rights that are, in some respects, similar, though less important: a right to wear gaudy socks while giving lectures, for example. If these two activities were prohibited to me, I should not thereby be stopped from doing anything that I wanted to do. I should, nevertheless, feel that my liberty was being encroached upon. I should feel that way, not because I was stopped from doing what I wanted to do, but because my autonomy had been infringed: people who had no business to do so would have taken away some of my rights. I want to take my proper place in the community, and I should be prevented from doing so were others improperly to remove some of the rights that, along with duties, constitute my proper place in the community.

That way of preventing somebody from doing what he wants to do, though, cannot be used to explain or construct the concept of liberty. So to use it would be to argue in a circle. It is not that I wanted to vote communist but was prevented. What I was prevented from doing that I wanted to do was simply to retain my proper liberty, and my want can be properly understood only if described in such terms. One cannot then go back and explain liberty in terms of the want.

Nor is it a sufficient response to broaden the description of the right and say that I have been denied the right to vote for the party of my choice if the Communist Party is banned, though voting for the party of my choice is certainly something that I want to do. So long as the party of my choice is not the Communist Party, it plainly remains true that I have not been stopped from doing what I want to do; I am still allowed to vote for the party of my choice. Others, who wanted to vote communist, may have been prevented from doing as they wanted, but I have not. Nevertheless, by excluding possibilities that I should not have taken up, the ban limits *my* liberty, too. It does not stop my doing what I want to do except in that I want to retain a right that I regard as important. The want can be explained only by reference to the right, so it cannot be that the right must be explained in terms of the want. It is not that I have been stopped from doing what I want to do, but that a certain matter has been removed from my sphere of judgment.

Where wants are at issue, we still need to be discriminating in considering which wants count. My wants will not count unless the decision is one that should be up to me. If I happen to enjoy molesting children or bashing cripples, my wants will not count in determining what should be done, and the refusal to consider my wants will not constitute an infringement of my proper liberty. Liberty is not simply a property of a person or the person's ability to do as he wants. If it is a property of anything, it is a property of a social system. It is a relationship between people, and we can discriminate between wants in terms of that relationship.

If my wanting X is taken to be a sufficient condition of my having a right to X, then the concept of a right will be useless. Rights will clash as wants do; they will not serve as a point of reference by which to resolve clashes. The acknowledged fact that I have a right to X will be of no special significance if somebody wants to stop me from exercising it, because it will follow from his want that he has a right to stop me. The concept of a right will be redundant. Nevertheless, rights frequently seem to be treated in this manner in public debates these days. Assertions about rights are commonly taken as starting points in arguments, not as claims that themselves need to be supported, even in contentious cases. Because the debate starts from conflicting claims, it becomes incapable of resolution. What is needed is, for example, argument about whether a woman really does have a right to do whatever she wants with anything in her body, or about whether a fetus really does have a right to life at the expense of inconvenience to the mother and, in each case, whether the rights are limited and if so where the limits lie. Since there is disagreement about all these points, the argument will get somewhere only if those involved in the debate cease to bypass the philosophical problems about how rights are generated and determined. Even many of the philosophers involved in the debate about abortion have often skipped over the issues of the nature of rights and how they are generated and limited, staying within a debate strictly about abortion. Moral philosophy is practical, not something tacked onto practical debate, but it does mean going into wider-ranging questions. Until we go into these wider-ranging questions we shall be unable to resolve properly a lot of the conflicts that bedevil our political lives. It is probably because of those unresolved conflicts, and the consequent attempts by some to force their wills on others, that individual liberty has become so much a rallying cry of recent political life.

Two questions started me on this inquiry into the nature of liberty. One was the very general question: How can I work out what is my business so that I know what I can properly object to or try to stop and what I cannot, particularly when it is a matter of stopping people from limiting my actions? The other question, arising from an amateur interest in nineteenth-century United States history, was: What did the slaves gain when they were emancipated? What was the liberty that they sought, and what was the liberty that they were given? These questions are clearly related. The question about the slaves, while it explains why I have undertaken some discussion of writings of George Fitzhugh and John C. Calhoun, both prominent among defenders of slavery, is not of merely historical interest. Another version of the question is: What have we that the slaves lacked, and why is it worth having? And this leads to some quite wide-ranging questions about political life. What must be the relationship between citizens, and between citizens and their government, if the government is to have the power to stop those who would be slave-holders from holding slaves or to restrain those who would hold others in peonage or wage-bondage? Governments have enormous powers. Can we, without handing over to a government powers that make us its slaves, stop those who would take improper powers over others they hold as slaves? And this comes out as a question about what proper individual liberty is and whether we can have it.

I shall argue that individual liberty is itself a community notion and a community relationship, not something opposing the individual to the community. In doing so I shall, I think, be following a line of argument pursued by Thomas Hobbes, though my reading of him on this matter is so different from standard readings that it is probably mistaken. Hobbes was clearly aware of the social nature of people: "to man by nature . . . solitude is an enemy."[3] One thesis that I shall be suggesting throughout my argument is that rights have a place in a virtues theory of morality. In fact, I think that rights are crucial in a virtues theory; a kind person will help the victim rather than the mugger, and could not make that choice without consideration of the rights of the people involved. Without consideration of rights, the community in which virtues have their place would be impossible.

The word "community" is used in a number of different senses, or at least so that it has a number of different flavors. Michael Taylor so uses the word that the existence of community excludes the existence of a state,[4] and that use of the word is not eccentric; it is at least very close to the use of the word involved in everyday talk of a sense of community. But the word also has a more official use in which a particular community might be marked off by a state, the use usually involved when somebody is officially honored for services to the community. Given the range of possible uses, I should explain that what I mean by the word is a group of people who can act and speak as one, a group of people such that we sensibly speak of what the group decided or what the group did. It might help in the creation or maintenance of such a group if relations between its members were direct and multifaceted; it might help if, or even be necessary that, there was a sense of community; but what I mean by the term is a group that is personated so that it can act and speak as one.

In Chapter 2 I shall examine the idea that there is a moral presupposition in favor of noninterference in the activities of another, and shall argue that the propriety or impropriety of interference depends not on its being interference, but on who has what rights. This emerges from consideration of conditions of competition. Hobbes was right, I think, in his claim that competition is the natural condition of people, though it should not be assumed that competition means ceaseless war or that people spend much of their lives in their natural condition. In the absence of conventions, people who have incompatible aims can only compete for goods; there is no right or wrong in simply taking what one can get. There can be right or wrong in the way one takes it—one can be considerate, cruel, and so on—but not in the taking as such. One's actions will not infringe the liberty of others. The area of protected liberty, where interference is improper, is created with rights and obligations. One well-known and influential argument in support of the claim that there is a presupposition in favor of noninterference is H. L. A. Hart's "Are There Any Natural Rights?"[5] I conclude Chapter 2 by showing that Hart has not established that there is such a presupposition. The best to be said for the idea that there is a presupposition in favor of noninterference is that any requirement in a cooperative enterprise is to be judged by its necessity for the enterprise to achieve its point; if what is required is not necessary, then it is unjustly required. The same point must be understood as setting the limits of possibility in the claim that the area of action left free for competition should be as wide as possible.

In Chapter 3 I shall proceed to develop an argument for a claim, suggested in Chapter 2, that all rights are conventional. Rights are determined by the ways in which communities are organized. The function of rights is to make it possible to resolve disputes peacefully, and it follows from this that rights are publicly determined and are definitive in disputes. The disputes that arise will be not only between competing wants, but between differing judgments, and the differences must be resolved if common action is to be undertaken in a community. Everybody's judgment, I shall argue, must, originally, enter the dispute on an equal footing with everybody else's. In that sense, nobody is naturally superior to anybody else, so a nonnatural or conventional means of determining which view takes precedence must be used if the dispute is to be resolved peacefully. Since we differ at the first-order level, we must make use of a second-order decision-procedure, and the important question then will be: What makes such a decision-procedure binding? This, I shall argue, requires that, at least at a very basic level, members of the community share a sense of justice. Any number of social arrangements may be possible within a shared sense of justice, and what rights anybody has will depend on which particular social arrangements are made. One recent and influential writer who has tried to account for rights in a nonconventional way from an individualistic standpoint is Alan Gewirth,[6] and I shall conclude the chapter by responding to his arguments in order to back up my own.

Setting up a state of the sort we know today is one way of having a conventional means of resolving disputes, but it is not the only way.[7] If my account of rights is correct, we should need some other conventional way of resolving disputes if it is to be possible reasonably to oppose the allocation of rights made by the state. This is one reason for the importance of the idea of community. False ideas of independence can lead to the breakdown of community and hence increase both the power of the state and its arbitrariness. The state becomes the primary and outstanding organization of the people and thus becomes the community, weakening the basis of claims against its allocation of rights as it structures more of the relationships between people. The family, for example, is commonly less of a community than it used to be. Changing ideas of independence, among other things, have made it less likely that adult members of a family (parents and grown children) will look first to each other for help in times of need or feel that they have duties toward each other, and more likely that they will look to the state with its provision of pensions and other services. The members of the family grow away from each other; they become more independent of each other, but they can do so at the expense of decreasing community and increasing the power of the state, making it harder to argue about the rights allocated by the state. It becomes more difficult to argue that there are established rights in the community that the state is ignoring. The state can become an instrument not for a community to achieve its aims, but for people who have no other social relationship to try to use against each other. This growth of state power, and thus the chance for its misuse, is urged along by the requirements of modern economic structures. This, and the manipulative relationships between people required by modern industrial economic structures,[8] both break down the feeling of community, and by breaking down the feeling break down community.

The claim that rights are definitive means that if X has a right against Y, then X can impose a requirement of a quite special sort on Y. In Chapter 4 I shall examine that special sort of requirement and what distinguishes it from others. This involves some consideration of the notion of a role, in terms of which the requirement is to be explained, and that, in turn, leads to further consideration of how rights are generated. Roles need not be taken on deliberately in order to generate rights, and I shall show this by investigating the roles of parent and child and the way in which children's rights are generated in an ongoing community. Problems about children's rights seem to appear when we try to explain them in terms of relationships in the community at one particular point in time, but those problems disappear if we regard the community as something historical that exists over a period of time.

In Chapter 5 I shall take up the issue of whether there could be a community that did not have the concept of a right, and shall argue that, despite the existence of apparent examples to the contrary, there could not be such a community. There could be languages with no word translatable into English precisely as "a right," but communities using such languages will still operate other concepts and institutions that are comprehensible only in terms of the concept of a right. This follows from the need for a binding second-order decision-procedure. This need is denied by anarchist writers, and I shall consider some of the arguments presented against it by R. P. Wolff,[9] whose arguments seem to be based on a misunderstanding of the role of the second-order decision-procedure. I shall then proceed in Chapter 6 to develop my points about the second-order decision-procedure and its role. The role of the second-order decision-procedure is to resolve disputes and make common action possible. It can do this without being infallible, and its bindingness (when it is binding) does not depend on its never making mistakes. This is just as well: if the role of the second-order decision-procedure is to resolve disputes, those ruled against in any given case will think that it is mistaken. The hard problem here arises when the dispute is one about justice. If the decision-procedure rules against me in that case, then, *ex hypothesi*, I shall regard it as having produced an unjust decision. If I regard the decision as unjust, how can I regard it as binding? I shall argue that what is required is that I be able to regard the decision as justly made, that is, that I regard the procedure as a just one even if I regard the particular decision as mistaken. This means that people can share a decision-procedure only if they agree enough to be able to agree on the justice of the procedure, but it is no surprise that people who cannot agree about anything to do with justice could not live together in a community. The role of agreement means that the idea of justice is not purely procedural.[10]

This brings to an end my first line of argument. One's liberty is one's rights. One has one's proper liberty, as opposed to having license or being repressed, if one has all the rights one should have. Questions about liberty must always be capable of being raised, because whatever community one lives in will have some allocation of rights. But why should these questions be raised? In Chapter 7 I shall consider the value of liberty. This, I shall argue, is not simply a matter of what liberty produces, and is not simply a matter of intuiting that liberty is valuable in itself. It is a matter of seeing the role of liberty in human life. This I shall try to bring out by considering two concepts that are aspects of liberty: toleration and autonomy. Neither is unlimited. Autonomy is not simply a matter of being able to do whatever one wants to do, and toleration is not a matter of putting up with everything. Autonomy is, primarily, a political notion concerned with the possession of rights. The primary case of autonomy is when a country becomes self-governing, that is, comes to be recognized as having certain rights and a certain status in the community of nations. A particular person's autonomy is his or her rights and status in the community. It is not simply a matter of psychological capacities, even if such matters are related. Autonomy is a status in the community, and toleration is recognition of the autonomy of others. Both autonomy and toleration are conceptually related to community, and it is this that explains their value in the lives of social beings. I shall develop the point by examining George Fitzhugh's defense of slavery,[11] granting all his claims about how well off the slaves were compared with free workers.

In Chapter 8 I shall make a similar point about the role of liberty in democracy. Democracy is misunderstood as being merely a matter of majority government, and to see what underlies our varied uses of the term is to see that liberty is conceptually linked to democracy. Democracy is a form of government attempting to recognize the proper autonomy of citizens. We recognize that there is a moral dimension to politics, but we all too frequently fail to recognize that the importance of rights and the second-order decision-procedure in morality means that there is a political dimension to morality. That political dimension is democratic, but is not merely a matter of majority rule. It is the truly social nature of morality.

There is no need to dilate on the evils of despotism with respect to liberty, but the idea that democracy is a defender of liberty is more complex than it usually appears to be in public debate. Letters columns in newspapers constantly reveal an assumption that the context of democracy allows a one-step inference from "the majority of people want this done" to "the government ought to do this." Lip-service is given the idea that it is necessary to guard against a despotism of the majority, but often no more than lip-service. Simply allowing a minority the power to determine when the majority is acting despotically will not solve the problem about liberty; it does no more than shift that problem to a new place. Fairly clearly, it will be at least difficult to institutionalize a guarantee that whoever has power, majority or minority, does not act despotically, and I shall argue that that is an abiding problem even though there are better and worse ways of organizing a community in terms of what the organization encourages about the protection of liberty. The problem will be avoided only by having a populace at large that argues in the right way, concerning itself not only with who has power and how to get it, but with the purpose of the power and, therefore, with its limits. It is not simply a matter of being concerned with whether one can do what one wants or with what one's group wants. If that is the concern, then the most that can be achieved is power over other people, and freedom for some becomes bondage for others. That sort of freedom becomes despotism. A different ground on which to argue, and a different account of liberty, are necessary if despotism is to be avoided and if democracy is not simply to be tyranny of the majority. The growth of undisciplined liberty and the loss of a sense of community lead to the growth of government control and generally to the growth of control by power and to coercive relationships between people. The populace at large will have to become, at least to some extent, philosophers.

This book sets out no program for institutional reform or change, and I have no idea what form such a program would take. My argument is addressed to particular people. If the social problems that lie behind the argument of this book are to be solved, they can be solved only by people arguing properly about liberty and rights instead of simply asserting them. My aim has been to bring out what is involved in such argument.

Notes

1. Cf. below, Chapter 3.
2. It seems to me an important right because of its relationship to the presupposition of equality dealt with in Chapter 3 below: even if I disagree with the other person's views, it matters that he gets a hearing and that his sense of justice enters the fray on a par with everybody else's.
3. Sir William Molesworth, ed., *The English Works of Thomas Hobbes* (London: John Bohn, 1834), Vol. II, p. 2.
4. Michael Taylor, *Community, Anarchy and Liberty* (Cambridge: Cambridge University Press, 1982).
5. H. L. A. Hart, "Are There Any Natural Rights?" *Philosophical Review* 64 (1955).
6. Alan Gewirth, *Reason and Morality* (Chicago: University of Chicago Press, 1978) and *Human Rights* (Chicago: University of Chicago Press, 1982).
7. See, for example, Michael Taylor, *Community, Anarchy*.
8. Compare, for example, what J. K. Galbraith has to say about economic planning in *The New Industrial State*, 2nd ed. (Pelican books, 1974).
9. R. P. Wolff, *In Defence of Anarchism* (New York: Harper Torchbook, 1970).
10. The second-order decision-procedure plays a role in my argument similar in some ways to that played by the Original Position in John Rawls's *A Theory of Justice* (Oxford: Clarendon Press, 1972), but the role is one in which real people appear, with all their differences and idiosyncracies, and thus avoids the objections raised by Michael J. Sandel in *Liberalism and the Limits of Justice* (Cambridge: Cambridge University Press, 1982). Though the second-order decision-procedure and the Original Position play similar roles in the two arguments, it should be clear that the differences between Rawls's position and mine are more extensive than the one just set out. Our accounts of justice and rationality are quite different, and, whereas Rawls appeals to independent principles about liberty in explaining what justice is, I shall argue that there are no such independent principles of liberty because liberty is to be explained in terms of justice.
11. George Fitzhugh, *Cannibals All! or, Slaves Without Masters*, ed. C. Vann Woodward (Cambridge: Harvard University Press, 1960).

Causing pain with no good reason is wrong, certainly, but if there is good reason (if, for example, this *is* the only possible cure for a serious disease), then the fact that pain is involved does not detract from that reason or make it a worse reason than it would otherwise have been. The agent must be conscientious in his assessment of reasons, but that the act involves causing pain is not a fact having a special initial weight meaning that he must discount the other reasons. If the disease is serious and the patient wants to live, the doctor's reasons for proceeding are no worse than they would otherwise have been simply because the cure is a painful one. If the cure is merely a prolongation of pain, and if the pain is extreme, we might worry about whether all of this were worth it from the patient's point of view. We might worry about the morality of having a doctor force onto the patient his own decision that the patient should live. But, setting that aside, and allowing that the patient does know exactly what he is letting himself in for and does want to live even in so unfortunate a world, that the doctor's actions will cause pain does not detract from his reasons for performing them.

We need good reasons for causing pain. We need good reasons not in order to counterweigh or justify or excuse a wrong, but in order to place it in the context of our activities. Causing pain with good reason is a matter neither of the end justifying the means nor of good outweighing bad in an organic whole; it is acting well in this imperfect world.

A similar point, fairly clearly, holds good of killing people. There is a moral presupposition against killing people, but not in any way that implies that killing people is wrong in itself or that the fact that one's action will kill somebody is something that weighs against it no matter what the reasons in favor. From the statement that A murdered B it follows that A did wrong, but from the statement that A killed B nothing follows immediately about the morality of A's act even if the two statements are used to describe the same incident. The concepts of killing and murder differ in this way, but there is still a moral presupposition against killing people. Somebody who can always contemplate the deaths of others without even a qualm is inhuman. A hangman who is glad that the world is (as he sees it) such that jobs such as his must be done, is inhuman. Somebody who would never infringe the rights of others might, nevertheless, take great pleasure in going into the toughest part of town because he knows that, when he gets there, somebody will try to kill him and, by his attack, give up his own rights so that our venturer can, with great glee at a successful plan, kill him without infringing rights. Such a person may be meticulous about recognizing people's rights, but lacks the warmer feelings and care for others that lie at the base of a sense of justice. He displays a raw form of the vice of injustice,[3] unstructured in terms of rights; were everybody like him, no cooperation or social life would be possible. It is this that makes the quality of character that he displays a raw form of injustice; he does not infringe anybody's rights, but it is a quality of character that gets in the way of the generation of rights. The structures that produce rights would not evolve if people were, by and large, like that. Killing people for no reason at all is vicious. If, however, one can save hordes of innocent people from death at the hands of somebody who simply likes to see people die, and if one can save them only by shooting him, then there is no particle of vice in shooting him for that reason, even if one knows that shooting him will kill him. That his death will follow from one's act is no reason to refrain, let alone a reason to which special weight must be given. One might regret that there are such people in the world. Given that there are such people in the world, one might regret that they can be stopped only in so final a manner. But that the world is, in some ways, constituted regrettably does not show that one's acts in that regrettable world are vicious. Again, the issue is not one of the end justifying the means, but of reasons placing an act in the context of an imperfect world.

From the fact that there is a moral presupposition against doing X, then, it does not follow that X is wrong in itself (even a little bit wrong in itself), or that there is always a weight against doing X to be balanced in the scales against the reasons for doing X, or that an agent, faced with a decision about whether to do X in a situation in which he does not yet know all the facts that he would need to assess in his reasoning about whether to do X, can properly infer from the fact that it is X in question that he would probably be wrong to do it. I believe that this is generally the case when there is a moral presupposition against some sort of act, and certainly it is sometimes so. Even if there is a moral presupposition against interfering with the activities of another, we cannot properly infer that interference is wrong in itself, or probably wrong, or has a weight that needs to be outweighed. It might be that interference for no reason at all is vicious, whereas interference for good reason has no particle of vice.

It seems quite clear that there are many circumstances in which it is perfectly proper to prevent somebody from doing what he wants to do even though he does not want to do anything that would infringe another's rights (such as murder or theft) and even though the interference with his planned action is not undertaken for his own good. Such cases are so obvious and so everyday that it is worth making the point in that blunt form first. Faced with obvious, everyday cases, we might assume that they cannot go against general principles that are commonly espoused. They show, perhaps, that the principle as it is actually applied is somewhat more complicated than the principle as we say it, but the way we express the principle in words affects the way we are likely to argue out an account of liberty and thus particular problems about liberty.

The class of cases that I have in mind comes out of the whole range of competitive activities. A wrestler who sits on his opponent and holds him pinned to the mat most certainly interferes with any attempt his opponent might make to do what he wants to do. The wrestler is not acting so as to prevent his opponent from infringing the rights of another, and he is not acting out of a self-sacrificing concern for his opponent's good. He has purposes of his own for preventing his opponent from doing what he wants, and is acting in pursuit of those purposes. There are certainly limits to what he may do in pursuit of those purposes—one wrestler, as far as I know, may not belabor the other with a corner stool—but that is a different point: it is simply the point that, if some forms of interference are legitimate, it does not follow that all are. In this case, he certainly does interfere with his opponent's planned activities by sitting sweatily on top of him, but he does so legitimately. Any misguided liberal who tried to remove him would be making a mistake.

It might be pointed out that the wrestlers are in a special situation: when each goes onto the mat, he effectively consents to his opponent's sitting on him. That is partly true; the context makes a difference. The loser cannot, with the same legitimacy, wait outside and attack his opponent as he goes home, and the winner cannot relive his victory by sitting on his opponent when he sees him in the High Street the next day. The wrestler, by going onto the mat, has put some of his rights into abeyance, so the opponent will do no wrong by treating him in ways that would otherwise constitute a wrong. But this point goes only so far; that somebody has given up his right not to be sat on does not mean that sitting on him fails to interfere with his freedom to do what he wants to do. That he has given up a right affects only whether his rights are infringed, not whether he can act as he wishes.

It should be noted, too, that wrestlers' consent, if they give consent, is of a special sort with respect to legitimating the activities in question. They do not consent specifically to being sat on, and they place themselves under no obligation to submit to their opponents. Their behavior on the mat is not such as could readily be construed as tacit consent to having their opponents sit on them. Their consent, for what importance it has in the issue of whether there is interference with their freedom to do as they want, is simply consent to competition.

Another case, equally obvious, is that of middle- or long-distance footraces. Where the race is against opponents rather than against the clock, it frequently depends on who can make whom run in a way in which he does not want to run. The runner with no finishing sprint will try to make the sprinter go fast in the middle stages, or somebody else will try to break away early. This is not quite the same as the situation of the wrestlers, because there is still an important place left for the runner's decision, though that place is not sufficiently important to affect whether the runner is being allowed to do what he wants to do. The wrestler stays pinned to the mat because he can do no other; if it were up to him, he would be on top with the other fellow worrying or, perhaps, if it were up to him after his recent experiences, he would rather be at home playing the role of a devoted family man. The Olympic middle-distance gold medal aspirant who finds another of his kind breaking away in the middle stages of the race can just leave the track and go home to his family. There was, nevertheless, something else that he would rather have done: he would rather have run in a race in which everybody took an hour and a half over the first 1200 meters, after which he showed them a clean pair of heels on the way to the tape. But that was not to be. What we can do (and this is part of the problem about noninterference) depends on what other people do, what they hinder us in doing, and what they will help us to do. The fellow who steps up the pace in the middle stages stops the sprinter from running the race he wants to run, but he does no wrong.

Again, it might be said that the sprinter has consented to the activity in which he is made to do what he did not want to do. And again, what he consented to was competition rather than specifically being made to go fast in the middle stages. But these references to consent are by the way. References to consent are misplaced in this argument, because consent will affect only the distribution of rights and not whether one is stopping somebody from doing what he wants to do. It is by no means unknown for people to want to do what they have no right to do. And, quite apart from that, consent is not necessary for competition. All the arguments about consent in politics can be brought into play at this stage, especially the arguments about tacit consent.

The business world of free enterprise is very competitive, but the fact that somebody competes in it cannot be taken as showing that he has consented, no matter how tacitly, to the way it works. It may well be true that he has committed himself to abiding by its rules by joining in the activity, and that he will do wrong if he breaks the rules and thus cheats, but consent is only one way of committing himself to abiding by its rules, and nothing but confusion is gained by distorting the notion of consent to cover all of commitment. Consent is itself a formal way of committing oneself; the performative utterance "I consent" is not magic, and the story of how it takes on the significance of placing one under an obligation explains also how other actions (such as joining in a cooperative enterprise) can do so as well. The businessman in a free enterprise system may be committed to the rules of that system, but we cannot properly infer that he has consented to them. It may be that he simply finds himself in a world run this way, a way of which he thoroughly disapproves, and decides to make the best of a bad thing. He might spend as much of his time as possible trying to reform the system but, in the meantime, he is stuck with it; if he is going to live, he must play, no matter how unwillingly, according to other people's rules. Such a person has not consented to the rules, even tacitly; he simply found the competitive situation forced on him as people find life under government forced on them. Such businessmen will, nevertheless, force each other to do things that they don't want to do; that is the nature of a competitive business world. They will, as part of competition to which they have not consented, interfere with each other's freedom to act as they want to act and, provided that they do not break the rules of the game, they will do so legitimately.

A businessman might even interfere with the activities of another in cases in which there is no immediate need to do so, and that behavior might be proper. Though he has nothing to gain in the particular case, the businessman who thus interferes need not be displaying wanton vice. The reason for this is that a private enterprise system puts him in a Hobbesian position about security: the only way that he can make sure that he gains the contract after this one is to make sure that his opponent is in a worse position to tender for it. What matters is that his interference is legitimate business practice and not, for example, blowing up his competitor's factory. He, or others observing, might object to the private enterprise system as a way of doing business and wish that the country were organized along some other lines; but as long as the private enterprise system is the one in operation, no matter how objectionable the system is, *he* does no wrong in interfering with his competitor in that context provided that his activities are legitimate.

We need to distinguish between different sorts of rights, or different senses of "a right." Running different sorts of rights together, or shifting from one to another, can cause a great deal of confusion in arguments about liberty. One fairly standard set of distinctions between different sorts of rights is that drawn by Wesley Hohfeld,[4] and that set of distinctions is worth setting out at this stage. Not all of Hohfeld's distinctions will come into play immediately, but they will be useful to us over the long haul. Hohfeld was concerned with legal rights, but I think that much the same sort of analysis might be applied to moral rights. We need not concern ourselves just now with the relationship between legal and moral rights.

Since he believes that fundamental legal relations are *sui generis* and that, therefore, no satisfactory formal definition can be given, Hohfeld proceeds by setting out the various relations in a scheme of opposites and correlatives and then explains their meanings by the use of examples. The scheme looks like this:

Jural opposites	right no-right	privilege duty	power disability	immunity liability
Jural correlatives	right duty	privilege no right	power liability	immunity disability

Each of the parties to any relationship between people has, with respect to each other party, one of each pair of jural opposites: he has either a right or a no-right; either a privilege or a duty; either a power or a disability; either an immunity or a liability. It might be that I had a duty to wear a three-piece suit while giving lectures but, if I have no such duty, I have the privilege of not wearing a three-piece suit while giving lectures. If any person has to some other person one of these relationships, then the other person has to the first the jural correlative of that relationship. If you have a right against me that I wear a three-piece suit while giving lectures, I have a duty to you to wear a three-piece suit while giving lectures. These are the two sorts of relationships set out in the two schemes.

Hohfeld takes it that the simplest way to explain what a right is in these schemes is by reference to its correlative, a duty. We do not always, just as a matter of fact, use the word "right" in this way (indeed, the point of Hohfeld's endeavor is that we use it in at least four ways, as marked out in his scheme), though we often take rights to be this sort of thing when we think about them. The sense in which we should usually say that I have a right to walk in the Hay Street Mall is not the Hohfeldian sense of "a right": if the Mall happens to be jam-packed with people, nobody has a duty to move out so as to make room for me. On the other hand, at least in normal circumstances, I have a Hohfeldian right to an ice-cream when I have paid the vendor for one: he would fail in his duty if he did not provide me with one. The sense in which I have a right to walk in the Hay Street Mall, though, is a Hohfeldian privilege: it amounts simply to my not having a duty not to walk in the Mall and means that others have no right against me that I shan't walk in the Mall. (It is this sort of right that makes competition possible. When the race starts, you have a right to try to win and I have a right to try to win, but not in any sense that implies that either of us has a duty to let the other win.) To *lack* a privilege is to have a duty, a point brought out by what is probably the most common use of the term "a right" in this sense. When, in a censorious tone of voice, I say to somebody "You have no right to do that," my point is not simply that I have no duty to help him, or anything of that sort; my point is that he has a duty not to do it.

It should be noticed that these relationships, like the others in Hohfeld's scheme, can vary from person to person. To take Hohfeld's example, if X, the legal owner of a salad, contracts with Y that he (X) will not eat the salad, but makes no such contract with A, B, C, and D, then with respect to Y, X has a duty not to eat the salad, but he has no such duty with respect to A, B, C, and D. As regards them, but not as regards Y, he has the privilege of eating the salad. (This does not mean that A, B, C, and D cannot properly judge X to be untrustworthy if he fails in his duty to Y.) Y has a Hohfeldian right against X that he not eat the salad, but A, B, C, and D have a no-right against him that he shan't eat the salad.

To have a Hohfeldian power is to be in a position such that, by means of conditions within one's volitional control, one can change rights and duties. Hohfeld's example: a traveler has the power, by making proper application and sufficient tender, to create in an innkeeper a duty to receive him as a guest. The innkeeper does not have such a duty unless the traveler takes the appropriate action (no innkeeper fails to do his duty simply in that not every traveler in the country stays with him on any given night), and the traveler lacks the Hohfeldian right unless he takes the appropriate action, but it all depends on the traveler's action. The traveler thus has a power over the innkeeper with respect to gaining accommodation, and the innkeeper is under a liability toward the traveler with respect to providing accommodation. My position is different from that of the innkeeper insofar as that the traveler has no such power over me. If the traveler applies to me for accommodation, he is asking for a favor and does not create in me a duty. When it comes to changing rights and duties by acts within his volitional control, the traveler is under a disability with respect to me, and I have an immunity with respect to him.

Areas of competition are areas in which people are at liberty or have Hohfeldian privileges, and the areas of competition, at least usually, will be bounded by areas of Hohfeldian rights and duties. Each runner in a footrace, for example, has the privilege of pacing himself as he sees fit; no runner is under a duty to run his race in accordance with the tactics of one of his competitors. The sprinter who sees somebody else step up the pace in the middle stages has no legitimate complaint; the runner who tries to break away at that stage is under no obligation or duty not to do so. A runner has a legitimate complaint, though, if one of his competitors spikes him or uses a motorcycle; each runner is obligated not to do those things and has a Hohfeldian right against the others that they not do those things. If one wrestler sits on another to pin him to the mat, then he interferes with the fellow's freedom to do what he wants to do, but there can be no legitimate complaint because, in the context of a wrestling match, he has the privilege of doing such things. If a spectator responds to this interference with the freedom of another by himself interfering, rushing onto the mat and trying to unseat the uppermost wrestler, then there can be a legitimate complaint. Spectators are not licensed as wrestlers are, and spectators are obligated not to interfere in that way. It is not necessarily the first piece of interference with the freedom of another to act as he wishes that ought to be stopped, but the interference that infringes a right. Competing properly with somebody does not infringe his Hohfeldian privilege. Cases of competition are always cases of mutual interference and thus allow for intervention on Mill's ground that the act in question will harm another. Mill's principle will, therefore, be useless as a ground for rejecting interference.

In general, people may do anything that they are not obligated not to do no matter what effects that has on the plans of others. When such plans clash, that may just be too bad. Perhaps such people simply push on with their plans and see who comes out on top, competing as the runners do. Provided that each is doing something he is not obligated not to do, neither can simply insist that the other stop and allow him right of way. That one's freedom to do what one wants to do is being interfered with is unfortunate and might upset one, but the alternative is that somebody else is prevented from doing what he wants to do and, with each at liberty to pursue his plans or having the Hohfeldian privilege of pursuing his own plans, there is nothing to pick out one as taking precedence. Or, to make life easier, such people might sometimes agree on a procedure for determining who shall take precedence without each pressing on with his plans. Whatever that procedure may be, it cannot simply be a matter of giving precedence to noninterference in the freedom of others to act as they want, because it is two such freedoms that are clashing. Once they have submitted to such a decision-procedure (tossing a coin, for example), the situation changes. The loser can no longer press on with his plans; in submitting to the procedure, each obligated himself to accept its result, so he is no longer at liberty to go ahead and do what he wanted to do. Where he was formerly at liberty, he is no longer; he has lost a privilege and gained a duty. His erstwhile competitor now has a Hohfeldian right, and a Hohfeldian right will ground a complaint about somebody's interference.

The area of protected liberty, where interference is improper, is created with rights and obligations. It is not simply the area of what one wants to do subject to certain bargaining or compromise limitations, and is misconstrued if it is taken to be constructed on the basis of an initial freedom for people to do what they want to do. That there has been interference with the attempt of one person to do what he wanted to do is not even a *prima facie* case for saying that there has been wrongdoing; to establish even a *prima facie* case, the person complaining must go on from there and give some ground for believing that he has a Hohfeldian or strong right to perform the act in question and that others have a correlative obligation to allow him to do so. Such a Hohfeldian right to perform an act is strictly equivalent to the correlative obligation; my failure to perform the act does not itself show infringement of the right, but it is a right that others not interfere with my attempt. We shall not get to those rights simply by considering frustrated desires and reaching compromises; we shall need to examine the nature of rights and how they are generated, which will force us back to consideration of cooperation and community life.

Somebody might say that the presupposition of noninterference still holds for self-regarding actions: when it comes to self-regarding actions, I may do as I see fit. That might well be true, but it will not resuscitate the presupposition. If my self-regarding act gets in somebody else's way, even if only by offending his sensibilities, what right have I that he not interfere? (The term "self-regarding act" is normally used for actions that can get in somebody else's way in at least that manner. If nobody cared about them nor ever wanted to interfere with them, there would be no clash of desires to resolve and no problem.) If it is a self-regarding action, there will be an answer to the question of what right I have: a self-regarding action will not affect the efficiency of the working of any cooperative endeavor, so the prohibition of the act is not necessary to the endeavor, and that I refrain from it cannot justly be required of me. Even with self-regarding actions, the issue is not one of whether I want to perform the act, but one of whether I have the right to do so. And to show that I could not justly be required to refrain from a self-regarding act, that I have no duty not to do it, is not sufficient to show that others must not impede me in my attempt; I might be licensed to try, but it does not follow that I have a strong right against others that they get out of my way.

To show just how these points apply, I now turn to H. L. A. Hart's "Are There Any Natural Rights?"[5] and his discussion of the idea that, if there are any rights, then everybody has the right to be free.

It is not clear exactly what Hart means by his general claim that if there are any moral rights, it follows that there is "the equal right of all men to be free" (p. 53). He seems to mean that provided one is not coercing or restraining another, one has a moral right to do whatever one wants to do without coercion or restraint from anybody else, that is, one has a basic moral right to do what one wants to do, subject to certain restraints, viz., that one is not coercing or restraining somebody else. That somebody is free to do what he wants to do is itself valuable, and one must not interfere without a special sort of justification.

Hart wants to rule out cases of competition as objections to his thesis. Clashes and contests between competing desires create a situation far too complex for everybody to get what he wants, so Hart tries to distinguish competition from coercion and restraint:

> all men may have, consistently with the obligation to forbear from coercion, the *liberty* to satisfy if they can such at least of their desires as are not designed to coerce or injure others, even though in fact, owing to scarcity, one man's satisfaction causes another's frustration [p. 53n]. *Coercion* includes, besides preventing a person from doing what he chooses, making his choice less eligible by threats; *restraints* includes any action designed to make the exercise of choice impossible . . . But neither coercion nor restraint includes *competition* [ibid].

The point that Hart trades on here is that the desires and plans of different people clash and cannot all be satisfied but, as long as people are simply going about their own business and not trying to hurt others, there is no problem. That seems to be the force of reference to "actions *designed* to make the exercise of choice impossible" (p. 53n, my italics), and Hart may well be right in believing that there are fewer problems with people who set about seeking their own ends without reference to other people than with those who take as their end the frustration of other people. Nevertheless, it is not clear that his point will stand; it does seem that there can be problems even though somebody does not aim at the frustration of others. Some people, for reasons that remain obscure to me, take great pleasure in catching and keeping inordinate numbers of fish, even though the fish will simply be left to rot and many of them are undersized. Over a period of time, this can result in an area's being fished out. Though he aims simply at catching lots of fish rather than at frustrating other people, such a person does interfere with the activities of other people: he interferes with the pleasurable activities of those who like to catch fish but keep only as many as they can eat and return the others, and he interferes with the livelihood of professional fishermen. It is not clear that right is on his side. Bag limits, size limits, and bans on amateur netting and dynamiting have been introduced, at least partly because it seems proper to stop such a person in so selfish a pursuit of his ends. He simply seeks his own ends and does not aim at the frustration of others but, nevertheless, he is judged (and rightly so) to be interfering improperly with their liberty and their pursuit of their own ends.

The reply here might be that, though the objectionable fisherman does not *aim* at coercion or restraint, nevertheless he is limiting the freedom of others, and that is what justifies others in aiming at restraining him. The limitation might be that we can *aim* at coercion only in response to coercion. But that cannot be the whole of the story. If there is a fishing spot with room for only one person, and if somebody else has got it, then he forces me to go elsewhere. He does not aim at coercing me, but his fishing there has that effect. This certainly does not justify me in aiming to force him out of the spot. At best, Hart's limitation does not enable us to distinguish where we should want to distinguish. He has not set out a sufficient condition for the justification of coercion, as would be necessary for the distinction to be drawn completely. Nor has he set out a necessary condition: a wrestler may have to wait for the bell to ring before he can attack his opponent, but he does not have to wait for his opponent to make the first move. What justifies the wrestler in attacking at the sound of the bell is not that his opponent has acted in a threatening manner by, for example, signing up for the fight: that threat will not play the role that Hart gives to threats, because it is effective only if it is accepted by the original wrestler's also signing up. And if all men have an "obligation to forebear from coercion" (p. 53n), then either the objectionable taker of hordes of undersized fish is coercing and thus failing to meet an obligation, as is the fellow who gets in first to the fishing spot, or he is not, in which case there is no coercion for the rest of us to respond to coercively.

Nor is Hart clearly right in his distinction between coercion and restraint, on the one hand, and competition, on the other. Competition, and legitimate competition, need not take the form of A trying to achieve X and B, quite independently, also trying to achieve X, so that any interference of one with the other is merely accidental. It can properly take the form of A and B each trying to beat the other to X. Bobby Fischer set out to crush egos. Over a chess board, without breaking any rules or even descending to sharp practice, he tried (frequently with success) to stop his opponent from doing what he wanted to do, to make his choices less eligible by threats, and to leave him with no choice about what to do. It is precisely because he was so devoted to these ends that Fischer was described as a very competitive chess player. It may be that "competitive" is used in a different sense here (though the sense is clearly not too different), but the main point remains clear: Fischer did things that plainly fit Hart's accounts of coercion and restraint, he limited his opponent's freedom to play the game as he wanted to, but he did not infringe his opponent's liberty and did nothing about which his opponent could legitimately complain. Fischer did not try to hypnotize his opponent, did not whistle while his opponent's clock was on, and did not resort to a foul-smelling pipe for purposes of distraction. Everything that he did was a proper competitive activity. And the problem is not simply one of scarcity, because Fischer's aim of winning was not an aim independent of frustrating his opponent.

If Fischer's activities are not allowed to count against Hart's thesis because they are in a context of competition, that cannot be because competition occurs only in such formal contexts as a game of chess. If one wanted to rule out any other case of coercion, one would have to show that it was not in a context of competition; that is to say, one would have to show that it infringed some specific right. That it was a case of coercion otherwise than in response to coercion would not, by itself, even start the argument to show that it was improper. It might raise the question, but would not do anything to show which of the possible answers was correct.

The problem might be about just how coercion is to be explained. On the face of it, either coercion is not simply pushing people, or, if it is, the problems about coercion are not solved simply by reaching a compromise or favoring the second pushing, that is, by saying that force is justified only as a response to force. If a violent robber attacks somebody who tries to fight him off, we should not think that the dispute was properly resolved by a compromise such as sharing the victim's money between the two of them. And if a boxer achieved a knockout with the first punch of a fight, we should not regard that first piece of pushing as justifying a spectator in leaping into the ring and starting to throw punches. We have already been through a number of such cases. Forcing people to do things against their will seems to be perfectly proper in a variety of cases. What is not proper is forcing people to do things I have no right to force them to do or forcing them by means I have no right to employ. To put the same point another way, coercion is wrong when it constitutes failure to meet an obligation, not otherwise. Only if we mark coercion off thus, in terms of invasion of rights, is it possible to regard coercion as something wrong in itself or needing special justification, and, if we do mark coercion off in that way, then we cannot refer to coercion as the test for who has what rights. By means of a pawn advance I may force my opponent to delay castling and no objection can be taken, but I do wrong if I force him to delay castling by holding a gun at his head. My taking my custom elsewhere may be the straw that breaks the camel's back and forces the corner grocer out of business. If so, I have forced him into a situation in which he is worse off than he might otherwise have been, and might have done so for my own gain if I think that his closing down will allow me to open a grocer's shop and make my fortune. Despite my having forced him into this situation, I have done nothing that would license him to attempt to force me to bear his losses. The story would be different if I forced him out of business at gunpoint.

Certainly, simple reference to who used force, or who used force first, or who used force to prevent another use of force, seems incapable of satisfactorily resolving the dispute. For a satisfactory resolution, we must consider the pattern of rights in the situation. It is not true that "in the absence of certain special conditions . . . any adult human being capable of choice . . . has the right to forebearance on the part of all others from the use of coercion or restraint against him save to hinder coercion or restraint" (p. 53). In the absence of certain special (though common) conditions, one has no such right: if you can force me to delay castling, then more power (unfortunately) to your arm. The Hobbesian natural condition, one lacking the relevant special conditions, is one in which anybody may do anything; nobody is obligated not to coerce or hinder anybody else. When obligations are created, they constitute the special conditions. In the absence of obligations, we are simply in competition and nobody has a right that others allow him to do what he wants to do.

Hart says:

> When rights arise out of special transactions between individuals or out of some special relationship in which they stand to each other, both the persons who have the right and those who have the corresponding obligation are limited to the parties to the special transaction or relationship. I call such rights special rights to distinguish them from those moral rights which are thought of as rights against (i.e., as imposing obligations upon) everyone, such as those that are asserted when some unjustified interference is made or threatened. [p. 60]

Hart gives as examples of special transactions or relationships promising, consenting, authorizing, and mutuality of restrictions (or the relationship between "cooperating members of the society" [p. 62]). Later (p. 64), he considers how general rights are related to special rights:

> Such rights share two important characteristics with special rights. (1) To have them is to have a moral justification for determining how another shall act, viz., that he shall not interfere. (2) The moral justification does

not arise from the character of the particular action to the performance
of which the claimant has a right; what justifies the claim is simply—
there being no special relation between him and those who are threatening to interfere to justify that interference—that this is a particular
exemplification of the equal right to be free. But there are, of course,
striking differences between such defensive general rights and special
rights. (1) General rights do not arise out of any special relationship or
transaction between men. (2) They are not rights which are peculiar to
those who have them but are rights which all men capable of choice
have in the absence of those special conditions which give rise to special
rights. (3) General rights have as correlatives obligations not to interfere
to which everyone else is subject and not merely the parties to some
special relationship or transaction, though, of course, they will often be
asserted when some particular persons threaten to interfere as a moral
objection to that interference. To assert a general right is to claim in
relation to some particular action the equal right of all men to be free in
the absence of any of those special conditions which constitute a special
right to limit another's freedom; to assert a special right is to assert in
relation to some particular action a right constituted by such special
conditions to limit another's freedom. The assertion of general rights
directly invokes the principle that all men equally have the right to be
free; the assertion of a special right . . . invokes it indirectly.

Hart is drawing a distinction here where there is, for his purposes,
no difference: the *only* difference between special rights and general
rights is that one holds special rights against one person or a few
people and general rights against a lot of people. Whence, for
example, my right to say what I think (p. 64)? One thinks of this as an
important political right. It is not simply the right to utter, but the
right not to be deliberately drowned out—if it were not, it could not
properly be used in the defensive role that Hart sees as its home. If it
is a political right, then one has it as a member of a community (even
if all members of all communities should have it) and not simply as a
human being. The basis of the right lies in cooperation (the mutuality
of restrictions that Hart correctly sees as underlying political obligation). We recognize no such absolute right, and it is interesting to
consider the sorts of circumstances in which we should deny the right
or be puzzled about whether the person who claimed it actually had
it. Suppose that what a person thinks is ill-founded, irresponsible,
and defamatory: must he then be accorded the right to say what he
thinks to a group of impressionable children? What if what he wants
to say is merely a pointlessly offensive demonstration of his freedom
from the shackles of courtesy and consideration? What if he happens
to think accurately about the defenses of his country in time of war?
Or suppose he has previously declared his intention to lie so as to
cause trouble? Most interesting consideration, what if he has consist-

ently drowned out others who try to say what they think, insisting that he has the right to state his side of the case while not allowing any other side to be heard? (Compare my saying "I have a right not to be hit" when somebody tries to fight back against my unprovoked assault, which would be a case calling on another general right.) It is an unfortunate society in which such things happen but, in such a society, it seems to me that no wrong is done in drowning me out. The justification for coercing me is not that it hinders me in coercing others; drowning my voice out when I speak does not stop me from drowning their voices out when they speak. The point is that, if I refuse to cooperate with others with respect to the right to speak one's mind, then I do not have the right; it arises from the special (though common) relationship of cooperation. It is an example of mutuality of restrictions. If I have not the right to speak my mind, then no wrong is done to me in drowning me out.

To come at the same point slightly differently, suppose that somebody says that he has the right to say what he thinks as he pleases, that what he thinks is that I should shut up, and that he says it loudly and often enough to drown me out. Some sort of procedure, involving mutual recognition of restrictions by the people concerned, is necessary here to resolve the contending claims to a right.

If the right is based on cooperation, does it follow that I can legitimately drown out any hermit I come across? By coming across him I establish some sort of relationship with him, and *pointlessly* interfering shows me to be unfit to have cooperative relationships with people or to live in a community. If we both simply start to sing, drowning each other out, there is nothing to pick out either of us as the one to stop until we cooperate in some agreement such that he sings in the morning and I sing in the afternoon, or that I sing tenor and he sings bass. If, with urban sprawl, I set up house next to him and he refuses to enter any cooperative relationship with me—he throws his rubbish over the fence, sings loudly while bathing at 3:00 A.M., uses my verandah posts when he runs short of firewood, and steals my crops—how would he base his claim that I stop practicing the trumpet to prevent him from listening to his favorite radio program?[6] In such a situation we might reasonably say that the hermit and I have a Hohfeldian power with respect to each other when we meet: each of us can, by behaving decently, create in the other a duty to behave decently and a right in ourselves that the other shall behave decently.[7] If we simply proceed to carry on as yahoos, though, neither of us will generate any rights against the other.

I have argued in more detail elsewhere that a general right not to be assaulted or murdered arises from cooperation.[8] The point can be seen fairly clearly by considering what is true of a situation in which there is no cooperation: the Hobbesian natural condition. When everybody else is a constant threat to me, acting as he or she believes to be necessary for self-preservation and believing my death to be so necessary, then I, too, may kill as I see fit. Any killing I do of other people will be licensed as self-defense. Since, in that natural condition, everybody is in the same position as I, the same holds true of everybody. Anybody may properly kill anybody else; there is no general right not to be wantonly assaulted or killed, because such a limitation cannot properly be required of one person without reciprocity from the others. It is when we have mutual recognition of limitations, cooperation, that such a right can come into being. The argument fairly clearly carries over to cover all the cases Hart is concerned with as general rights. General rights are simply special rights against a lot of people. I have them against each and every person with whom I have cooperative relationships;[9] each one of them has an obligation not to assault me wantonly and not to interfere with my exercise of the right to freedom of speech. As part of the same cooperative system, I have the same obligations to them. General rights are simply special rights against a lot of people, not specific instances of a basic right to be free from all interference. They are rights arising from cooperation, not simply from one's being human. There is a connection between being human and possession of these rights, but it is a somewhat more complicated connection than Hart suggests. People in a Hobbesian state of nature would be justified in killing far more frequently than we would be in civil society: they would be so justified because, with complete lack of security, each other person constitutes a threat in such a way as to justify preemptive action as self-defense. But people in a Hobbesian state of nature would not be justified in killing for fun. Killing for fun would exhibit a vice, a quality of character making them not apt for social life. Social life makes presuppositions about human nature: it presupposes that people, by and large, are inclined to cooperate and are capable of entering cooperative relationships. Possession of the rights that Hart is concerned with as general rights is not unrelated to whether certain creatures are human beings with human nature, but the rights arise from the cooperative relationships that those human beings enter as an expression of their human nature. The rights are generated by the cooperation, and, as suggested, it is no accident that people cooperate. To some extent, the content of the rights will depend on the detail of the cooperation, a point we can see worked out in different possible property systems.

We come down, then, to what Hart says about special rights: "unless it is recognized that interference with another's freedom requires a moral justification the notion of a right could have no place in morals; for to assert a right is to assert that there is such a justification" (p. 65). The argument is that there must be a basic right to be free if the notion of a special right (with corresponding obligation in the person against whom one has the right) is to make sense. I hope that the examples I set out earlier explain what is wrong with this argument. I have a right against somebody if I may interfere in his activities by determining what he shall do and if he must submit. Hart's argument assumes that there is only one alternative to this: that I may not interfere. Only then is noninterference the norm, with interference requiring the special justification of a special right. In fact, there is another alternative: that I may interfere but the other person need not submit; that is, that each of us is at liberty to pursue his own plans even if, for one reason or another, it is impossible for both plans to be successful. This is the situation of competition, and I hope that the examples presented earlier are sufficient to defend the claim that competition is the norm, that is, that competition is proper wherever special rights are not infringed. The claim here is not a statistical one that competition is the most common relationship between people. It is the claim that, in the absence of convention, competition is proper: people may do whatever they are not obligated not to do. Special rights do not presuppose that the norm is noninterference; only if one has a special right is one in a position morally to insist on noninterference.

Hart's argument does not succeed in showing that interference is improper except as a response to interference, so it does not demonstrate any truth in the presupposition of noninterference. His argument falls down at two points. The first is that general rights are not, in the relevant way, different from special rights. The second is that special rights do not make sense only on the assumption that noninterference is otherwise the norm. In the absence of special rights, we are in competition: in the absence of special rights, and thus of obligations, each is at liberty to do as he or she will, even if that involves impeding or interfering with others. The area of protected individual liberty is the area in which one has special rights, and the story determining the bounds of that liberty will be the story of how the rights are generated.

Notes

1. One could produce an enormously long list of people making weaker or stronger claims of this sort. Three fairly recent examples will suffice. Robert Nozick, "Coercion," reprinted in *Philosophy, Politics and Society*, 4th ser., ed. Peter Laslett, W. G. Runciman, and Quentin Skinner (Oxford:

Basil Blackwell, 1972), p. 101, says "making someone unable to perform an act needs justifying." John Passmore in *The Limits of Government*, Boyer Lectures, Australian Broadcasting Commission (1981), p. 48, says, "By its very nature, coercion is in itself an evil." W. N. Nelson in *On Justifying Democracy* (London: Routledge & Kegan Paul, 1980), p. 10, says, "If there is reason to believe that an individual might decide an issue in a way which would lead to serious harm for someone else, there is some reason to take the decision out of his hands." Much more important than mere brief quotations is the role that the idea plays in people's arguments, but displaying that is far too long a job for a footnote. The idea seems to be very common not only among philosophers, but in discussions of, and arguments in terms of, liberty carried on by nonphilosophers.

2. Again, there could be an enormous number of examples, but two will do. John Stuart Mill, in *On Liberty* (Totowa, N.J.: Everyman, 1910), pp. 75, 152, says "The only freedom which deserves the name, is that of pursuing our own good in our own way . . . Liberty consists in doing what one desires." Paley (quoted by George Fitzhugh, *Cannibals All!*, ed. C. Vann Woodward, Cambridge: Harvard University Press, 1960, p. 73) says: "To do what we will is natural liberty: to do what we will, consistently with the interest of the community to which we belong, is civil liberty; that is to say, the only liberty to be desired in a state of civil society.

"I should wish, no doubt, to be allowed to act, in every instance, as I pleased; but I reflect, that the rest also of mankind would then do the same; in which state of universal independence and self-direction, I should meet with so many checks and obstacles to my own will, from the interference and opposition of other men's, that not only my happiness, but my liberty, would be less than whilst the whole community were subject to the dominion of equal laws." Paley's liberty is constructed by compromise from the basic notion of being able to do whatever one wants to do, and is so constructed in terms of maximizing one's actual opportunity to do what one wants to do. Again, this view of liberty is not peculiar to philosophers. Versions of it are very commonly found in nonphilosophical discussions of liberty.

3. This idea of a raw form of the vice of injustice is taken up in Chapter 6.

4. Wesley Newcomb Hohfeld, *Fundamental Legal Conceptions*, ed. Walter Wheeler Cook (New Haven: Yale University Press, 1964).

5. H. L. A. Hart, "Are There Any Natural Rights?," appeared first in *Philosophical Review* 64 (1955). References are to the reprinting of the paper in A. Quinton, ed. *Political Philosophy* (Oxford: Oxford University Press, 1967).

6. Not all of morality is concerned with rights and obligations. My responding in such a spiteful way to his nastiness might show that I was an unpleasant fellow, but that is not what is at issue. What is at issue is whether *the hermit* can make any claim on me.

7. It is useful to consider the possibility that a number of commonly claimed rights might actually be Hohfeldian powers. The right to life is one example. Certainly the claim that people simply have a Hohfeldian right to life is wildly implausible: people can have such a right only if they behave appropriately, and somebody who, for example, makes a hobby of killing other people will not possess that right. We might consider, though, the possibility that everybody has a Hohfeldian power to life, that is, that by behaving decently they can generate in others a duty not to kill

them. The point seems of limited use, though. It does not help to answer questions about whether a fetus or somebody in a coma from which he will not recover is a possible holder of Hohfeldian powers.

8. In *Cooperation and Human Values* (Brighton: Harvester Press and New York: St. Martin's Press, 1981).
9. And I have the Hohfeldian privilege of doing whatever is not precluded by the terms of the cooperation.

3

All Rights Are Social Rights

P EOPLE WHO READ Hobbes's moral and political philosophy always pick up the point about people's interests clashing, but
often miss the equally important point about people's judgments
differing. Many people agree about many matters, but it is in the
nature of things that people often disagree. They disagree about
many sorts of things: witnesses in court differ about what happened;
physicists disagree about questions of physics; critics disagree in their
judgment of a particular piece of music; people who agree over a
wide range of moral matters may still disagree about the finer points
of justice or about what behavior would be proper in given circumstances; and so on.

These disagreements often cause no trouble. If we differ sufficiently
in our judgment of a piece of music, one of us will listen to it and the
other will not. If we differ about the best way of preparing soil to
grow fuschias, then we shall prepare our soils differently if we grow
fuschias. When our actions are quite independent of each other, our
differences cause no problems.

Where what is at issue is common action, though, what each of us
does is the other's business. If we go off on a picnic, you taking the
food and I the drink, we shall not have much of a time if we go to
different places. If we are jointly building a town hall and differ on the
construction, you thinking that wood is cheap and strong enough
and I thinking that only brick would be strong enough, we have a
problem that must be resolved. If we agree that wood is strong
enough but I think that it would be improper to use it because the
town council deserves a more prestigious building material, then,
again, though we may be differing about a different sort of thing, we
have a problem that must be resolved before we can go ahead and act.

We cannot resolve the problem by agreeing to do what is best,
because we differ about what it would be best to do. If we are to act
jointly despite our differences, one must somehow submit to the
other or both submit to something, or somebody, else. If you disagree
with me about what would be the correct building material, then you

36

will differ with my further judgment that, when we disagree, my view should prevail because I know best. Why should either of us submit to the judgment of the other? There may, in particular cases, be particular reasons: you are a master builder and I have made no more than a paper airplane that would not fly anyway. But it is difficult to imagine a world in which differences of judgment would be restricted to such cases (they certainly are not in this world), and it is difficult to see what general reason could be given for one to submit to the judgment of the other when such particular reasons are not available. Having already presented all my reasons in favor of brick and having failed to persuade you, what extra reason could I give for you to submit to my judgment? At the "natural" as opposed to conventional level, there seems to be no way of resolving the problem and providing ourselves with a town hall. If we are to build the town hall without this disagreement deteriorating into a brawl, we shall need to move into the field of convention to resolve our differences and determine which view is to prevail. In the way that is important here, neither of us is naturally superior to the other.

There is a general point to be made here about equality. The claim that all people are equal, as a matter-of-fact claim rather than as a misleading expression of some rather vacuous prescription, is often regarded as nonsense simply because people are not all the same in every, or perhaps any, respect. People differ in weight, height, intelligence, athletic ability, and so on, but it does not follow from this that there is no sense to the claim that people are, in fact, equal.

If I say "Do the same as I do," what must you do to comply? Move your right arm vigorously from the elbow, but with the wrist stiff, through an eight-inch arc? Or swat a fly, which you can do with your left or right hand, with stiff or loose wrist, with or without a newspaper, but only when a fly is present? Or swat a fly right-handed? What does the word "same" mean? (And if there is some temptation to say that in only one of those cases would you really be doing exactly what I did, consider this; if you are teaching me to play golf and say "Do exactly what I do," *must* I use your clubs?) "Same" is a formal word and must have its criteria supplied for it: we must know under what description we are to do the same. Usually the context will make plain the description under which the act comes: it will be clear whether we are exercising or getting rid of flies.[1]

"Equal" is also a formal word and must have its criteria supplied. Nothing could simply be equal or unequal independent of the context in which the question was raised or the point of raising it. Before we can say whether two things are equal we need to know the respect in which equality is being claimed (is it a matter of their height or their weight?) but, more than that, we need to know the point of the inquiry. What is equal in respect X in one case need not be equal in respect X in another case.

- *Case 1.* I am judging a sprint race, and I decide that it is a tie. The two runners reached the finish at the same time.
- *Case 2.* I have a tutorial in my room each week, and I explain to the members of the class when I want them to arrive: not some early, because that would disturb my writing, and not some late, because that would disturb the tutorial. I want them all to arrive at the same time. But that does not mean that I want them to get jammed in the door. They arrive at the same time if they come in one after the other.

The criteria for "same time" are different in cases 1 and 2. The criteria are determined by the point of bothering in each case about whether people arrived at the same time.

- *Case 3.* The instructions say "Take two pieces of equal length," and the two pieces that I have differ in length by one millimeter. I am making a Rolls-Royce engine, so I send the parts back.
- *Case 4.* The instructions say "Take two pieces of equal length," and the two pieces that I have differ in length by one millimeter. I am making a rabbit hutch, so I take up the two pieces and get on with the job. I have followed the instructions.

The respect in which equality was required (length) was specified, but the criteria for equality of length differ in cases 3 and 4. The criteria are determined by the point of requiring equality. In these cases, the pieces are equal in length if the difference between them does not matter for the job in hand. The specific context gives the criteria for equality.

Equality, then, is compatible with difference: differences will sometimes matter and sometimes not. The simple attack on egalitarianism, pointing out that people differ, is not sufficient for the job; it does not show that people are not equal. To deal with the matter, we need to know the context and the point of the inquiry.

When Hobbes made his claim that all people are equal, the context that he had in mind was that of entering and remaining in social life, so the question here is: are the differences between people such that some need social life (not necessarily sociable life, and not life in high society) and others do not? Could anybody live in the complete absence of help from others? The argument about man's natural condition is, partly, an argument that each of us needs at least restraint from others (and is partly an argument that the necessary restraint can be provided only with conventions that Hobbes believed must be coercive). This is the import of Hobbes's egalitarian claim:

each of us needs something from others; nobody can survive without the social contract. Our activities depend at least on forebearances from others: hence Hobbes's remark that the strongest, when asleep, can be killed by the weakest. Each of us needs to enter the cooperative enterprises in which obligations are generated, and each of us can, therefore, have claims made on him. Nobody can properly claim to owe nobody anything. At some level, recognition of this point is required if there is to be a community.

Each of us, then, enters social life on the basis of equality with others in this respect, and that is quite compatible with differences between people such that people are not always equal in particular contexts within social life. But that point about equality is at the base, and the point applies not only to physical hardihood but to other attributes as well. It applies to our needs to resolve differences in our private judgments.

At the foundations of communal life, people must treat on the basis of equality. We cannot assume from the start that somebody is a fool, a point that emerged from our consideration of building materials for the town hall. To call on the Hobbesian model, people treated in that way would have no reason to make the contract. Where X and Y have a disagreement, we cannot simply start from the *assumption* that X is superior and that his views must, therefore, take precedence. The views of each must be given a fair hearing (which might require enough common ground for them to agree on what counts as a fair hearing and a fair way of resolving their dispute).

This same point is reflected at a different level, too. I may be firmly convinced of the justice of A and you of its injustice, but we ought to be able to agree on the injustice of either simply forcing his views on the other. If you take responsibility for the joint enterprise and I am merely a paid employee then, of course, your views prevail,[2] but that is not simply one person forcing his views on another. It is not simply a matter of your views prevailing because you think you are right; your views prevail because you have to take the responsibility. This is a reason why your views should prevail, and a reason different in kind from those that either of us would have given in support of our primary views about the justice of A. "I take the responsibility, so what I say goes" is at least a plausible argument. "I take the responsibility, so brick is stronger than wood" is a rotten one.

So we need to move into the field of conventions. Our first-order decision-procedure, discussion of the strength or prestige of building materials, or of the justice of an arrangement, having failed to resolve our differences and make joint action possible, we refer to a second-order decision-procedure, which enables us to get on with the job. That decision-procedure cannot start from the assumption that one of the conflicting views must be given precedence simply because of who holds it; such a procedure would not resolve disputes peacefully. The function of this second-order decision-procedure, to which I shall refer from now on as the public procedure, is to resolve disputes definitively, which is why Hobbes required that his sovereign be unitary and absolute: the sovereign must be unitary so that there cannot be conflicting decisions about the dispute, and must be absolute because there must, in the end, be a final decision that cannot be overthrown. If each of the disputants is subject to the public procedure, then the disagreement can be resolved and joint action will be possible. In cases in which there is such dispute, only a public procedure can make joint action possible.

I shall use the term "public procedure" with some misgivings, since the term, taken out of context, could be misleading. With the same misgivings, I shall use the term "private procedure" as its pair. The terms "first-order decision-procedure" and "second-order decision-procedure," though I have used them initially because their meanings should be clear, are quite long enough for frequent use of them to be tedious and, perhaps, excessively formal. Both procedures, in fact, are public or at least publishable. The reference to *discussion* of building materials should make this clear; discussion is a public and interpersonal activity. Even when I reason out in my mind the justice of a situation, without talking to anybody else or even to myself, the moves that I make, if I am reasoning properly, are moves the tests for the rationality of which are public rather than a matter of my own personal standards. Nevertheless, if people who disagree manage to sort the matter out themselves by discussion rather than, say, going to court or calling in an arbitrator, then we commonly say that they sorted it out privately, so I shall use that term. A warning is necessary, though, that these more readable terms could be misleading if the way they have been introduced is forgotten: if the two in dispute solve the problem by tossing a coin, then we should usually say that they have solved the problem privately, but, as I shall be using the term, they have changed their method of solving the problem and are using a public procedure. The first-order decision-procedure, or private procedure, is a matter of discussion in which each tries to persuade the other by rational means to change his view. The second-order decision-procedure, or public procedure, operates by the imposition of authority, even if it is only the authority imposed by the toss of a coin. If we cannot agree on where to go for our picnic, and we resort to tossing a coin, then the fact that the coin so falls as to favor you decides the issue by giving authority to your preferences, not by changing my private judgment about which would be the better place to go.[3]

The primary function of the public procedure is to determine which view prevails. It is not simply to add one more view on the same level as those already involved in the dispute, but to determine the issue. This does not mean that first-order views must be irrelevant: the public procedure might take the form of tossing a coin, but it might also take the form of appeal to a group of wise people who would be expected to consider the first-order views and try to judge which was the more soundly based.[4] But even if the public procedure does work by having people consider first-order views, it does not itself simply produce another first-order view to be considered on a par with all the rest: it determines the dispute, otherwise it is pointless and cannot serve its function. Those going before the public procedure have taken on an obligation to submit to its decision, and each has a right against the others that they shall do so. The point of the activity depends on the allocation of those rights being definitive no matter what the private judgments of the people involved may be.[5] If those rights are not definitive, then the dispute is not settled; joint activity and the communal life requiring it would be impossible. The rights take precedence over private judgment of right and wrong; the person who has the right makes the decision.[6] There can be no question here of the right's being overruled on grounds of kindness or the common good; what is at issue is who makes the decision, not the grounds on which it is made.

Sometimes one does not willingly submit to a public procedure, but is made to submit to it. The same things will follow as long as the decision-procedure is binding, and that is a matter I shall deal with later.

Rights are definitive in disputes. That, indeed, is their point: there would be no content to the notion of a right if my having a right implied nothing about the propriety of others' preventing me from exercising it. Rights can operate in this definitive way, when there are disputes between people, only if they are settled and agreed on by the community in which the dispute occurs.[7] A mere claim to have a right settles nothing if it is not, in the end, accepted by the relevant community, even if some members of that community finally accept it only as a result of appeal to a public procedure used to resolve disputes about who has what rights. If some will not even accept that, then coercion may be necessary to uphold the rights and keep the community from collapsing, though whether coercion is necessary will depend on facts about the frequency of refusal to accept decisions, the vehemency of the refusal, and the significance of the particular decisions not accepted. Widespread and common refusal to accept decisions will make common action and community impossible.[8]

If there is one cucumber sandwich left and both of us are hungry, recognition that it is mine settles the issue of who may grab it and who may not (and, indeed, the issue of who may give it to the other). This does not, of course, prevent the other fellow from grabbing it, bolting it, and running away, but various social consequences follow from that act: we can sum them up by saying that he is a thief. He is liable to punishment when caught, may be required to make restitution (of something equally good if not the original), and will not be trusted by others who know of the incident. (If he acted *in extremis* those consequences might not follow, but that reflects less on our notions of rights and responsibilities than on our notion of responsibility.)

A mere claim is not sufficient to produce the same consequences. Saying that the sandwich is mine is not enough to make it mine, and is certainly not enough to make a thief of the fellow who runs away with it. If he thinks that my claim is correct but grabs the sandwich anyway, he is as bad as a thief (and in the same way as a thief) even if my claim is, in fact, mistaken. He shows unwillingness to restrict his pursuit of his own interests by consideration of other people's rights, and is the sort of person whose activities can be limited only by coercion. The same sort of point applies if he does not even bother himself about whether my claim is true or false; he does not care about the rights of others, and his subjection of others to his own judgment of how to behave will recognize no limits other than those of coercion. In either case, he displays a quality of character that gets in the way of cooperation or common action.

A different point arises if he does not believe that I am serious in my claim. I might not believe that I have a right to the sandwich, or even have thought about whose sandwich it is, but might mouth the words as a verbal ploy in a game of grabs, a not uncommon move. If the issue is simply who can make the most effective grab, then he does nothing reprehensible in making a direct grab while I beat about the bush. If we are both simply grabbing, then we are playing a different game and rights do not come into the question. If he believes that the cucumber sandwich is his and that I am merely uttering words in an attempt to grab the sandwich, he betrays no vice in eating it. If he accepts my claim as a serious one, believes it to be false, and thinks that the sandwich is actually his, then he is playing the game of rights and should not simply run off with the sandwich. Simply running off with the sandwich might not show that he had no care for the rights of others and was a thief, but it would show that he had limited care for the recognition of the rights of others, expecting them to be subject to his judgment, and was trying to take to himself the rights of a tyrant. He would show the vice of arrogance in lack of toleration for the views of others, ignoring the presupposition of equality. If each of us recognizes the other's claims as serious and takes rights seriously, the appropriate line for us to follow when we find that our claims conflict is to try to work out the rights. We might do so through discussion, or we might submit to arbitration. In the end we might be reduced to simply making grabs for the sandwich, but rights have then disappeared from the picture because they were ineffective.

Rights make a peaceful life possible with people who are willing to live a peaceful life, people inclined to resolve disputes without recourse to fighting. The test for rights is not the determined selfish person or malefactor who ignores them or simply asserts his own judgment over that of others, because he can be controlled only by coercion. Good will does not lead him to fit in and allow a peaceful life for all, so force or threats of force must be used if we are to have that peaceful life while he lives among us. The claim that rights disappear when they are ineffective, or that an ineffective right is no right at all, should be understood in this light. It is not the case that I no longer own what is stolen from me, though my right to it is then, in a clear sense, ineffective. In that case, I retain the right, and that is why the taking of whatever is in question is a case of theft. But a right that cannot be agreed on by people willing to settle disputes in terms of rights cannot serve the function of a right, so it is ineffective and no right at all unless it is made definitive by, for example, reference to a public procedure.

Somebody who steals from me may not act in a manner appropriate to the recognition of my property rights, but the social consequences that follow—recognition that he is a thief, may be punished, may be made to restore what he has taken, and so on—do follow because my property rights are more generally recognized by the community. Those rights may not have been effective in stopping him from taking what was mine, but they have been effective, among those willing to settle disputes in terms of rights, in producing those social consequences and thus in upholding those rights and keeping them in existence.

Rights must resolve disputes in which they can be appealed to; they would be pointless were they not definitive, because they are not commensurable with other considerations that might be brought to bear. My hunger might be compared with your hunger, but not with the fact that you paid for the apple pie or baked it yourself and take great artistic pride in its unsullied beauty. Reference to rights must work in a different way, determining the relevance of such facts as that both of us are hungry or that I am hungry and you want to keep the pie to show to others.

There must be something to settle cases of dispute if those disputes are to be settled, and what does the settling must be different in kind from the considerations working against each other in the dispute. Producing more reasons of the same kind might lead one person to change his mind so that the dispute disappears, but an ongoing dispute can be resolved only if a reason of a different type is brought to bear. As the world is, something must play that role if people are to be able to live together in peace. The problem is not merely one of clashing wants, problems such as that it is a small apple pie and each of us wants all of it. Honest and intelligent people of good will can differ about what would be a good use for X, or about what would be the best use for X; even after they have reached agreement about that, they can differ about how most effectively to put X to that use. Kind people can differ about whether the best thing to do is to help Bill build the fence he is building, or to leave him to it, disconsolate at our standing back, so that he will develop his independence and cease to have his future plans so limited by his need for help from others. These are not clashes of interest, but differences in private judgments, and it is at least difficult to imagine a human world in which such differences did not appear. That would be to imagine a world in which everybody was infallible or, even more implausibly, a world in which people were fallible but all made exactly the same mistakes.

Disagreements are part of our lives, and those disagreements must be resolved where there is to be common action or community. Considerations of kindness, effectiveness, and generally of what is best have failed to resolve the dispute. We must move from that sphere of considerations to a different way of making the decision, a way that takes precedence over the primary considerations involved in the dispute and must do so if it is to achieve its point. This way of resolving the matter will contribute nothing at all unless it is definitive, but it plays a role that must be played if there is to be community. What this new way of resolving the dispute determines is not which views are the best; that is what the disagreement is about, and simply applying a public procedure would not give anybody a reason for changing his mind on that point. What must be determined, and what this new procedure determines, is which views prevail. This is the home of rights. If you have a right to the remaining apple pie, then your views prevail no matter how poorly reasoned I believe them to be. If we cannot agree on where to go for a picnic and resolve the matter by tossing a coin, then, when the coin favors you, I may agree that I am now committed to going to Balga. That does not mean that I have changed my mind on the point of primary dispute: I may still think that it would have been far better had the coin so landed as to favor Albany.

There is some playing down of the importance of truth in all of this, and rightly so. To insist that the truth always prevail is, to put it crudely, to insist that I have my way. It would, no doubt, be nice if the truth always prevailed, but what matters among people who must live together peaceably is that different people have different ideas of what the truth is. If I insist that the truth (as I see it) prevail in community action, then I am insisting that my views (which need not be selfish views) prevail, but there is no reason at all apparent in the story so far why those who differ from me about the truth should be forced to fit in with my opinions any more than that I should be forced to fit in with theirs. If one of us must submit to the views of the other because of disagreement, what matters is that there be a fair decision about who is to prevail in the allocation of rights. No more can reasonably be looked for. Truth is much less important; insistence on it as primary in such cases is inconsistent with life as a community. This does not mean that honesty is not a virtue; it means that toleration is a virtue too.

The idea that rights must be definitive is not one that everybody would accept without argument. Some people are quite happy with the idea that one can have rights that may be overridden for one's own good or for the public good, a view that depends mainly on examples for its plausibility. It may not be contested that somebody owns a particular block of land but, especially if he has made no use of it and intends to make no use of it, there seems no impropriety in the community's being allowed to resume it, even against his selfish wishes, for some worthwhile project. It seems quite proper to override his property rights. The same sort of point holds true if somebody buys land in a residential area and wants to use it as a testing ground for explosives or to build a factory that will pollute the immediately surrounding air very badly: it does not seem at all improper for the community to limit his use of what is his. In general, it seems that we are prepared to allow such cases of interference for the good of others or for the public good. If somebody finds himself overweight and responds by such masochistic courses of action as taking up diet and exercise, that is, no doubt, his own business; he has a right to inflict such pain on himself if he wants to. If, however, his weight-reducing program consists of chopping off one of his legs, we might well feel that others were justified in interfering for his own good.

In general, though, interfering with somebody else for his own good is regarded as justified only if he is incapable of exercising his rights for himself.[9] What we are faced with then is not the problem of justifying a deprivation or overriding of rights, because the person is not deprived of his rights; he retains his rights, but somebody else exercises them for him because he is incapable of exercising them for himself. How we are to judge that somebody is incapable of exercising rights is a problem, but not the same problem as how to justify overriding somebody's rights. If a person's rights are overridden, then his interests may also be neglected, but if I exercise somebody else's rights for him, I must do so in terms of his interests.[10] The model for paternalism, the relationship between father and child, brings this out. It is not the same as the relationship between master and slave.[11] The slave lacks many legal rights, and many of his moral rights are overridden by the interests of his master. The child is not there, as child, to serve the interests of the father, and does not lack rights in such a way as to make proper toward him behavior that would be (legally) proper toward a slave. A child's rights are built into the social structure, but must be exercised by somebody else as agent until the child is capable of exercising them.[12]

The standard case of paternalism is not one of overriding somebody's rights for his own good, but one of acting in a gap left by the fact that the person treated paternalistically cannot exercise a right that people standardly can exercise. Perhaps he cannot exercise it because, as in the case of a child or a madman, a lack in him makes him incapable of exercising any or many rights. Or perhaps a condition of his having the right is no longer met, as a criminal gives up some of his rights by infringing the rights of others and makes proper toward him treatment that would not be proper toward others. Things may properly be done to change his ways that may not be done to change the ways of people who refrain from infringing the rights of others. Or there may be limits on the person's rights, and the act that interferes with his doing what he wants to do (and lays claim to do) may not, in fact, overstep those limits and infringe or override his rights.

To exercise the power of eminent domain is a case bringing out the limits of somebody's rights. Eminent domain appears to override rights because we think, typically, that a person can do whatever he wants to with his own property and, in particular, does not have to give it up unless he wants to. This general idea seems to live quite happily beside the quite incompatible recognition that there are limitations on people's property rights and on what they can do with what they own:[13] somebody who buys a block of land in a residential area is not entitled to make life unlivable for everybody else around by using it to test explosives or pollute the air with poisonous chemicals; that the block is in a residential area means that there are limitations on the property rights. I can do what I like with my own money insofar as I can save it or splurge, but I may not deface coins of the realm or use them to buy heroin or hire killers. There are severe limitations on what I can do with any guns that I own: if I start using them to shoot at people then the guns are likely to be confiscated, and quite rightly so.

Acquisition of land through the power of eminent domain is carried out legally. That brings out that it is not a case of overriding somebody's rights, but of acting outside the limits of his limited rights. We might argue about the rights and wrongs of such an action, but that is not an argument about the propriety of overriding somebody's rights; it is an argument about whether his rights are or should be so limited. If the right could be overridden, then the right would become irrelevant; that I had a right in a given situation would not entitle me to act and would not matter at all. I should have to show that my right was not overridden in that case, which is to say that I should have to show that my proposed act was justified in quite different terms. A court's determination that George has a right to keep the land settles in his favor the legal question of whether it may be acquired, or the court may determine that he has no right to keep the land in opposition to the public interest, so that one condition of his right's not being limited in the relevant ways is no longer met. Analogous moral points will hold.

If a sane man could decide to cut off his leg for no good reason (and it is, at least, hard to imagine such a case), then we might want to argue about whether he had a right to do whatever he wanted to do with his body. The community might well have a proper interest in what he does with his leg, since whether or not he has two sound legs might well affect the contribution he can make to and the claims he makes upon the community. Whether he has a right to chop his leg off or others have a right that he keep it and perform certain tasks to which his leg is necessary is a matter to be argued out, and that is what must be argued out in such a case rather than simply arguing about the advantages of allowing or prohibiting his self-mutilation. What is needed is not simply an argument about the advantages to us of so limiting him, but an argument of reciprocity showing that he *owes* us such advantages because of what he takes in the cooperative endeavor in which we have joined with him.

Arguments about who has what rights and what limitations there are on them are different from arguments about what is to be gained by overriding somebody's rights. The actual activities that are justified—legally acquiring a piece of land, having a father look after his son's investments, stopping somebody from chopping his leg off in a fit of madness—may frequently be the same, but that they are different forms of argument matters. It matters because rights must be definitive if there is to be community life. If there is no peaceful way of resolving disputes there can be no community, and definitive rights are the only plausible candidates. It might seem that universal agreement on the truth of Utilitarianism, or some other such formula for resolving disputes, would do the job of settling disputes peacefully, but that is an illusion. If the job is to be done, then agreement is required not only about the formula but also about all of its detailed application. When we disagree, as we will under any such system of fact-finding, calculating, and forecasting, we must have some way of determining who has the right for his views to prevail, and others must recognize an obligation to fit in with it. A declaration of or agreement about what is to happen can be definitive; a finding as to fact cannot be.

There can be disagreement about who has what rights as much as about other things, and those disputes must be resolved in the same definitive way: the decision-procedure must determine who has the rights and who was falsely (dishonestly or mistakenly) claiming to have rights. Merely saying that one has a right is not the same as having one. Nor is sincerely believing that one has a right.

Rights can serve their function only if taken away from merely private judgment. Private judgments are what differ, and those differences can be resolved so as to make communal action possible only if there is a shift to the public, interpersonal sphere. If each person is the judge of his own rights, then substantively, as Hobbes pointed out, all men will have a right to all things. No honest and reasonable person, perhaps, will be able to persuade himself that he has a right to all things, but that I judge the facts to be thus and interpret the applicable principles in this way is no guarantee that everybody will do so. There is no act such that we can reasonably say that nobody (no matter how silly he might be) could think that he had the right to do it, and if each person is his own judge then nobody can overrule the fellow who is silly. In this sense, each person has a right to all things, nothing is excluded, and what follows from widespread failure to resolve disputes is the impossibility of communal action and a shift toward the Hobbesian natural condition. We can see hints of this today, despite widespread agreement about a lot of rights, in the recognition of confrontation and demand as fairly standard relationships between people. Contemporary lauding of a remarkably inadequate notion of private conscience undercuts rights and the role they play in such a way as to make them pointless, so that claims to rights are roughly equivalent to no more than expressions of wants.

Natural rights must be subject to definitive interpretation. They will become positive rights, or they will be useless. Rights that go with private conscience apart from the sphere of public determination can have no point. Disagreement between people is, then, a sound objection to the idea of natural right.[14] Rights act interpersonally and must be recognized to achieve their point.[15]

If my right is not definitive and does not justify me in rejecting interference, how can the interferer's right be definitive and justify him in interfering? We should simply be in contest to see whose will prevailed. It was the introduction of rights of the sort in question that constituted the change from the Hobbesian state of nature to civil society, and, indeed, without the recognition of such definitive rights we should have universal competition, permanent possibility of conflict with one's own strength and guile as the only way of defending one's interests against attack, and the Hobbesian state of nature. This was the equality that Hobbes required be recognized by those meeting to make a contract setting up civil society: an area of autonomy for each person, an area in which each person has a right not to be subject to the judgment of others but to enter into the contract-making on equal terms. The rights are definitive: where one has them one acts on one's judgment, taking advice as one sees fit, and is not subject to the dictates of others. In the absence of a natural right to control others, this must be recognized if there is to be a community. There is a political aspect to morality, and that aspect is democratic; as each person has his say, each person has his protected area of personal sovereignty, and within that system will be an impersonal way of determining the grounds on which somebody can properly be judged to be unfit to exercise his rights. My rights to do various things may be limited, and somebody else's right to interfere with my activities may be limited, but whatever the rights are, they must be definitive if recourse to coercion and contest is to be improper.

Definitive rights carve out our place in the community and give us a moral independence of others. Within the area of my rights I am subject only to my judgment, and in this way rights create the area in which we can be individual people. That people are agents and not merely patients is important to their being people: they act purposively, think, respond to situations, initiate courses of action. Even having a concept of oneself involves viewing oneself in this way as an agent,[16] so the notion of autonomy has come to be accepted as an important notion when considering both people and morality:[17] autonomy is the recognition of one's agency and the condition required if one is to be responsible for one's acts.

The importance of autonomy has led many people to stress the individuality of people at the expense of their social nature, thus distorting relations between people. The correct model for autonomy is not that of an isolated person standing against all others, capable of beating them down and making interference impossible. Autonomy is a political notion. The primary case of autonomy is that autonomy given to a country formerly governed by another, which is a matter of granting it rights rather than of somehow giving it abilities. Autonomy is conferred on the former colony by its former colonizer, giving the colony a new place in relations between nations. No country can be autonomous in isolation, because autonomy is a matter of recognition by others and does not mean that that country is capable of doing whatever it wants or will be allowed to do whatever it wants. Autonomy is a status in a community, whether of a nation in a community of nations or an individual person in a community of people. It is the status of having rights and stands against social life only insofar as rights do—the status can occur only in a community, but enables one to reject interference by others in that context.[18] If one must have autonomy to be a person, then one must have rights to be a person. To enslave somebody and ignore all his rights is to treat him as something other and less than a person.

Rights can be definitive in the required way only if they are public and agreed on by the community, determined by a community procedure. If two people are involved in a dispute and an arbitrator makes a judgment to the satisfaction of one of them, the dispute is not resolved unless the other, too, is prepared to abide by that judgment. A dispute is not settled if it is settled for only one of the contending parties. Resolution of disputes, the determination of whose claims stand or of who actually has what rights in the matter, must, therefore, be by means of a generally accepted and binding procedure (such as submission to an agreed adjudicator). This mutual acceptance of limitations is cooperation, and it is from this cooperation that rights, as opposed to mere claims, arise. So rights, even the rights of individual people, are determined cooperatively by the community or, if the whole community is not involved in a particular dispute, will be determined cooperatively in relation to all the contending parties. In the face of this, one can assert claims, but claims are not rights; shouting very loudly that something is mine does not make it so.

Use of the public procedure in the form of legislation or courts is an obvious example of the way in which the community operates to generate rights, but that is not the only way it can do so. Frequently we have no need to refer to the public procedure; we simply accept the rules of a cooperative endeavor and the roles it allocates as determining the rights. Rights are determined by cooperation in general, not only by cooperation in terms of the public procedure. There is no problem as long as we agree on the interpretation of the rules of the cooperation. It is disagreement about such matters that makes the public procedure necessary.

Claims certainly do come into conflict and, when they do, require use of the public procedure. It is possible that rights may sometimes clash. They should not come into conflict; whenever they do, they reveal an imperfection in human arrangements, but humans are fallible and human arrangements are imperfect. What is at issue here is not Hohfeldian privileges, which do not actually come into conflict even though the people acting in the light of them might come into conflict when they compete, but full-blown Hohfeldian rights. Different enterprises might be set up generating different rights and, the world being what it is, might not run into each other for a long time. When they do run into each other and the Hohfeldian rights come into conflict, those rights cannot serve their function of peaceably resolving disputes by determining who takes precedence; either can take precedence over the other, but it is impossible for each to take precedence over the other at the same time. Those rights cannot be effective. In practical terms, those rights enter a suspended existence, and "rights" is a practical term. A public procedure must be referred to in order to determine which right stands in the case. When that is done, the loser in the debate is not the possessor of a right that has been ignored; it has been determined that he has no right in that particular matter.

Another sort of problem can come up, though it is not really a conflict. I can be cruel, inhuman, or generally nasty, not only *while* acting within my rights, but *in* asserting my rights. It might be cruel, inconsiderate, or inhumane for me to insist that my tenant pay the rent today rather than next week, but that does not affect my right to collect the rent when it is due. It certainly does not mean that I have no such right. What it means is that, since I am that sort of person, you should be careful and not expect mercy if you undertake obligations to me.

Rights are not simply something that one has on one's own. One has them in relation to and in community with others; all the contending parties are involved. If the community has an interest in whether or not I chop my leg off, then we must argue out whether I have a right to do so; the fact that it is my leg is not enough to settle the issue without recourse to argument. Similarly, if a woman claims a right to her own body (and there is still a step to be argued from that point to rights over a fetus in the body, as there might be to her rights over a diamond that she swallowed), the fact that it is her body does not rule out argument about whether she has such a right. It is clear that what rights I have over my leg are limited: I am not entitled to belabor people with it, for example. Requirements within cooperation are imposed in terms of what is necessary for the cooperation to achieve its point, since the basic requirements arise in terms of the possibility of common action. If I could show that my chopping my leg off would affect nobody else and thus would not affect the cooperation, nobody would have a base for a right against me that I refrain. Showing that nobody else has an interest in the matter is one way of showing that I am at liberty to do as I please, but it is something that has to be shown and not merely said.

One recent and influential writer who has tried to account for rights in a nonconventional way and from an individualistic standpoint is Alan Gewirth.[19] I propose to back up my own arguments by dealing with his in a little detail before making some quick comments about the idea of human rights. Rights, as I have been explaining them, are always conventional. They depend on, and emerge from, particular arrangements that people make or particular ways in which people cooperate,[20] so there will be no rights apart from such arrangements or cooperation. Rights arise interpersonally or communally, not from individual people considered discretely. The conventionality of rights, at least apparently, means that there is a problem about the idea of human rights. If "human rights are rights that all persons have simply insofar as they are human" (*Human Rights*, p. 41), then my thesis has the consequence that there are no human rights: there are no rights that everybody (or anybody) has simply because they are human without consideration of how they behave and how they are cooperatively related to other people.

That somebody has rights will not follow simply from the fact that he is human, and it will not follow simply from any property of humans. Somebody who kills at random, lies, cheats, and slanders will at least weaken his rights, and if he behaves badly enough will give them up altogether,[21] but he will still have interests, so interests cannot be a sufficient condition of the possession of rights. Such a person will also have desires, so desire cannot be a sufficient condition of the possession of rights, either. Indeed, one of the points of rights is that they discriminate between interests or desires, determining which interest or desire takes precedence in cases of conflict. Nor will possession of rights follow simply from what is necessary for people to survive or to live their lives to the full. It is clear that rights depend, at least to some extent, on reciprocity. I cannot, with any legitimacy, go around infringing other people's rights on the many occasions on which it suits me to do so and claim that my own rights are unaffected by that behavior.

The form of argument that Gewirth uses about rights is what he calls the dialectically necessary method.[22] This method starts out from beliefs that any agent must hold simply because he is an agent, and it proceeds from within the standpoint of the agent. This last point is crucial. Gewirth stresses several times that some of the moves in his argument can be made only because the argument proceeds within the standpoint of the agent, and I shall try to show that that same point prevents Gewirth from successfully reaching out from the agent to other people. He finishes with a solipsism of reason that possesses features similar to the difficulties in moving from a Hobbesian state of nature to civil society. Having started his argument about rights with a discrete, individual person, Gewirth is unable ever to place him in a community.

Gewirth's argument starts from the claim that, when an agent acts, he necessarily acts for some purpose that he regards as good, and "hence, he implicitly makes a value judgment about this goodness" (p. 49). Presumably Gewirth means that he makes a value judgment about the action or its purpose rather than about its goodness, but, even so, the claim is somewhat obscure. Where an agent acts habitually, as I sometimes find when I am writing that I have been smoking for a while, it is not clear that he acts for any purpose, let alone for a purpose that he judges to be good. It is fairly commonly appreciated that people do not always understand their motives and that they can deceive themselves about what they are trying to do. If I am jealous, then I may persuade myself that I am merely insisting on my proper rights when, in fact, I am trying to make the object of my jealousy pay for my suffering. That is not a purpose that I judge to be good; if I judged it to be good, I should have less need to deceive myself in trying to attain it. In some sense, making the object of my jealousy pay for my suffering must be something that I want to do, but that is a far cry from anything that we should normally mean if we referred to a value judgment. It is by no means uncommon for an agent to feel that his act or purpose is not so much good as forced on him by the circumstances. We should bear in mind that when Gewirth refers to an agent's value judgment, he can mean no more than the agent's want or purpose. That his making a value judgment follows from his having a purpose depends on this being so. If the reference to a value judgment carried any more weight than that, then further argument would be needed to show that that move can be made. And as long as we are dealing with a discrete individual not considered as part of a community, there is no reason why he should take as his standard anything more public than his own wants and purposes. In that condition, "whatsoever is the object of any mans Appetite or Desire; that is it, which he for his part calleth *Good*."[23]

Gewirth's agent regards as a necessary good any essential features of his action, such as the voluntariness or freedom without which he could not act, and sees any threat to these as a threat to his getting "what he regards as good," or what he wants (p. 52). "The basic goods, which are the general necessary preconditions of action, comprise certain physical and psychological dispositions ranging from life and physical integrity (including such of their means as food, clothing, and shelter) to mental equilibrium and a feeling of confidence as to the general possibility of attaining one's goals" (p. 54). If the agent has wants or purposes, then, if he is to be consistent and efficient in pursuit of them, he had better see to it that he has all those things necessary for him to achieve them. If his purpose is important to him, then he will regard as important what is necessary for him to attain it.

What Gewirth wanted to show was "that all purposive action is valuational, and that agents regard as good not only their particular purposes but also the voluntariness or freedom and purposiveness that generically characterise all their actions" (p. 57). In fact, he has not shown that in any ordinary sense of the words "valuational" or "good." It is worth reiterating that if an agent's judging something to be good means any more than his having a want or a purpose, then we cannot simply infer from his having a want or a purpose that he judges something to be good. If we keep that in mind and substitute references to an agent's wants for references to his judging something to be good, then Gewirth's argument looks a lot less persuasive than it does the way he sets it out. What Gewirth's argument so far amounts to is the point that an agent cannot act unless certain conditions are satisfied. As long as we remain within the viewpoint of a particular agent, we might say that his purposes are good to him, since there is no more public or interpersonal test for goodness. This would be the sense that Hobbes said "good" would have in man's natural condition. But we are not in man's natural condition, and that is not a meaning that the word has for us. Part of Hobbes's point was that the word could not have in the natural condition the meaning that it has for us. We should remember, too, given where Gewirth's argument is heading, that Hobbes stressed that there is no morality in the natural condition and that nobody has what would now be called Hohfeldian rights in that condition.

The importance of Gewirth's rewording becomes clear with his next move, because it becomes clear that he is playing on more ordinary senses of words such as "good" and "right." "Since the agent regards as necessary goods the freedom and well-being that constitute the generic features of his successful action, he logically must also hold that he has a right to these generic features" (p. 63). Now, even in a quite ordinary sense of "good," it does not follow from my judging something to be good that (I think) I have a right to it. If my son were to forego his game of cricket, do his homework early, and then make dinner and do the housework so that I can get on with my writing, that would be an excellent thing: it would show great kindness on his part. Nevertheless, I should not dream of saying that I had a Hohfeldian right that he cook dinner or that he had a duty to cook it. His share of the work is the washing up. Nor does the reference to necessity evade this problem. If we are wrecked at sea with only one lifebuoy between us, it would be an excellent thing (self-sacrificingly kind) if he were to give it to me. The lifebuoy is necessary for me in that I shall drown and be incapable of acting without it. Nevertheless, I cannot, on those grounds, seriously claim to have a Hohfeldian right to the lifebuoy. For a start, it is just as necessary in the same way for him to have it.[24]

If the judgment that I have a right does not follow from the judgment that it is good that I have certain things, it certainly does not follow simply from my wanting them. For a start, my wants may clash with those of others. As in the lifebuoy case, or in other cases of scarcity, my purpose of staying alive may, in fact, be incompatible with other people's purposes of staying alive.

Gewirth says:

(a) If a rational agent is to claim any rights at all, could anything be a more urgent object of his claim than the necessary conditions of his engaging both in action in general and in successful action? (b) If he regards these conditions as indeed necessary for the very possibility of his agency and for his chances of succeeding in his actions, then must he not hold that all other persons ought at least to refrain from interfering with the conditions? Since this "ought" entails correlative rights insofar as it signifies what the agent regards as his due, the latter question may also be put in the following equivalent form: Must not the agent hold that he has rights to these necessary conditions of his agency? [pp. 63–64]

Now, the answer to (a) clearly is that nothing would be more urgent for the agent, but that really does not help Gewirth's argument at all. If he has any rights at all, then they will be pointless if he is never able to exercise them, but that does not show that he has any rights at all. And the answer to (b), on the face of it, is no. I may need the lifebuoy if I am to survive, but I cannot reasonably conclude from that that others ought to let me have it, especially in a sense of "ought" that entails correlative rights. Gewirth stresses that the argument operates within the standpoint of the agent, so we might want to say that from my point of view they ought to give me the lifebuoy, that it would be a good thing for me if they did. But this sense of "ought" carries no correlative rights; it gives nobody else any reason for acting at all, and certainly does not show that they are under a duty. If the agent regards the lifebuoy as his due in any ordinary sense of the word "due," then he is simply confused. There may be senses of the words "good," "rights" and "due" in which we can proceed in this way from one to the other, but they are not senses restricted to the viewpoint of the agent; they are senses that apply interpersonally and deal with reasons for different people to act.

The crucial point here is that nobody but the agent is given any reason to act, which is unsurprising given that we stay within the agent's viewpoint. Simply the fact that I want or need something is no reason for anybody else to do anything, especially if they might want or need it as much as or more than I. That nobody else has a reason to act means that "others ought to refrain," "I have a right that others refrain," and "others' refraining is my due" are not used in their ordinary senses. For Gewirth's argument to work, these phrases must be translated in terms of the agent's viewpoint, and then they are equivalent. (They were all introduced in terms of something's being good for me or my wanting it, and each of them is equivalent to that.)

Gewirth explains a right as a reason-based demand (p. 74). There is a sense of "demand," as when I receive letters with the words "final demand" at the top in red, in which one who demands must have authority in the sense of the right to insist. This sense, clearly, would be question-begging, so we must take it that Gewirth means something like reason-based insistence. But not just any reason for insisting will serve as a ground for a right. Perhaps you have done the washing up, for the last week, but I might nevertheless try to insist that you do it again. If my reason is that the housework is divided up so that I do the cooking and you do the washing up, then I have a right that you do the washing up instead of leaving it for me. It would be unfair of you to leave the washing up for me. If my reason for insisting is that, though we agreed that you would do the cooking and I the washing up, now that the time has come I should prefer to continue reading my book, then I make a reason-based insistence that you do the washing up but I have no right that you do it. Rights are backed by reasons about certain sorts of interpersonal relationships, such as the making of an agreement or promise, though agreement and promise do not exhaust the field. It is because rights arise interpersonally that they can settle interpersonal disputes, which is their point.

Gewirth, though, simply means a reason-based demand in general.[25] A right may be interpersonal in that one makes the demand of somebody else, but the reasons need not be concerned with anything interpersonal. A demand based solely on my interests will be a right.

I have reasons for making the demand, but they are not reasons for you to respond. That is, in any ordinary sense, they do not show that you have a duty, and thus the right will fail to resolve any dispute between us. Indeed, you would have a right contrary to mine if you have reason to reject my demand. One might introduce the word "duty" as a correlative of a right explained in Gewirth's way, but one would need then to be clear that "X has a duty to Y" means simply "Y has reasons for wanting X to behave in a certain way." It does not imply anything about the propriety or reasonableness of X's not behaving in that way. With rights and duties introduced in this way, strictly within the viewpoint of the agent, Gewirth has not yet managed to get the agent in touch with other people or *their* reasons for acting. The rights to freedom and well-being for which Gewirth has been arguing so far are "prudential rights," based simply on reasons about the interests of the agent and not reaching out at all to touch other people's reasons for acting.

Gewirth supports the claim that rights are no more than reason-based demands by reference to a list of what he calls intellectual or logical rights (pp. 69–71), which he takes to show that the reasons need not even be moral or legal. These intellectual or logical rights are rights to assert, believe, assume, consider, infer, and so on. He stresses elsewhere, though, that the rights he is concerned with are Hohfeldian rights that have correlative duties, and his list of intellectual and logical rights certainly does not fit that pattern (though one might note that Ayer takes it that his "right to be sure" has to be earned). A point about Hohfeldian privileges will not do for Gewirth: that his agent, considered from his own isolated point of view and completely apart from relationships to anybody else, is under no obligation to anybody else, is a fact that would neither surprise anybody nor help Gewirth's argument.

In all but one of the cases that Gewirth cites, though, what is at issue is that it is permissible, or generally okay, to make certain moves, and this is an analogical extension of a Hohfeldian legal privilege. To have a Hohfeldian privilege to do X is to be under no duty not to do X, so that one is permitted to do X. One can see easily how that construction can be taken over and applied in terms of what is permitted by, say, the laws of logic, but that application implies nothing whatsoever about duties or Hohfeldian rights. To say that we have a logical right to the use of teleological concepts, for example, is simply to say that their use is not ruled out by the laws of logic. If the skeptic insists that we have no right to assume that other things are known, then he is insisting that such an assumption is not logically permitted. In neither case is anything implied about duties or Hohfeldian rights.

The one exception to this pattern in Gewirth's list is "The right to have one's conjectures taken seriously must be earned by prolonged immersion in the historical sources," where what is at issue is a claim that others have a duty to take one's conjectures seriously. This example will not serve to make Gewirth's point, though. It is not simply an intellectual or logical right: it is a moral right, concerned with the morality of life in the intellectual community. What is at issue is not a right to assert or believe, but a right to take up people's time. The point of the remark is that it is improper to insist that people simply waste their time on you. If you want them to have to take you seriously, then you must earn that right by doing your bit. Again, the point is that rights have to be earned; they must be won from other people, interpersonally. That is a severe limitation on the sort of reason on which a Hohfeldian right can be based, and a limitation that, at least apparently, rules out prudential rights based simply on what I want or need considered without any question of my relationship to other people.

Gewirth writes:

> if any agent denies that he has the generic rights, then he is caught in a contradiction. Suppose some agent were to deny or refuse to accept the judgment (1) "I have rights to freedom and well-being." Because of the equivalence between generic rights and strict "oughts," this denial of (1) would entail the agents' denial of (2) "All other persons ought at least to refrain from interfering with my freedom and well-being'. By denying (2), the agent would have to accept (3) "It is not the case that all other persons ought at least to refrain from interfering with my freedom and well-being." But how can any agent accept (3) and also accept (4) "My freedom and well-being are necessary goods"? [p. 80]

Now, Gewirth stresses that what he is concerned with are Hohfeldian rights with their correlative duties, and it seems perfectly clear that I can think it a good thing that I win a competition (that is, I can want to win the competition, or have that as my purpose) without thinking that others have a duty to let me win, and thus without thinking that I have a Hohfeldian right to win. That the goods at issue for Gewirth are necessary goods (that is, goods that I must have if I am to have various other goods, and perhaps goods that I must have if I am even to remain alive) does not change the case. In times of scarcity we might have to compete for necessary goods, such as food or the one remaining lifebuoy. The only way in which Gewirth can avoid this problem is by redefining all the relevant words in terms of the agent's point of view: that something is necessary for the agent to act is equivalent to its being a necessary good; its being a necessary good is equivalent to his having a right to it; his having a right to it is equivalent to its being his due. But it must be recognized that these are redefinitions. Words such as "good," "rights," and "due" take their meanings publicly from relationships between people, not from the point of view of one particular person. Because of the way in which Gewirth has had to redefine the words, they never take him beyond the viewpoints of the particular agent. Reason of this sort cannot relate people to each other; it remains solipsistic.

What Gewirth says about competition (p. 92) reinforces this point. There is competition between, say, bank robbers and police, he says, and this might appear to pose a problem for his argument in that it seems that the robbers must say "We ought to rob this bank," a prescription based on the justifying ground of their own interest, and conclude from this that other people (including the police) ought at least to refrain from interfering with their robbing the bank. The robbers will recognize, though, that the police will try to interfere on justifying grounds of their own. How can the speakers hold, then, that each ought to be free to perform his actions? The entailment still holds, however, so Gewirth claims. "I ought to rob this bank" does entail "We ought to be free to rob this bank without interference" when the same criteria (the robbers' interests) are applied. When we change to other criteria, legal criteria, we get the conclusion that the police ought to stop the robbers. That is to say, Gewirth's response is simply that it remains true from the robbers' viewpoint that they ought not to be interfered with and true from the police's viewpoint that they ought to be stopped. This shows the vacuity of this notion of "ought," the way in which it fails to tie up with reasons for others to act. References to what ought to be done or to rights will not remove the competition or settle any dispute; the participants will remain in their own quite separate spheres of reasoning.

Because of the way he has set this up, Gewirth's attempt to get people together and to set up human rights is doomed to failure. As long as one is a prospective agent with purposes one wants to fulfill, he argues, one must hold that *as such* one has rights to freedom and well-being and hence that everybody else who satisfies that description has those rights (p. 108). But just as my having these rights implied nothing about others' having any reason to act in any particular way, so recognizing that they have the same rights gives me no reason to act in any particular way. The individual people are still not rationally related to each other and do not form a community. The same point applies to Gewirth's claim that "Their right to freedom means that just as the agent holds that he has a right to control whether or not he will participate in transactions, so his recipients have the right to control whether or not they will partici-pate. Hence the agent ought to refrain from interfering with their

freedom by coercing them" (p. 134). The most that would follow is
that the agent ought, *from the point of view of the others*, to refrain from
interfering; it does not follow that he ought to refrain from his own
point of view or that he simply ought to refrain. Those sorts of
conclusions would follow only if words such as "ought" and "right"
were used in their more normal senses, and that, as we have seen,
would mean that the early steps of Gewirth's argument collapsed.

So, having started out with an isolated individual, Gewirth has
ended only with a lot of isolated individuals and with no rights that
will relate them to each other. Such rights can be explained only if we
start with consideration of community and the relations between
people.

This does not mean, though, that reference to human rights must
be completely pointless. There is a problem here, even if talk about
rights is not a precise way of dealing with it. There are no human
rights, but common talk about human rights has, even if mislead-
ingly, located problems of moral importance. Rights may depend on
convention and cooperation, but some sense can still be given to the
idea of human rights in a vague way that cannot be translated into the
precision required of real rights. It is really a point about virtues,
rather than about rights, and especially about the raw form of
injustice. Perhaps any particular convention can be dispensed with,
and it might even be a mark of a convention that it can be dismantled
and cease to exist simply as a result of agreement between people, but
it does not follow that all conventions could be dispensed with so that
there would be no conventions. Perhaps disposing of some conventions can be done only if we replace them with others. There might be
classes of conventions such that any community must have some
member of each class even though there is no particular convention
that every community must have. Perhaps every community must
have some sort of property system, for example. It seems plausible to
say that every community must have some way of allocating goods,
even if not all communities have the same way. Every community
must have some prohibition on killing people, though the prohibition
will be partly determined by convention and will differ from one
community to another. I have argued that every community must
have some public procedure, though one community's decision-
procedure need not be the same as another's. This possibility might
allow us to talk in a general way about human rights, provided that
the way of talking was sufficiently general to reflect its dependence
on classes of conventions rather than on particular conventions. We
could not talk about human rights to private property and certainly
could not talk about a human right to four weeks' paid holidays a
year, but we might sensibly be able to talk about a human right to a

fair return for one's work. Such a remark would be very general and would have to lead to argument about such things as what counts as a fair return, but there could be a point to it nonetheless. Its point is that it locates the areas for argument. In a similar way, we might be able to make sense of talk about a human right to life. Reference to such a right would not settle any arguments, but it locates where the arguments have to go on and points toward the presupposition against killing people. And while we might not be able to talk sensibly of a human right to trial by jury, it might make sense to talk of a human right to an impartial hearing when accused of crime.

I referred earlier to the presupposition against killing people,[26] and that point can be called on again here to explain part of the significance of talk about human rights. The presupposition against killing people is different from and stronger than the presupposition against causing pain: the presupposition against causing pain is concerned with cruelty and callousness, which are vices the nastiness of which is unaffected by reciprocity and which are not concerned with rights. In that way, the claims imposed by the notion of cruelty may be more wide-ranging and longer-lasting than those imposed by the notion of injustice: that somebody has behaved abominably may mean that it is no longer unjust for me wantonly to hurt him, but it does not affect the cruelty of my wantonly hurting him. The morality of the presupposition against killing people centers much more around the idea of rights. Infringing against that presupposition is displaying the raw form of injustice.

One might conform to the requirements of justice out of a variety of motives: because one has a sense of justice, for example, or because one is afraid of the consequences of not doing so. Somebody who conforms simply out of fear is likely to be more concerned with the mere letter of the law and finding loopholes to defeat its point; such a person is lacking in a sense of justice.

There are, I have suggested, areas in which any community must have one of a class of conventions, even though there is no one convention that all communities must have. It is in these areas that one can display the raw form of injustice even though no convention has yet grown up; one does so by acting in a manner contrary to the point that the relevant class of conventions has. In the absence of specific conventions, nobody has specific rights (is euthanasia, defense against rape, or defense of property an adequate defense against a charge of murder?), but one can still so act as to display an inadequate sense of justice and a lack of aptness for social life. Somebody who kills people for the sheer joy of it displays this. He might, out of fear or prudence, conform to the conventions in a community constituted by others, but he cannot be the norm or there would be no community and no chance to set up rights. He can display the relevant and objectionable quality of character even where there are no conventions: if, as an explorer to previously uncharted lands, he comes across a community that has had no previous contact with his own, then there will be no established conventions governing behavior between him and these people; nevertheless, he will display the raw form of injustice if he proceeds to kill them for fun. He will display a quality of character that, if common, would make community and the generation of rights impossible. Because of the relationship between the quality of character and the possibility of generating rights, and because of the absence of conventions in such a case, we might want to think of the case as one involving infringement of a natural or human right to life. This, I suppose, is unobjectionable as long as we recognize that we cannot list specific natural or human rights in such a way that they can be called on to settle any complex and detailed argument about propriety. A natural or human right not to be killed just for fun would not affect debate very much, because it has no real bearing on the actual cases in which an appeal is made to a right to life: cases concerning abortion, political killings, the place of civilians in wartime, and so on. If somebody did approach me with a view to killing me for fun, I should not expect to gain anything of practical value by engaging him in a debate about theories of natural or human rights. Specific rights are determined by specific cooperative ways of doing things, but the presupposition against killing people has an important part to play in the overall argument.

As well as the point about classes of conventions, there is the possibility that there are necessary conditions for cooperation such that one can sensibly talk of people's having a human right to them. One cannot cooperate without some rationality, but it makes no sense to say that people have a human right to rationality. On the other hand, it can be argued that one cannot cooperate properly if one is starving among wealthy people, so that it could be argued that people have a human right to welfare services.[27] Just what welfare services anybody had a right to would depend on facts about such matters as how much wealth the community had, but again the area for argument has been marked out.

Human rights as necessary conditions for cooperation still depend on convention and cooperation. People have them, not as human beings, but as communal beings. And not everybody need have the rights. In conditions of great scarcity it may be impossible for everybody to live, and thus impossible for everybody to live as a member of a community. Human rights could not operate in such conditions, which approach the Hobbesian state of nature. And if somebody behaves sufficiently badly it may be impossible for others to live with him as a member of the community, in which case he will not have human rights. Even these human rights are alienable.

It might seem that there are some rights that we must have, and even some legal rights that we must have. There is more than one reasonable legal system, so perhaps nobody *necessarily* has a right to a jury trial, to payment of legal expenses from the public exchequer, and so on. Perhaps, in some small communities, one might reasonably not have the right to a formal trial at all: we do not normally regard formal trials as being necessary within a family. But, surely, no matter what the legal system, one has a right not to be framed? One has, indeed, a right not to be framed, but it is not really a right that one has quite apart from membership of any community. To frame somebody is, essentially, to put on a show of trying him, but not to follow all the rules. Trying somebody is treating him as a member of the community, bound by its public procedure. Framing somebody is treating him as a member of the community and denying him the rights that he should have in that capacity. Framing somebody necessarily infringes his rights because it involves the procedure of trying him, which requires that he be regarded as a member of the community.

Human rights, if we are to make even vague sense of that notion, must be expressed fairly generally as, for example, the right to a proper return for one's work rather than as a right to have "rest and leisure, including reasonable limitation of working hours and periodic holidays with pay,"[28] a right that would make no sense at all in a subsistence farming economy. Ordinary rights are often, at least popularly, expressed in a similarly imprecise way. "I have a right to do whatever I want in my own home," I may say. If I am responding to attempts by others to persuade me that I should do better to have somebody competent paint a mural in the kitchen rather than to take on the job myself, then others may readily agree with my assertion of that right. They may also say that that was not the point: what was at issue was not whether I had the right, but how good my judgment was in choosing to exercise the right in a particular way. It seems fairly clear, as we ordinarily live our lives, that I have a right to paint a mural in my own kitchen even if I should not make a very good job of it. Because the point seems obvious, and because it depends on the house's being mine, rather than on its being a mural that I want to paint, my audience would probably accept quite readily in that context that I had a right to do whatever I wanted in my own house.

If I have a right to do whatever I want in my own house, then, clearly, it is a right that can clash with other rights and a right that can properly be overridden. My right to do what I want in my own house will clash with my neighbor's right to do what he wants in his house if he wants to sleep after a hard day's work and I want to practice the trumpet at 3:00 A.M. If rights are to settle that clash of interests, then somebody's right to do what he wants in his own house will have to be overridden.

Anybody who defended his playing the trumpet at 3:00 A.M. by saying that he had a right to do whatever he wanted in his own house would be regarded as frivolous and irresponsible. "Perhaps," we might reply, "but not to play the trumpet when everybody else is trying to sleep." And what this shows is that that particular expression of a right, under which clashes of right would be unavoidable and overriding of rights necessary, is imprecise. Such an assertion of a right usually appears to be unobjectionable because there is a range of things that it is proper for me to do provided that I do them in my own house, and because the general claim is usually employed in a responsible fashion to draw attention to this fact. But when we get down to the nitty-gritty, nobody would take seriously as a precise claim that one had the right to do whatever one wanted in one's own house. That I am careful to lure my victims inside before battering them to death does not mean that I am within my rights in killing them.

This particular class of apparent clashes of rights and proper overridings of rights is easily dealt with. It is merely apparent, arising from imprecise expression of the rights. My neighbor has a right that I not play the trumpet at 3:00 A.M., and I have no right that clashes with that. There might be harder cases of this sort (we might need to refer to a public procedure to determine whether my neighbor has a right that I not paint the outside of my house puce with pink spots), but the principle is the same.

Another way in which imprecision can suggest clashes and overridings of rights is suggested by Judith Jarvis Thomson's example:[29]

> Surely you do have a right that people will not break into your freezer and take a steak. If you had no such right, why would I have a duty to compensate you later for having done so? The fact that compensation *is* owing shows (and it seems to me shows conclusively) that I did do something you had a right that I not do.

A right that people not break into my freezer and take a steak is, in some respects, like a right to do whatever I want in my own house. If that particular steak has been discovered to contain a bomb, set to explode in ten minutes and capable of demolishing the whole apartment building, it would be irresponsible to suggest that others have no right to remove the steak to a place of safety. That people are, by and large, responsible about the assertions of such rights as the right not to have somebody break into the freezer and take a steak sometimes hides quite a bit about the detailed limitations on such rights. We tend to accept their assertions in a general form because they are not asserted where they would cause trouble. Nevertheless, slighly bizarre examples bring out that the rights are limited and that people who assert them in the very general form cannot be taken seriously as meaning exactly what they say.

That a government compensates somebody when it uses the power of eminent domain to acquire his land for a new airport or a new highway does not show, despite Thomson's suggestion, that the government recognizes that it had no right to acquire the land or that the previous owner had a right that the land not be acquired. Nor does it suggest that the land did not really belong to the previous owner beforehand. What it shows is that the previous owner's property rights in the land were limited in a fairly complex way. Along with limitations on his using the land as an explosives-testing site or as a trumpet-practicing area at 3:00 A.M., there was a limitation that he could not retain what rights he had to the land if the public interest required that he give them up. And because the acquisition of his land by the government means that he bears an especially heavy burden for the benefit of the community, justice requires that that last limitation itself be limited by a requirement that the government pay compensation when it acquires the land. It is not that the previous owner's rights were merely a disjunctive right either to have the land or to be compensated, because not just anybody can compulsorily purchase his land, and the government cannot do so merely at whim, but only on grounds of public interests. The right is a very complex one. Payment of compensation is recognition of one part of that complexity, not recognition that a right has been violated. Thomson's example of the steak and the freezer fits the same pattern.[30]

That there are such limitations on property rights need not be a random matter. If the institution of property has some particular point, such as the point of enabling people to have reasonable security by giving them the chance to provide today for needs that they will have tomorrow when they might be ill and unable to work or when famine might strike, then such a point would itself suggest limitations on property rights.[31] If everybody will have more such security if a particular piece of land is acquired through eminent domain, and if provision of compensation will protect the previous owner against loss, then the point of having the institution of property suggests a limitation on property rights by the possibility of compulsory purchase in certain circumstances. That is not a random limitation, but a rational working out of rights.

I referred earlier to the possibility that rights might come into conflict when they arise in different institutions that grow for a while without coming into contact with each other. If such institutions do eventually run up against each other, then we might find that rights in one clash with rights in the other. Such clashes reveal imperfections in human arrangements, but imperfection in human arrangements is a common matter. Such clashes need to be resolved, and the line of argument that I have just been following suggests a rational way of resolving them without moving outside the sphere of rights and having either of the clashing rights overruled by considerations of, say, public interest. If the institutions have managed to come into conflict, then they must have some common ground. It is within that area that the clashing rights will have to be limited if they are to fit together so that the clash is resolved, and within that area it will be possible to argue in terms of the points of the institutions.

Notes

1. Stephen Davies has drawn to my attention that Wittgenstein made a similar point about "same" in Part I of *Philosophical Investigations* (Oxford: Basil Blackwell, 1958).
2. Though you might take the second-order view that your employees' views should be considered.
3. There is a logical relationship between private and public procedures: the public procedure can be understood to be binding, and thus effective, only in terms of private procedures. There is some sort of chronological parallel to this: procedures for resolving disputes can be called on only after disputes have arisen. In both ways, the private procedure is primary. This does not imply, though, that government must be restricted to an umpiring function. I shall take this point up in Chapter 8.
4. That coin-tossing is a possible way, even if not the ideal way, of resolving disputes seems to undermine the dependence thesis advanced by Joseph Raz in "Authority and Justification," *Philosophy and Public Affairs* 14, 1 (Winter 1985), according to which a legitimate authority ought to act on reasons that could have been reasons for those subject to its decisions. That is not a possibility in the case of coin-tossing. Lest it be thought that in a case such as coin-tossing there must be nobody in authority, consider the case of the Victorian State election in March 1985. The last seat to be decided for the Legislative Council was Nunawading; after the votes were counted, two candidates were tied. Mrs. Kath Leonard, the divisional returning officer for the province of Nunawading, exercised her casting vote by drawing a name from a hat. It was an appropriate method in those circumstances precisely because the job of the returning officer in such a situation is to resolve the dispute about who is to sit in the seat. She might achieve that end by taking sides on the merits, or by a method such as she employed.
5. What goes before the procedure might be conflicting private judgments

about who has what rights. Such a case of conflicting views about rights is not the same as a case of conflicting rights. Other apparent cases of conflicting rights appear in Chapter 6.

6. This point about the role of rights in the settlement of disputes is completely overlooked by R. G. Frey in *Interests and Rights* (Oxford: Clarendon Press, 1980), pp. 10–12, in his argument for the superfluity of rights. Loren Lomasky's interesting paper "Personal Projects as the Foundation for Basic Rights," in *Social Philosophy and Policy* (Spring 1984) brings out the role of rights in dealing with conflicting aims of different people, but does not notice the underlying significance of more basic cooperation in the distribution of rights.

7. The idea of a community is a movable one. It may be a family in one case, a neighborhood in another, a whole nation, or even, in some cases, humanity. Actions that could affect the whole world, such as starting a nuclear war, make common action to achieve or avoid some outcome necessary, and can lead to thinking of everybody as one community in those contexts.

8. This need not be a bad thing, given the movability of the idea of a community. A community's collapse would not necessarily have us in our Hobbesian natural condition. People might appeal to a wider international community, for example, to justify attempts to cause the collapse of the state under which they live if they thought that state was infringing rights of the wider community. Success in such an endeavor would mean the collapse of one community in favor of another, not the collapse of community as such.

9. The hard argument for taking this interpretation of paternalism is the argument for saying that community is possible only if rights are definitive.

10. See Griffiths, "Representation," *Proceedings of the Aristotelian Society*, Supplementary Volume, 1960.

11. I set aside for the moment arguments that the system of slavery served the interests of the slaves much better than emancipation would and made them better off than free laborers, arguments common in the antebellum southern United States.

12. This point is taken further below. See Chapter 4.

13. See also earlier in this chapter.

14. Contra John Finnis, *Natural Law and Natural Rights* (Oxford: Oxford University Press, 1980), pp. 29–33.

15. Natural law is different. It is common to distinguish between descriptive and prescriptive laws: between laws such as "$e = mc^2$" on the one hand, and laws such as "A port-tack yacht shall keep clear of a starboard-tack yacht" on the other. The one sort of law is true or false, the other is obeyed or disobeyed. Hobbes, though, ran these two notions of law together. His laws of nature set out ways in which people were required to behave, but the test for what was a law of nature was what was necessary for people to live in a community (or, as he put it, what was required for people to emerge from their natural condition and enter civil society). Hobbes's laws of nature, therefore, could be discovered by empirical investigation, and are not dependent for their effectiveness on people's accepting them or believing in them. The disagreement objection does not hold against this sort of natural law.

16. See below, Chapter 7.

17. The term "autonomy" has come to be used, especially by those concerned with the philosophy of mind, in a sense very close to what I mean
by "agency." It is used to refer to somebody's will, capacity to reason and
make decisions, and so on. It is easy to see how this shift has occurred,
but I should stress that I use the word "autonomy" to refer to somebody's independence, not to his psychological capacity to make use of his
independence. Psychological autonomy is sometimes taken to justify or
require the sort of autonomy I am concerned with, and the two are
closely linked, but they are not the same thing.

18. R. P. Wolff, *In Defence of Anarchism* (New York: Harper Torchbook, 1970)
consistently takes autonomy to be something asocial and runs the notion
of political autonomy into that of psychological autonomy. He assumes
that capacity to reason is a sufficient condition for possession of rights,
but he is mistaken. Capacity to reason, by itself, lacks the element of
reciprocity. One might use that capacity to work out plans for being nasty
to people, and being nasty to people means giving up one's rights rather
than generating more of them. This asocial notion of autonomy also
commits Wolff to a strange idea of the political, taking political freedom
to be decision-making isolation as though the Hobbesian state of nature
were a state of political freedom. Politics is a replacement for war,
including a war of each against all. It is not a matter of isolation, but of
dealing with competing views and interests and trying to resolve the
disputes peacefully. The individualism that stresses isolation is a nonpo-
litical position. It may free one from various things (taxes, conscription,
etc.), but it does not constitute a *political* status.

19. Alan Gewirth, *Reason and Morality* (Chicago: University of Chicago Press,
1978) and *Human Rights* (Chicago: University of Chicago Press, 1982).
Unless otherwise specified, page references in the text are to *Reason and
Morality*.

20. This does not mean, as Gewirth (*Human Rights*, pp. 70–71) seems to
assume in his reply to Golding, that they depend on agreements reached
by all the people involved. Sometimes people do not realize all the ways
in which they cooperate, let alone consciously agree to them, and the
parties with rights need not themselves be (full) members of the cooperative enterprise (see Chapter 4).

21. This does not mean that those responding to the problem of containing
him could not be cruel, humane, merciful, or display any number of
virtues or vices in the way in which they dealt with the problem.

22. He sets this method out on pp. 42–47 of *Reason and Morality*.

23. Thomas Hobbes, *Leviathan* (Harmondsworth: Pelican, 1968), p. 120.

24. And if there were nobody else there, so that this problem did not arise,
then reference to rights would be pointless.

25. The position is slightly more complicated than this, since Gewirth allows
that something's seeming good to somebody is not a sufficient condition
of his claiming a right to it. The criteria by which it seems good to him,
the agent might acknowledge, may be outweighed in importance by
other opposed criteria, as when one considers stealing from a widow in
order to be able to buy a transistor radio (p. 77).

26. See Chapter 2.

27. See below, Chapter 8.

28. Universal Declaration of Human Rights adopted and proclaimed by the
General Assembly of the United Nations on 10 December 1948, Article
24.

29. Judith Jarvis Thomson, "Self-Defense and Rights," The Lindley Lecture, University of Kansas, 1976.
30. Herbert Morris raises similar points in his discussion of the tort doctrine of incomplete privilege. See Herbert Morris, "The Status of Rights," *Ethics* (October 1981), pp. 48ff.
31. I have no intention of trying to argue out here the point of the institution of property (if it has one point). My unwillingness to argue out the detail of that particular example does not undercut the importance of argument about the point of an institution in attempts to determine rights reasonably.

4

Roles and Requirement

ONE OF MY AIMS is to show how rights fit into a virtues theory that explains morality in terms of qualities of character. Rights go with justice, so my thesis that rights must be definitive means that justice must impose requirements in a way in which the other virtues do not. This is a thesis that is likely to strike any decent person as strange, so it needs to be explained and defended. To explain it I shall need to distinguish between first-person and third-person cases, a distinction that might be expressed as being between the subjective feeling of requirement and the logic of requirement, because there can be no question that the subjective feeling of requirement can be the same in the cases of justice and, for example, of kindness.

It seems clear that there is a difference between justice and, say, kindness when it comes to requirement. This comes out in several ways. One is that kindness involves something beyond the call of duty: somebody who restricts his helping of others to what can strictly be required of him, who pays his debts but will never make a gift or a loan, is not kind. Kindness operates in a different dimension from the sort of requirement involved in debts (and, though monetary debts are the simplest example to take, the point applies to any proper debt, or debt of justice). Another difference, related to the first, is in the role of motivation. Whether a person is just or unjust is a matter of his character, but justice is special among the virtues in the way in which it attaches to the act: somebody can be forced to pay his debts, and he has then paid his debts, though unwillingly; justice has been done even if he was not just. One cannot, in the same way, force somebody to be kind and thus have kindness done. Kindness is very much a matter of motivation; it is more a matter of motivation than of the act. A kind act is, among other things, an act performed out of concern for the other's plight and out of warm feelings toward him; that, more than what the act amounts to on some more impersonal assessment, is what makes it a case of kindness. That is why a kind attempt to help, even if unsuccessful, can have such significance for the recipient. An act performed because of coercion or requirement, therefore, is not an act of kindness even if the beneficiaries are as well off, and in the same way, as they would have been had it been an act of kindness. (If I perform the act because of a requirement I impose on myself that I behave like a decent person, the act might be conscientious or in some other way meritorious. Nevertheless, I have not been kind if the act had that motivation.)

There are reasons why there should be such differences between justice and other virtues such as kindness. The life that people live is ineluctably cooperative. It is not simply that cooperation is a good thing for people; it is necessary for them. In this context of cooperation we can see why justice and kindness are different, and also why each of them is a virtue. The point is not merely one about helping with the washing up, or anything of that sort. The most basic form of cooperation is in the recognition of mutual limitations in the form of decision-procedures (be the procedure a shared concept of justice or a formal second-order procedure) to resolve disagreements of judgments or clashes of interests. Without that we should be in a Hobbesian state of nature in which human life could not have lasted beyond one generation. Without a sense of justice, cooperation is impossible: people must, by and large, be prepared to recognize the mutual limitations as requirements. If somebody will not do his bit or pay his debts, then we cannot cooperate with him. So justice is the basic virtue for people: if people were not, by and large, naturally willing to do their bit or to keep their covenants made, then community would be impossible and human life would be impossible. If somebody will do his bit and keep his covenants made, then we can cooperate with him. If he recognizes the mutual limitations, refrains from wantonly killing others, and so on, then we can get by with him, but life with somebody who would go no further than that would not be very pleasant. It is in the nature of things that cooperation is easier, and is likely to be wider-spread, with people who are kind, generous, tolerant, and so on. All of these are virtues, too, though they play a different role from that of justice.[1] A sense of justice is a quality of character necessary in people, by and large, if they are to cooperate. Because it is necessary, it also attaches more to the act, and its requirements can properly be imposed by coercion on those whose sense of justice is deficient. Kindness helps cooperation and makes for a better life, but it is not necessary to cooperation and community as justice is, so it does not impose requirements in the same way that justice does. Nevertheless, that is not the way things feel when we are working out what to do, and if it does seem clear that the requirements of kindness are of a different sort from those of justice, it is not clear what the nature of each sort of requirement is.

My main concern in this chapter is to explain the differences in these sorts of requirements so that I can explain the sense in which claim-rights can be the basis of a strong requirement. I shall examine sorts of requirements that come up in friendship and a sort of requirement that appears in private but not in public judgment to explain what sort of requirement is involved in having a right. This will lead into a little more consideration of how rights are generated, since the strong requirement comes from the considerations of justice that generate the rights. I shall begin with the claim that the requirements of kindness are of a different sort from those of justice.

My thesis is likely to strike a decent person as strange because, for such a person, the subjective feeling of requirement is likely to be much the same in the cases of justice and kindness. If such a person promises to turn up at 10:00 A.M., in the absence of special circumstances, he will feel bound to turn up at 10:00 A.M. If he comes across somebody who is very upset, and if he can, by an innocent action and without very much trouble, relieve that distress, then he will feel just as much bound to do so as he did to keep his promise. In ordinary, everyday cases of kindness, no decent person would feel that he was doing something supererogatory or especially laudable. Such an act would strike him as one than which he could not do less, as an act about which he had very little choice. (That one feels that one has little choice about such matters is something that shows that one is a decent person, not something that shows that one lacks "free will" and is not responsible for what one does.) In a lot of everyday cases, failing to be kind is not acting neutrally, but is itself enough to count as being cruel, or at least callous, and no decent person would consider that prospect with equanimity. Cases of great kindness would, no doubt, be different. If one had to go to a lot of trouble to relieve another's distress, then one might feel that one was being self-sacrificing or that a lot was being expected of one. One might feel the burden. This will not do the job of distinguishing the subjective feelings, though. In the same way, when justice requires that one go to a lot of trouble, one might feel that one was being self-sacrificing or that a lot was being expected of one, and if one had felt a temptation not to be kind, then one would probably feel a similar temptation not to be just.

If, in order to be kind or decent or just, one must do X, then kindness or decency or justice requires that one do X, and there is no obvious difference between them in that respect. Nor is there obviously anything special about them, because, in exactly the same way, unkindness, indecency, and injustice will require that one do not-X. There seems to be nothing special about the requirement. The only apparent difference between the cases is that one ought to be kind, decent, and just.

Nor is the difference that, whatever one may require of oneself, in the third person one can properly take notice of somebody else's injustice but should ignore other failings such as unkindness. One may quite properly note the whole range of human failings in somebody else. If one will have a great deal to do with somebody, or is in the position of deciding whether or not to have a great deal to do with somebody, one would be foolish to ignore his callousness, lack of consideration, and cruelty. Nor need one keep these points to oneself. Knowledge that somebody is cruel might quite properly be passed on to others, especially if it will help them to avoid harm, and there need be nothing improper in trying to persuade somebody to do the kind thing. Sometimes it might not be my business to try to persuade somebody to do the kind thing, but sometimes it is not my business to try to persuade somebody to be just. If the person to whom the promise was made wants to make no objection when it is broken, it is simply no business of mine to interfere unless it was somebody such as my son who broke the promise. And it is not always clear that justice is more important than kindness, either. Certainly some injustices can be forgiven more readily than some unkindness and would be taken to reflect less badly on somebody's honor or decency. A minor injustice performed in favor of my son when he was gravely threatened would not reflect nearly as badly on me as my failure to perform a major kindness for somebody who had helped me in the past when I could have done so with little trouble. Anybody can succumb to great temptation, but it takes a thoroughly nasty fellow to care so little for everybody else.

Because it is traditional for moral philosophers to emphasise the impersonality of moral judgment, it is worth pointing out that there can be differences between first-person and third-person cases. We readily recognize that it makes sense to say "He is honestly mistaken" or "I was honestly mistaken" but not "I am honestly mistaken," and similar points come up elsewhere. Some things might quite properly be considered in third-person cases that cannot properly be considered in the first-person. If I see somebody performing, or contemplating the performance of, some reprehensible action, then, in the standard case, there could be no objection to my making due allowance for extenuating circumstances or even passing moods. Perhaps, depending on the action in question, I should still try to stop the person from acting, but making due allowance for extenuating circumstances shows understanding, proper concern for the person, and, in some cases, toleration. If I find myself performing, or contemplating the performance of, some reprehensible action, then my making allowance for extenuating circumstances shows self-indulgence and moral laxity. In reflecting on what I have done and

wondering whether I can live with myself I might make such allowance, but not when dealing with present or prospective action. Such
considerations are proper when making judgments, but not when
making decisions about what one will do. This sort of asymmetry
between first-person and third-person cases is important to the idea
of friendship. It also shows fairly clearly a way in which I must
require things of myself but need not require them of others.

A similar point, though not the same point, can be raised about
private and public judgment. I can certainly require that I meet my
own standards, but there is an important sense in which I cannot
require that others do so. I do not mean to suggest that my own
standards are something that I set for myself at whim: my standards
exercised in private judgment are my own judgment of the application of quite public notions such as justice and kindness, notions
determined by the nature of the world in which we live. They are
quite public notions, and I cannot, simply by fiat, make it the case
that any old thing counts as a reason for judging something to be just.
Nevertheless, people can differ in their judgments of how those
notions apply in particular cases or classes of cases, as I have already
pointed out in arguing the need for a public procedure. My private
judgment, taken by itself, does not give anybody else a reason to act,
so it does not provide any basis for a demand made on them. That
somebody else does something that is, in my private judgment,
unjust, does not by itself give any reason for saying that he displayed
the vice of injustice; it might show only that we differed in our
judgments of the situation and that the other person scrupulously did
what he thought was right. That I did something that was, in my
private judgment, unjust does give a reason for saying that I displayed the vice of injustice whether or not my private judgment was
correct.

We have cases of private judgment if each is his own judge, so the
point can be made by reference to a judge. The home plate umpire is
the sole judge of balls and strikes. He may ask a base umpire about
whether a batter swung, but he does not have to ask, and the final
judgment is his. Each of us stands to the subject-matter in cases of
private judgment, as the plate umpire does to judgments of balls and
strikes. He takes responsibility and he has the final say; nevertheless,
he employs quite public criteria that can be looked up in the rule book
(and appeal can be lodged against his knowledge of those criteria,
though not against his judgment in applying them), and he can make
mistakes even if he cannot be overruled. In the same way, in cases of
private decisions about what to do as much as in cases of public
decisions by a public procedure, public concepts such as justice are
employed. That each is final judge for himself does not mean that

each gets to set the rules for himself any more than does a plate umpire (though people and plate umpires can cheat or be incompetent). Because public notions of justice, kindness, or whatever are employed in both private and public judgment, the difference between private and public judgment with respect to requirement cannot show the difference between justice and kindness with respect to requirement. There is a sense in which I can require things of myself in a way in which I cannot require them of others, because I can require things of myself on the basis of my private judgment. But this will not explain the different sorts of requirements imposed by justice and by kindness, because *both* of these notions occur within private judgment as well as within public judgment.

The suggestion here, clearly, is not that private judgment or conscience is crudely opposed to publicly determined standards. Apart from the point about the use of public concepts, that there is a public procedure in operation is one thing that I ought to consider in making my private judgment of what it would be just for me to do in a case in which there has been disagreement on which the public procedure has ruled; the situation is not at all the same as it would have been had there been no public procedure. If the procedure is a properly binding one, it might impose restraints on me in directions in which I should not otherwise have recognized restraints: it might make it unjust for me to do what I should otherwise have regarded as just for me to do. Or it might release me from restraints: whereas I might have privately judged a particular restraint to be required by justice, determination by the public procedure that it was not required might quite properly lead me to make another private judgment that I should be foolish and, in a clear sense, unjust to myself if I imposed that restraint on myself when nobody else recognized it.

I can and do make judgments of others in the light of my own standards; that is, I can and do make private judgments of others. To do so is perfectly proper, and it would be foolish not to do so were I considering how far I could trust them in some particular enterprise or whether I wanted to mix with them. My private judgment by itself, though, gives nobody else a reason for acting, so it will not serve as the base for a requirement to be made of them. That I privately believe X to be just is something that others might consider in deciding what to do, but it is not something that I can properly force on them as a basis for action contrary to their own judgments. A justified demand on others, given that justification is distinguished from whim partly in that it is a public and interpersonal matter, depends on public judgment and a public decision-procedure. In that way, I cannot require that others fit in with my private standards. Addition of a public decision-procedure or a public role can be the basis of such a requirement: a parent dealing with an infant can properly require that the infant behave as the parent thinks right.

Friendship requires various sorts of action and attitudes, but that does not mean that friends can require those actions and attitudes of each other. Friendship, in the terms that I have just been using, is very much a first-person affair and not a matter of one person making demands on another. Good friends will be tolerant of each other and will make allowances for each other's moods and ways, so one might very well put up with some improper behavior and demands from the other. Though putting up with such demands in that way might be part of friendship, making the demands is not; if one demands things of one's friends as friends, then one is displaying a failing as a friend even if it is a fairly common example of human frailty. Friendship is a relationship in which one acts out of care for one's friend, not simply (and certainly not grudgingly) because one has debts. If one is acting only because one owes something and the other is calling in debts, then the relationship is not one of friendship. It is something far more impersonal in which one has been cast in the role of a debtor whose interests are not particularly to be considered.

This, of course, is a simplified picture, but it is at the core of the relationship between friends. One might have mixed motives, acting partly out of care for one's friend and partly because one feels one owes him something. If the friendship grew out of one doing some unowed service for the other or making some sacrifice for him, then the other may well feel a debt and look for the chance to repay it. But that is not at the center of the relationship, and the relationship does not end when the debt is paid, as does the relationship between me and a taxi-driver when I pay for my journey. Nor does friendship grow if the one who provided the original service immediately proceeds to treat it as the basis for a debt, insisting that the other cut his grass or read his proofs in return; that is much more like the commercial relationship that I have with the taxi-driver. If I owe him that debt for his service, then I do not owe him the special sort of debt that one owes friends. When my friend does me a service, I owe him a special, unquantifiable sort of debt based on the fact that the act was not performed to gain some specific service in return, as commercial acts are performed, but simply out of care for me. That the act was not performed to create a debt makes it the basis of the special sort of debt that one owes friends.[2]

Apart from such cases of mixed motives, one might act out of consideration for the long term. My friend might have displeased me recently, perhaps by telling me some important home truths; this is one of those helps for which one looks to friends, but it is not always pleasant and I might feel no inclination to help him at the moment.

My desire to further his interests for their own sake might be, temporarily, negligible. Nevertheless, realizing why he did what he did, and recognizing the importance of the friendship, I might manage to turn my thoughts away from my immediate inclinations and act as a friend should. Or, having joined in and helped me to do something last week, he might now call that in as a debt simply because he is, at times, an ill-tempered so-and-so. Being his friend, caring about his well-being, and realizing that he will think better of his attitude later, I may put up with the vagaries of his temper and go along with what he says. He might call in a debt from me because he sees that I am becoming ungrateful in my relationships with people and wants to help me stop my decline. Or, in a wider context, he might call in a debt from me because, apart from being my friend, he is a professional gardener who does my gardening and needs to be paid if he is to feed his family.

Behind all these complications to the original simplified picture lies the idea that friendship is a matter of acting out of care for the other, not out of a desire to repay debts of the sort for which repayment can be demanded. Demanding repayment changes the relationship, or at least shifts the focus to a commercial relationship that may exist along with the friendship but is not the same thing. The virtues shown toward each other by friends are virtues such as kindness and compassion, not justice.[3] Justice is a virtue shown in a relationship between people who can demand things of each other, even if such relationships often work better when polite requests, or a little leniency, replace the demands. Justice is a virtue shown in relationships such as that between employer and employee, not between friends.

The word "friend" is used very broadly, but friendship is, in the central case, a moral phenomenon.[4] The claim that somebody is not much of a friend is a remark about his character, and much more of a condemnation than the remark that he is not much of a carpenter. Failing as a friend is letting somebody down, and is a display of moral deficiency. One might develop an acquaintanceship with somebody because he is witty or cultivate somebody else because he is useful, but at the core of friendship is trust, and trust with a special basis. It is because of this trust that one can look to one's real friends to be told home truths even though they are unpalatable. The basis of my trust in a friend is not simply that I have some hold over him so that he fears me; that gives me a lackey rather than a friend. It is not simply that the person likes me and favors me over others; that might be somebody who made me feel good and might be pleasant company, but would not be somebody I could trust to tell me unpleasant truths that I need to know. Either of those relationships would be, at best, an imperfect friendship. In the ideal case, in terms of which we understand actual cases of friendship and can see why failing as a friend is a moral failing, I trust my friend because he is trustworthy. A good friend is a decent person: kind, honest, and so on. That, though not to the extent of perfection, is why friends are trusted. (Friendship in many ways usually falls short of the ideal simply because people are imperfect, and it is that that allows some of the ideal friendship to be shown by the friend of the one who falls short.) These are virtues that will be exhibited toward people who are not one's friends, too, but because friends know and understand each other better than do strangers, the virtues will have more chance to come into play between friends. They will have more chance to come into play between friends in another way, too: friends care about each other, so a friend's plight will move one sooner than somebody else's.

One cannot demand or require things of one's friends as friends, but one can expect things of them and in more than one sense. One might simply think it likely that they will behave in such a way as to help one, but one might also expect such behavior in a sense like that in which I might tell my son that I expect him to play with young Johnny when the guests arrive, the point of my remark being that I think it proper that he should do so and quite likely that he would not do so if left to his own devices. In this latter sense, somebody who fails to do what is expected of him does less well than he should have and is less good a person than he might be. He might have paid all his debts as they were called in, and it might be a matter of his having failed to do so with a smile. He might have returned a favor where no return could strictly be required, but he might have done so with poor grace. He might have failed to take an opportunity to help somebody when he could have done so with no great trouble. Whatever it was he did, it somehow showed a moral failing in him, and the moral failing need not be that of being unjust.

Friendship is, in the central case, a moral relationship, and failing as a friend is showing a moral failing. One can, therefore, expect things of one's friends in the strong sense; one can believe that they will show a moral failing in not acting so as to help one even if one could not expect that behavior of somebody else, no matter how decent he might be, who was not a friend. One's friends act out of special care for one, and can therefore be expected to be prepared to go further out of their way to help one than can ordinarily be expected of a decent person toward a stranger. Failure to be so prepared shows that one is less of a friend, that one's kindness, compassion, and so on are not as strong as they should be even in cases of special care. But because qualities such as kindness or compassion are at issue, performance cannot be demanded of a friend. One might befriend a lesser being or act as a friend toward a lesser being, but if we are friends we are equals and treat each other that way; the relationship is not that between patron and protégé, nor between master and servant. There is a difference between saying "Any decent person would do this" or "If you are any sort of a friend you will do this" on the one hand, and, on the other hand, "You owe me this." The person who owes is not treated as an equal, but as somebody subject to the decision of the other in this matter: he has the obligation and the other has the correlative right. The relationship is one of authority.

One can properly say such things as "You are supposed to be my friend" or "If you are any sort of a friend you will do this," because such remarks will draw to the attention of the other the importance one places on the matter at hand, but one can go no further. His being my friend, which is the basis of my hope and expectation for his help, is, in the relevant parts, his being prepared to act for my good for its own sake and off his own bat; if he is not prepared to do that, then I have nothing on which to base any demand. (It should also be borne in mind that, if we are friends, I should be prepared to act for his good for its own sake and to consider his wishes, so that I should be prepared not to press the point unnecessarily once it is clear that he disapproves or otherwise does not want to act. Friendship is more complicated than doing simple sums or applying simple formulae.) The situation is different if he is a tradesman who has accepted payment for promised services. In that case it does not matter that he now does not feel like doing the job or that he aesthetically disapproves of my having a pergola where I have paid him to build one and that, without being chivvied along, he would not do the job. The relationship between us is a much more impersonal one than friendship, and is such that it provides me with a basis on which to demand that he get down to work.

Friendship is an interesting and important phenomenon too little considered in moral philosophy, but the point here is about requirement rather than about friendship. Justice requires as one can require services from somebody whom one has paid for them. Kindness, compassion, benevolence, and so on, require as one expects something from a friend. This is clear from the role of motivation in these virtues. One cannot coerce kindness as one can coerce justice, because kindness is in the agent rather than in the act. In a very important way, justice is a matter of what is done and kindness a matter of how it is done. A sense of justice, the virtue, is in the agent, but justice is a matter of what is owed and whether it is paid, which means that it attaches to the act. That the act was coerced, or was performed in a surly manner, does not change the fact that it was performed and that justice was done. *How* the debt was paid does not affect *whether* the debt was paid. On the other hand, how the act was performed, with what motivation, is crucial to the question of whether it was kind. One's own failings with respect to kindness, compassion, benevolence, and so on, can and should leave one feeling guilty, ashamed, and dishonorable. The failings of others in those respects can leave one feeling let down or even contemptuous. But kindness, for example, is a warm and immediate response to the distress of others; it consists of an inclination to help others for their own sakes. If somebody lacks that inclination then he has a moral failing. But there is nothing else in kindness on which we could base a demand that he perform. Justice is the basis for such demands. Kindness, compassion, benevolence, and so on, are different, though failings in those respects may leave one feeling just as dishonourable or indecent as failings with respect to justice. They may leave one feeling that one has failed to live up to the requirements of a decent life. In the first person one feels and recognizes requirement, but in the third person there is no basis for demand.

Requirements, strictly speaking, or requirements that one person can make on another, depend less on the feelings and inclinations of those involved. Such requirements are impersonal. They go with roles; they depend not on who the people involved are and how they feel about each other, but on the relationships between them. The impersonality of the requirement comes out in the fact that these are the cases in which impartiality is proper and partiality wrong. There is no impropriety in my being partial in deciding whom I shall take out to dinner or with whom I shall spend Saturday afternoon, but when I mark students' essays in my role or capacity as lecturer, I must be impartial. One's role or capacity might require that one give special treatment to a particular person or group of people, but the require-ment is impartial rather than personal and it comes out of the relationship. I am required to give special treatment to this person, not because he is Adam and I happen to quite like him, but because he is my son. In the same way, quite impartially, any other parents will be required to give special treatment to their offspring. If I had another son, I should be required to give him special treatment in the same way. And if I happened not to like the son I have, I should still be required to give him special treatment in the same way. Such roles go with getting a specific job done, the job of raising children, directing traffic, or whatever, and the nature of the requirement is that the job must be done if the enterprise in which the role is played is to achieve its point.

Friendship, at least in the central case, is not nearly as specific.

"Friend" does not refer to an official position such as that of a paid home companion or companion for the Grand Tour, a position with specified duties that can be demanded in return for payment (even if the duties are to act like a friend). Friendships usually grow from some common interest, but go beyond that. It is true that one might have chess friends, sailing friends, fishing friends, and so on. It is also true of an oak table that it is a table, omitting the original adjective. Nevertheless, it is not obviously true that a chess friend is a friend. An XY is not always a Y: an imaginary friend is not a friend, and neither is a false friend. The point of referring to somebody as a chess friend, rather than as a friend with whom I play chess, is to indicate severe and important limitations on the relationships. We have an interest in common and we enjoy each other's company; we might even exchange information about the doings of our families; but there is not that deep trust and personal relationship transcending the particular activity that is characteristic of the central case of friendship and that enables a friendship to survive untouched even if the friends have no contact with each other for a period of years because, say, one moves away and they are poor letter-writers. Friendship is much wider-ranging and much less defined than a role.

Another indication of the difference between friendship and roles, and an important indication for my present purposes, is that one can perform very badly in a role and still be playing that role, whereas if one performs very badly as a friend one is not a friend at all. Even if I never show up to classes and do no research, I am a member of the philosophy department (though probably not for long); if I cheat you, tell false and nasty tales about you, and so on, then I am not your friend at all. This indicates the way in which duties and requirements go with roles but not with a relationship such as friendship: one can perform poorly in a role and still be playing it, because the fact that one fails to do one's duty or to meet the requirements made of one does not mean that those duties and requirements do not exist. The fact that one will never act simply out of concern for the other does mean that the more personal relationship of friendship does not exist.

Roles are concerned with jobs to be done by joint action, and the requirement in the role is the necessity that the job be done if the enterprise in which the role is played is to achieve its point. It must not be forgotten here that there are a lot of complications laid on top of that initially simple point. The jobs to be done will be within the wider context of communal life, which has the point of making it possible for people to live peacefully side by side and is an enterprise in which people have jobs or bear burdens largely in the form of forebearances from actions that might, one way or another, break the peace. One of the things about which people can dispute is what is necessary if a given enterprise is to achieve its point, and those disputes must, when necessary, be resolved by reference to the public procedure; we must be able to have common action about them if we are to have common action about anything, and thus to have community. References to what is necessary if a job is to be done or an enterprise to achieve its point must be read in this context.

Roles are defined largely by reference to the jobs involved: we define parenthood in terms of the job of bringing up children; the role of a policeman in terms of the jobs of capturing criminals, directing traffic, and so on; and the same for other roles. Along with these jobs or duties, though, go various rights. Some of the rights one has as part of the job, because one's duties cannot be carried out without them. Parents could not carry out their responsibility to raise a child if they had no right to discipline him or make any decisions on his behalf. A carpenter could not do his work if he were not allowed to use a plane or hammer. Other rights one has because of the way roles fit together in an enterprise. One has a right that others in the enterprise do their job so that the enterprise can achieve its point, a right determined by the point of the activity. Doing one's own job is pointless if others in the enterprise ruin everything by failing to do their jobs so that the enterprise cannot achieve its point no matter whether one does one's own job or not. Requirements are reciprocal and depend on the point of the enterprise. Claims made on one depend for their validity on others' meeting the claims made on them, and one's claims on others depend on one's meeting one's own responsibilities. Apart from exceptional cases such as that of infants (which will be dealt with later), rights and responsibilities go together.

The nature of the requirements that one do one's duty shows the relationship between efficiency and justice. What is required is, subject to the proviso about the role of the public procedure, what is necessary if the enterprise is to achieve its point. What is not necessary cannot properly be required: using a position of authority to make underlings do things that do not contribute to the point of the enterprise is unjust. Inefficient requirements within the enterprise are, to that extent, unjust requirements.

Cooperation is more than a matter of simply all doing the same thing and more than simply all helping each other. If four of us spend the summer going swimming together, there need be nothing cooperative about that. If, to save fuel costs, we decide that we shall take it in turns to provide the transport rather than each driving his own car to the beach every day, then we have cooperation for mutual benefit:

each has his share to do, and that share can legitimately be claimed of him by the others. It may be cheaper for me always to ride with the others and never to take my car, but when it is my turn to provide the transport I have to do so. I have a role in the enterprise, the others have a right that I play that role, and I am unjust if I try to cheat them by taking the benefits without playing my role. The ideas of cooperation, justice, rights, and roles all go together. It is not that one is more basic and the others explained in terms of it: they form a mutually dependent group. The argument about the necessity for cooperation in human life, as brought out in the argument for the necessity of a decision-procedure, is an argument that we must have these structures and that the whole group of concepts is necessary for communal life.

I have heard it said that elephants are cooperative animals that help their relatives. I know next to nothing about elephants and want to make no claim about whether or not they cooperate, but I do want to point out some questions raised by this claim. We need to know more than that elephants help their young. Do elephants have second cousins twice removed and consider their interests because they stand in that relationship? Do they look after a decrepit and unpleasant elephant simply because that one is their brother-in-law, so that looking after him is their job? What happens to orphans? Are foster-parents appointed with the appropriate duties?

An elephant calf is likely to have emotional ties with its mother that lead it to fit in with its mother. It is not uncommon for mothers in the animal kingdom to have special ties with their own young but to ignore the destitute orphaned offspring of others. Action of the sort that seems to be exhibited here, springing directly from emotional ties, is not cooperative any more than is the relationship between a human mother and her newborn baby. The same applies to relationships between human adults whose actions spring directly from emotional ties. Not all help is cooperative; some is given selflessly, seeking no return, and help is sometimes returned in the same way. The help becomes cooperative when it is recognized that somebody has a job to do that can be claimed of them because of their place in the structure. We cooperate to provide ourselves with security, so it is recognized that when police help us to keep that security, they are doing a job that can be claimed of them because they are police.

If people were not so constituted that they were sometimes prepared to help each other outside a cooperative context, with no expectation of return, it is hard to believe that they would get together to cooperate. Nevertheless, such selfless action cannot be the whole of the story even if it is a very good thing that it is part of the story. The argument for the necessity of a decision-procedure shows that it cannot be the whole story. People differ in their judgments, and because of the more complicated things that people do, and plan to do, they have more opportunity to differ in their judgments than do, say, sheepdogs. People's interests clash, and, because of their intelligence and knowledge, people are more often aware of clashing interests than are some other types of animals, and their actions are more often likely to be affected: man (though not, perhaps, man alone)[5] is famished even by future hunger. Good will alone will not resolve disputes, because undifferentiated good will to all would not help us to choose between the mugger and his victim in deciding whom to help. Good will might mean that people will find a way to resolve a dispute, but is not itself the way. If we differ about whose turn it is to do the washing up, good will may lead to our settling the matter by discussion, or by having one offer to do it and the other accept, or by tossing a coin, but until some such method is added to the good will, the difference remains unsolved. That there can be, and is, selfless action does not undercut the importance of cooperation.

All of this touches on areas of moral psychology and metaphysics that are interesting and important, but that cannot fully be dealt with here. People identify and recognize themselves in a variety of ways, and the current tendency in moral and political theory to identify them as individuals, as though "individual" were clearly a noun rather than primarily an adjective, involves confusion that leads to an invidious individualism. Individuals are individual Xs. People can be identified in a way that separates them from each other when it matters: if we want to know which member of the family should be given medical treatment, we can pick out the one who has whooping cough. Sometimes other sorts of identification are more important: under some economic structures, what matters is the family unit rather than the separate identities of the members of the family. My self is what I identify myself as being, and I identify myself as being many different things in different contexts: a father, a brother, a philosopher, a sailor, a wordworker, an Australian, and so on, but always in terms of quite public concepts gained in a social context. People identify themselves in terms of families, countries, traditions, places in social structures, interests, occupations, and other things. These identifications give people selves that, so to speak, extend beyond their own bodies and unite them with people. It is part of what is involved in the claim that people are communal beings, and it explains how the notion of self-interest can move: it explains how I can be selfish just as much by unfairly favoring my son over somebody else as by unfairly favoring myself over my son. It also helps to explain why self-interest, with an appropriate identification of the self, need do no harm in social relationships: sympathy, for example, need not be a matter of putting oneself in the other's shoes, but might be a matter of recognizing part of oneself in the other.

Some of the importance of this comes out in a version of the Prisoners' Dilemma argument commonly used in moral philosophy. What the argument shows is that people cannot, by and large, be purely self-interested with the self of invidious individualism. This argument arises in the context of an attempt to base morality on self-interest. There is no real problem in this attempt if the self that has the interests is that of a social being, a family member, or something of that sort; the problem arises if the self is that of invidious individualism, where all the wants and interests attach to the body and mind of the person concerned, with no desire for friendship (which involves some concern for the friend's good for its own sake) or any other such relationship, but regarding other people as merely hindrances or irrelevant. If people resisted as little as trees do, such a person would as readily chop down a hindering person as he would a hindering tree. But people do resist, and are inclined to take preemptive action when they see it as necessary, so life would be solitary, poor, brutish, and short for such beings. None of them would satisfy many interests. Attempting to satisfy an interest that would allow somebody else the opportunity to get behind me would be too dangerous. Building a house to protect myself in the cold weather would be pointless if everybody else felt free to use it as firewood. And so on. In pursuit of his own interest, each person might well feel it worth his while to trade off with each of the others by making a contract that imposed mutual limitations. The contract might forbid my pursuing my own interests as wholeheartedly as before but, because others interfered less, I might achieve a lot more. In that case, it seems, the price of my submission is worth paying in return for the good of the submission of others. The same would be true of each of the others, so the contract would be made, and that contract of mutual limitations would constitute morality with reasons of self-interest for fitting in with its requirements.

It is clear that, if these people were different from what they are in that they had a sense of justice, they would regard the fact that they had freely made the contract as a reason for keeping it. But they are not different from what they are; they act only in terms of invidious self-interest and, because of that, they will not keep the contract. At the stage of making the contract, relations will be one-on-one; there will be no multiperson group until a contract has been made. So consider the contract for two people, A and B, and what self-interest leads to when each considers whether to conform to it.

A

		Keeps		Breaks	
B	Keeps	2	2	1	4
	Breaks	4	1	3	3

The numbers give the preferences, with B's preferences on the right-hand side of each pair. A's first preference is that he gets the good of B's compliance without paying the price of his own; his last preference is that he pays the price without getting the good; and the reasons that brought the contract up in the first place mean that he prefers both complying to both breaking the contract. The same sorts of points explain B's preferences.

But then A can see that if B keeps the contract and A breaks it, A will get his first preference rather than his second. And if B breaks the contract and A breaks it, A will get his third preference rather than his fourth. B will either keep or break the contract, and, either way, A is better off breaking it. The same sort of reasoning holds good for B. So reasoning purely in terms of self-interest will lead each to break the contract; such beings cannot, in effect, make a contract at all.

What emerges from this is the necessity of a sense of justice, or willingness to cooperate, if there is to be social life (or human life, given Hobbes's arguments about the state of nature). That is, we can see here the necessity that people have the selves of social beings. (This is Hobbes's point when he says that people must follow the laws of nature, which is part of his account of human nature: the laws of nature, until they become civil laws, "are not properly Lawes, but qualities that dispose man to peace.")[6] They must have at least some care for others for their own sake.

It is tempting to think that the Prisoners' Dilemma argument cannot make its point because it assumes the short term, treating the contract as though it were a one-shot arrangement. A ought to be able to realize, it might seem, that if he takes a short-term advantage by breaking the contract now, he will, in the long term, lose B's compliance forever after. But it would be a mistake to take this line: the contract *is* a one-shot arrangement. Remember the type of being that A and B are: totally self-interested with the selves of invidious individualism, regarding others only as instruments, hindrances, or irrelevant, willing to chop down hindrances whenever it is safe to do so whether the hindrance be a person or a tree. If B thinks that the contract makes him safe in taking up an interest that allows A to get behind him, it takes but one blow for A to put himself in a position where B no longer hinders him and A no longer has to pay the price of limiting his own actions. That makes the contract a one-shot arrangement.

There might be some people who are totally self-interested in that way, but once there is a community, it can coerce the oddities so that they do find it in their interests to comply. The war would no longer be of each against all, but of most against a few, and the odds would be quite different in that battle.

We do not have this Prisoner's Dilemma problem, because we have the selves, feelings, and inclinations of social beings. The argument shows the importance in human life of cooperation and of willingness to get on with others, and it shows that this willingness must be structured in terms of cooperation and justice, that is, in terms of mutual limitations recognized as binding. Good will by itself is not enough. Rights are necessary to a virtues theory: we must be able to distinguish between the mugger and the victim.

Justice and cooperation are matters of requirements and relationships between roles rather than of emotional ties and personal relationships. That is why considerations of rights within cooperation can sometimes seem so cold and impersonal. It need not be so, though. For one thing, people play the roles. For another, it is easier to cooperate with somebody whose attitude is that anybody who necessarily bears a burden in the production of a benefit should receive some return for it, and with somebody who takes the attitude that, if he gains benefit from the activity of others, he should repay them rather than simply get away with whatever he can for himself. This brings out the closeness of kindness and gratitude to the attitudes that get a sense of justice started, all reflecting the social nature of people. I cannot run off here onto the subject of moral psychology, but there are interesting lines to be followed that way.

Not all roles should be played, and not all enterprises should be carried on, so the simple fact that something is required in a role is not, by itself, enough to show that it is justly required even if it is necessary that that task be performed if the enterprise is to achieve its point. If the Mafia is to achieve its point, then it might have to employ hit men, but it certainly does not follow that what a hit man does in carrying out his duties is just. The whole enterprise is unjust, so the requirements made of people playing roles in the Mafia are unjust, and their duties should not be performed.

The Mafia can exist only in a wider context: thieves need people to steal from, and no criminal organization can make a profit simply by taking in its own laundry. The injustice of the Mafia's activities, of course, lies in its relationships with its victims, so it is in the place of the Mafia in community life in general that we see that injustice. The state may take money in taxation and may even execute people as punishment, but, at least on the theory used to justify those activities, it infringes no rights in doing so; people are obligated to pay taxes, and only those are executed who have forfeited their right to life. The state, if acting properly, structures our rights and acts within that structure. The point of the Mafia, though, depends on its infringing the rights of others as they are determined by the general conditions of communal life, so there is no problem, on the account that I have been setting out, in explaining the injustice of the Mafia's activities. But that account also explains why it makes sense to talk of the duties of a hit man and why members of the Mafia could recognize claims that they made on each other as well as explaining why those duties should not be carried out and those claims should not be met; the sorts of structures required to set up duties and roles are present within the Mafia. Duties and requirements are morally binding insofar as they are generated justly, and these duties and requirements are generated by an unjust enterprise.

The case of the nearly desert island, in which ten people are marooned on an island with exactly enough food for ten, nine agree to ration the food, and the tenth insists that he will take whatever he wants, will make clear that it is possible to have obligations or duties without having deliberately or voluntarily taken them on, and the same sort of point applies to roles. Failure to recognize this point has led to significant misunderstandings of what obligations lie where, so I want to take the discussion further. One has a role, and its duties are binding on one, if it has been justly allocated to one by a binding procedure. If one is obligated to play a role, then refusal to do so exhibits injustice and does not free one from the grip of its duties. One's place in an endeavor might obligate one to take on a role: having been a member of the club for fifteen years, I might find that it is now my turn to take on the unwelcome role of secretary under a well-established convention that such jobs are to be passed around. Nor does the fact that somebody does not deliberately play a particular role mean that he has not the rights that go with it. There is an argument that capitalism depends for its effectiveness on the existence of a pool of unemployed people. I am not concerned with the truth of the conclusion of that argument, but with an inference that might be drawn from it. If the conclusion of the argument is accepted, then unemployed people in a capitalist society are making a contribution to the effectiveness of the life of their community, and, if they would rather be employed, they are bearing a burden in order to do so. They have been cast in a role not of their own choosing, one that they may try their hardest to leave. Indeed, the harder they try to leave the role, the better they will be playing it. Given the argument, one can see that this is a role: they are doing something (holding themselves available for jobs) without which the community's economy would not work. And their playing that role, no matter how unwillingly, would be a basis for their claim to rights. It would base an argument that payment of unemployment benefits is a matter of justice rather than of charity, for example, no matter what the actual history of payments to the unemployed may have been. Again, let me stress that I am not concerned to argue that capitalism does depend on the existence of a pool of unemployed people: my concern is with what would be implied by such a claim and with what it shows about whether roles must be willingly taken on. But the best example of a role that is not willingly or deliberately taken on is that of a child, and for the rest of this chapter I shall concentrate primarily on that role.

It is easy to misunderstand a relational concept that applies to things that usually stand to each other in two sorts of relationships at the same time. It is sufficiently easy for Hume to have made the mistake in one well-known passage. The concept of a parent applies to two quite different sorts of relationships that commonly go together, and we can see the two different sorts of relationships if we consider that, while it makes perfect sense for Hume to write about an acorn and its parent tree,[7] the acorn could not have a foster-parent or a step-parent; trees stand in biological relationships, but not in social relationships. Hume was straightforwardly wrong in his implication that there is, between human parent and child as we know them, no relationship that does not also hold between the oak tree and the acorn. *Parent* and *child* are social roles, and there are social relationships between the humans in those roles that do not hold between oaks and acorns.

Children are not merely young human beings; the notion of *child* can be understood only in relation to the notions of *parent* and *adult*, and is to be understood, ultimately, in terms of responsibilities. This is suggested by consideration of changing life expectancies throughout history: a world in which life expectancy was three and nobody lived beyond twenty would not be a world populated entirely by children and would not be a world in which fifteen-year-olds were children, because the responsibilities of adulthood would have to be taken on much earlier than they are now if those people were to live at all.

Because the biological and social relationships between parent and child commonly go together in the case of people, it is often implicitly assumed that the relationship between parent and child is simply a matter of biology. It is consequently inferred (by ungrateful children or uncaring parents as much as by philosophers such as Hume) that any rights or duties between parents and children must either follow from the biological relationship or not really exist.[8] That the assumption is false can readily be seen. It can be seen in talk of, say, George Washington as the father of his people, a metaphor that would not be at all apt if it referred only to a biological relationship. From a mere biological relationship, taken by itself, nothing whatsoever of any moral interest follows. So far, Hume was right. Morality enters with social relationships.

The first problem to be tackled here is how childhood can be a social role. It is clear that a child of twenty, or even of ten, can be a social being, interacting and cooperating with others, following rituals, and demanding some things as of right, but the point is a lot less obvious about infants newly sprung from the womb. The actions of such infants, may, indeed, have social consequences. If an infant pukes on the vicar's vestments, that might have the social consequence of embarrassing the parents, and if its mewling keeps the Prime Minister awake all night and impairs his temper, it might even plunge the country into war—but it does not seem clear that such infants can play social roles. They lack self-consciousness, they lack awareness of the social consequences of what they do, they lack the capacity for decision-making to such an extent that their mewling and puking can count only marginally as actions, and, in general, it seems improper to describe them as *taking on* a social role. An infant may take on a rosy hue when put by the fire, but does not knowingly, deliberately, or willingly take on any tasks.

Roles are not played only by people. Sacred rocks might play a social role in the life of a tribe, and the public procedure plays the role of determining rights. Sacred rocks and public procedures are as incapable of knowingly taking on tasks as children are. If they can have social roles, then, why should there be a problem about infants' doing so?

The problem appears to be that the role of child, if it is important, is concerned with rights and duties. The problem about the social role of child arises because of worries about what rights and duties children have and what rights and duties parents have. Children enter the story as terms in social relationships, as items standing in social relationships to other people, and not merely as structuring social relationships in which other people stand to each other. Sacred rocks and public procedures are not like that; they structure social relationships between people but are not themselves terms standing in those social relationships toward people. I may have a duty to you not to cheat when I take legal action against you, and the content of that duty, what counts as cheating, may be determined by the public procedure, but I have no duty to the public procedure as such any more than I have a duty to the coin we toss to resolve a dispute. Reference to sacred rocks and public procedures will not explain how *child* can be a social role in such a way that those entering the relationship in which that role has its home (the relationship between parent and child) take on rights and duties. Children might be playing a social role as sacred rocks play a social role when the children are used as an excuse: "I can't stay late because I have to take the baby-sitter home." In these cases, but not in the ones that interest us, the child can readily be replaced by something else: I might have to water my pot plants or put the garbage out for collection. The only thing special about children in this context is that excuses referring to them are more readily accepted.

There are roles that people play (though we should not normally say that people took on those roles) in which rights and duties are plainly involved even though the role is not voluntarily assumed. The obvious case is conscription into the army. The conscript, whether he likes it or not, is simply put into the army, and that he is in the army, as well as what he is in the army (private, sergeant), is determined by his rights and duties.[9] If such roles do not have to be taken on deliberately or voluntarily, why should there be a problem about the role of *child*?

The point cannot be raised fairly this way, since it is often thought that there is a problem about conscription, too, precisely because it puts somebody into a role with no consent on his part. It is often felt that one cannot have obligations or duties that derive in no way from one's consent: the conscript may have a formal or a legal duty to polish his boots or stand and fight, but he has no such real duty, that is, no duty he has reason to take notice of as such, though he might be imprudent to ignore the coercion supporting it.

Coercion and conscription certainly affect the responsibilities of those involved. If I coerce or conscript you to do something, then I at least share the responsibility for that something, and the decision shows something about my character rather than about yours, neither of which points would hold had you performed the action of your own accord. But to say that you have no responsibility in the matter, or that one person can never rightly coerce or conscript another, is a far different claim that overlooks the significance of the public procedure. If the conscription were justly imposed by a binding decision-procedure,[10] then I should be bound to accept it, and its requirements could justly be made on me. This would be the case, for example, if I were a thief and were coerced or conscripted to return my booty.

Words have no magical properties. Saying "I consent" or signing one's name to a contract can have the significance they have only because of a context including human conventions, and other things can be effective in that context. Consenting is a formal way of bringing about a state of affairs in which we have an obligation; had we not been capable of recognizing that state of affairs quite apart from that particular way of bringing it about, we should not have been able to institute that formal way of bringing it about. Formal ways of undertaking obligations or duties cannot be the only ways.[11]

That there must be nonformal ways of taking on duties and obligations, though, does not mean that there must be nonvoluntary ways. Suppose that I go to settle new land with a group of people who, while I remain very quiet, agree that all will help to build each homestead rather than leave each to build his own. If they notice my quietness and decide to build mine first to get over my shyness and make me feel at home, the fact that I did not explicitly or formally agree to the system will not relieve me of a duty to help to build other homesteads. They would not be unjust in expecting me to do my bit, and I should be unjust in refusing. They proposed a cooperative system in which there were rights and obligations, and, reasonably in the context, they assumed that I was going along with them. For me to leave them labouring under this misapprehension so that I can make selfish use of their efforts is to cheat them, since I can reasonably assume that they would not do the job unless they had expectation of return. I have accepted a role in the system when it grants me benefits, but that role requires also that I pay when my turn comes. Given their beliefs about the rights-structure of the situation, beliefs they hold because I have misled them, they would not show injustice by infringing rights as they believed them to be should they force my compliance.

Suppose, on the other hand, that in my search for land to settle, I come across a community of which I know nothing and, being a trusting fellow and exhausted after my long journey, immediately go to sleep. While I am asleep the others rapidly build me a house, because they have a convention that any newcomer who has a home built for him must repay that debt by serving as slave to that community until some other newcomer arrives to take his place. It could hardly be thought that I should be under an obligation when I had no idea what was happening. Nobody could think that I was cooperating with those people in terms of that convention. If the benefit were forced on me in this way, I could not justly be required to pay the price for it any more than I could be required to pay for an ice cream that a vendor pushed into my face as I passed his stall. There is no need for cooperation with respect to housebuilding between these other people and me, and there is nothing on which they could base a claim that I am obligated to join their community. There is no good to which they would otherwise be entitled from which they are excluded because of my nonmembership. I am not taking the easy-rider position, as I might with something such as the provision of security against bomb-attack from another group, by accepting the benefits that inevitably flow to me from their cooperating in bearing necessary burdens among themselves (to provide antiaircraft defenses, for example) while I refuse to contribute to the cost of those benefits. In the absence of such bases, they have no proper claim that I must join their community. Their convention is binding only in the community within which it is a convention, and they have no reason to assume my membership of that community. Given the price that they charge for membership, they could most reasonably assume that I shall not want to be a member.

The same sort of point holds if, instead of sleeping, I sink back, exhausted, against a tree and watch in wonderment at what I take to be the extraordinary kindness of these people, not realizing that they set a high price on their action and take my enslavement to be its consequence. I could not reasonably be expected to know the significance of the action, so it cannot justly be held against me. I should, perhaps, have wondered at how helpful these people were and thought about how high their expectations of mutual helpfulness seemed to be, but I could not be expected to see my future slavery as part of that and could not be taken to seek membership of a community the structure of which involved my slavery. But if I should have known, though I did not, or if others could reasonably expect me to have known, though I did not, then the situation might well be different.

If I was negligent in what I did, or negligent in my investigation of the likely outcomes or possible mishaps in what I did, then, even if the actual outcome is accidental, I may be responsible for it. I may have a duty or obligation to make good any damage I do, even though the damage was done accidentally. What is at issue in this question of duties and obligations is what can justly be required of somebody, and that is not always a matter of his consent or voluntary acceptance. If, through my own stupidity, I accidentally shoot the secretary's hands off, then, much as I hate the job, I might owe it to others to keep the minutes from now on and they might justly force me to do so. That I have a role and can properly be required to play it need not depend on my consent or voluntary action.

My shooting off the secretary's hands was accidental, but something else (my playing with a loaded shotgun) was not accidental and was something of which I should have seen the possible consequences. Infants cannot see the possible consequences of playing the role of child, and cannot be expected to. But then, infants do not take on that role, and they do not create it. The roles of *parent* and *child* are created by activities of the community at large, not simply by the actions of parents and children. The role of *child* is not one simply in the family, but one in the community.

Rights inhere in social roles and structures, not in individual, asocial beings. Their nature is to be understood in terms of an ongoing community, not simply by taking a time-slice of the community. Taking a time-slice of the community means, not only that one misunderstands how the conventions, roles, and social structures arose, but that one does not see their point, and thus what they are.

Children are the *continuing* life of a community. They, therefore, play a crucial role in the life of any historical community; without children, the community dies. There is a lot for almost any person to gain from living in a community: increased security of various kinds, pooling of knowledge, and so on. But there is more to it than that. Hobbes's arguments may not have been sufficient to establish the necessity of a legally unlimited sovereign, but they are sufficient to show that if people cannot live in communities then people, and not merely communities, will die out. In an important sense, people are naturally social animals, and were they not so they would have died out with the first generation. People cannot live in communities without some conventions, so it is natural for people to form conventions. It might be true of any particular convention that we need not have had that convention in that particular form, and that might even be one of the marks of a convention, but it does not follow that we might have had no conventions at all. Some *sorts* of conventions are necessary, though the details of content might vary: there must be some concept of murder; and the roles of *parent* and *child* must be recognized (and usually played) in any ongoing community. The role of parent might be played by the biological grandparents while the biological parents, being younger and stronger, work in the fields; or it might be played by a Platonic creche. There are several ways in which the job might be done, but it must be done in some way.

Infants may make no time-slice contribution to a community, but no historical community can survive without infants who will become adults and do the work that must be done. Infants have no responsibilities, but they will grow into adults who bear responsibilities,[12] and how they bear those responsibilities will affect others in the community. The community at large has an interest in the upbringing of children; it has needs that are met by the upbringing of children and, in the standard case, can be met only in that way. The role of parent is one that a community must have, and with that role goes the role of child.

The point of parenthood is the bringing up of children, helping children to grow into adults. The point of children is that they are incipient adults, not slaves, and not dolls for their parents to play with. The role of child leads on to another role that is ready and waiting, and that second role informs the role of child. All of this is part of any historical community.

The story so far might explain something about the duties or obligations of parents, but it might seem to imply nothing about rights of children. The upbringing of children is the community's business, so it seems that the parent's duties will be to the community and the correlative rights will be held by the community against the parent. Parenthood is a role set up by convention in the community at large, not specifically by cooperation between parents and child (especially when the child is too young to cooperate). This might be part of the reason why we usually speak of parents having rights over their children rather than against them. And there is truth in this: communities do have rights against parents, and parents do have duties to the community, these usually being reflected in legislation. But the point of parenthood, and the new role for which childhood is preparing a child, bring in rights for the child. At one time a parent might have to act as agent for the child with respect to all the child's rights, and for a long time the parent might have to act as agent for the child with respect to some of the child's rights, but the fact that the child needs an agent does not mean that the child has no rights. Parents must teach children to handle responsibility, to exercise rights properly, to take up a place in the community with attendant rights and duties. One cannot teach children these things while keeping all decisions out of their hands; children must practice taking responsibility in order to learn how to do so. The only rights that they can be taught to exercise or can practice exercising are their own, as a matter of logical truth, so rights must be part of the role of child if the role is to serve its function. So must increasing acceptance of responsibility as the child's capacities develop, because learning to exercise rights is learning to take responsibility. The detailed content of the role of child, and just what rights go with it, will be determined by the community's cooperation just as other roles and the rights that go with them are determined, but that does not make the rights any less the child's.

A lot of this depends on the fact that children are incipient adults, but it should be noticed that no attempt is made to derive rights simply from potential personhood or any other quality of the child. The rights are derived from social relations and points about how communities must be organized.[13]

It might seem that my argument about children's rights is open to a straightforward objection:[14] it does not show that children must have rights, but only that they must be treated *as if* they had rights. Children play and are taught to play role-type games, such as doctors and nurses or shopkeeper. They have fictional rights within that fictional context. It is a crucial part of their upbringing that sometimes we treat them as if they had rights, as if they had a say in the decision, and so on, but that is not the same as saying that they really have rights any more than "Pickwick is fat" is really true outside the context of Dickens's novel.[15]

The objection, appealing though it looks, is not, I think, sufficient. If the conditions of social life require us to treat children as if they have rights, then they have rights. Rights are conventional, and our behaving in the appropriate cooperative way is what constitutes their existence. The children are not in the same sort of position as a gang of thugs who move into our little town and force us to treat them as though they had the rights of rulers when in fact they have not: in our relationship with the thugs we are being coerced, but in our relationship with respect to the children we are cooperating. That we so cooperate (at least in general terms) is forced upon us, but not by any alien will; it is forced upon us by the conditions of human life.

Children's games, though, are conventional, so why are not the rights within them genuine rights? When children play doctors and nurses, those playing the parts of doctors have, within the game, the rights of doctors, but they have not really the right to go around operating on people. Why not? Children's games, of the relevant sort, are indeed conventional, but the question to be asked is: they are conventional ways of doing what? Rights are generated by cooperative relationships, and cooperation is understood in terms of its point, or what it is cooperation for. The point of a children's game of doctor is the enjoyment of those playing, not the healing of the sick, so the rights appropriate to those involved in the activity of healing the sick are not generated.[16] Participants in a children's game of doctors and nurses do have rights. For a start, they have a right that the "doctor" not really remove their appendix, but that is a right generated by more general social relationships. Because the point of the game is enjoyment, the rights generated specifically by participation in the game are appropriate to that: rights that the others play their parts in the sense that they not cheat, not simply break the conventions so as to spoil the game for everybody else, and so on.

This means that, when there is dispute about rights, a lot of weight will be thrown onto arguments about the points of the institutions in which the contentious rights are or are not generated, but the weight simply does lie there. That is one of the reasons why arguments about who has which rights can be so very difficult, as important matters often are.

Notes

1. This thesis about the nature of the virtues and the primacy of justice, stated very bluntly and briefly here to place what follows in context, is argued out in my *Cooperation and Human Values* (Brighton: Harvester Press, and New York: St. Martin's Press, 1981). The general thesis holds good, but might be misleading if taken to imply that the virtues are really independent of each other so that somebody could have one of the virtues without having any of the others to any degree at all. In fact, as is to be expected given their common focus on cooperation in my account of their natures, the virtues seem to be closely tied together. Somebody who completely lacks a sense of justice would be deficient in kindness: simple willingness to help others would not enable him to choose between the mugger and his victim as the one to help, and helping the mugger would not be kind; it would not display a quality of character that could simply be regarded as a virtue. Somebody completely lacking in courage or fortitude, who gave up at the first obstacle, would find it difficult to exhibit any of the virtues. And so on.
2. Special but not unique. This is the sort of debt of gratitude owed in response to a supererogatory act, and one would owe such a debt if, for example, one received help from the Good Samaritan. For a discussion of this sort of relationship, see David Heyd, *Supererogation* (Cambridge: Cambridge University Press, 1982). The point toward which I am arguing is that friendship is a relationship of supererogation.
3. This point can be overplayed, as it is by Michael Sandel in his argument in *Liberalism and the Limits of Justice* (Cambridge: Cambridge University Press, 1982), Chapter 1, that consideration of friendship shows justice not to be a necessary and basic virtue. Friendship is not all the relationships in life. Even if my gardener is my friend, he is still my gardener and must be paid for his work if he is to live. Even if my friend is not my gardener, he earns his living in some other way. Being a jolly good chap and very sociable does not free one from obligations and duties even if one lives in a community that does not recognize private property. On top of that, the fact that one does not insist, and does not need to insist, on one's rights with one's friends does not mean that one has no rights or that they do not play an important part in structuring the relationship. One can forgive or overlook a friend's invasion of one's rights (and friendships are not always sweetness and light) only if one has the rights. My friend may well borrow my possessions without my permission, but he needs to be aware that the possessions are mine, and therefore needs to be discriminating: he may light the fire with whatever he likes of his own, but if he does so with the typescript that represents my life's work, he is not at all acting as a friend. That friends do not overstep such boundaries does not mean that the boundaries do not exist or that the friendship is not structured, in part, by awareness of them. Justice matters between friends, but friends do not usually need to insist on it and are ready to forgive lapses.
4. This claim, too, is argued out in *Cooperation and Human Values*.
5. Cf. Thomas Hobbes's *De Homine*, trans. Charles T. Wood, T.S.K. Scott-Craig, and Bernard Gert, in Bernard Gert, ed., *Man and Citizen* (Clifton: Humanities Press, and Brighton: Harvester Press, 1972), p. 40.
6. *Leviathan*, ed. C. B. Macpherson (Harmondsworth: Penguin Books, 1968), p. 314.

7. David Hume, *A Treatise of Human Nature*, 1888, ed. L.A. Selby-Bigge (Oxford: Oxford University Press), p. 467.
8. None of this is meant to suggest that the relationship between parent and child must be simply one of duty. One reason for giving biological parents the social role is that they commonly care about their children and are inclined to act for the children's good without having to be impelled by considerations of duty.
9. And his rights and duties are determined by whether he is a private or a sergeant: his role is equivalent to his rights and duties.
10. The idea of a binding decision-procedure is discussed in Chapter 6.
11. On this, see P. S. Atiyah, *Promises, Morals, and Law* (Oxford: Oxford University Press, 1981).
12. If one becomes a medical student, one's education has the point of making one a competent doctor. That is the point of the role of medical student, even if some people become medical students for other reasons. It retains that point, and is structured by it, even if one is unemployed on graduation and had good reason to believe that one would be unemployed. A similar point applies to the role of child. The rights and duties inhere in the role, not in the particular person playing it, and that role is structured by the point that it has—even if some children do not reach adulthood and even if there is good reason to believe that they will not.
13. The same points might be brought to bear on a number of arguments about abortion.
14. The objection was suggested to me by Stephen Davies.
15. On make-believe, see Kendal Walton, "Pictures and Make-Believe," *Philosophical Review* 82 [1973], pp. 283–319.
16. Also relevant to this is the discussion in Chapter 6.

5

Community and Rights

SEVERAL PHILOSOPHERS RECENTLY, notably Hart and Feinberg,[1] have been prepared to entertain the idea of a society of people with no rights or idea of rights. Feinberg's claim is a little weaker in that he tries to imagine a society in which "no one, or hardly any one . . . has rights," since he believes that the difference between the two positions is unimportant for his purposes, so, like Hart, he does not defend the claim that there could be a society without rights, though he is clearly prepared to entertain it. The difference between the claim that there could be a society with few rights and the claim that there could be a society with no rights at all is plainly crucial for my purposes, so I want to argue that there could not be a community of people that did not have and operate the concept of a right. One point that emerges from this, I think, though I shall not draw the point out in detail, is that Feinberg has undervalued rights.

If a community need not have and operate the concept of a right, then it would be necessary to argue about whether it is a good thing that it do so. If all communities necessarily have some distribution of rights, then the only proper argument is about which distributions are the best or which is the right one, and it is clear why investigation of rights should be important. At first glance, it seems a plausible claim that there could be a community which, though it had rules and requirements and values, did not have any distribution of rights, but I shall show that the rights are merely hidden: the story of such a community involves a background in which there are rights. As I shall show, the idea of binding law involves the idea of rights; the resolution of disputes, as is necessary if there is to be community life, involves the idea of rights; the second-order decision-procedure cannot be understood without reference to the idea of rights; and the role of police and courts in giving sense to our idea of legal requirement, or, more generally, the ideas of application and enforcement of the law, require reference to the idea of rights.

I should be careful to point out here that my claim that there could not be a community of people who did not have and operate the concept of a right is not the same as the claim that every language contains a word that can be translated into English simply and precisely as "a right." It is enough if it is impossible to explain certain phenomena in the community without reference to the notion of a right.[2] A group of people might have no word translatable as "a right," but if their community has the institution of property then they have and operate the concept of a right. Similarly, if they have contracts then they have the concept of a right. It might be impossible to explain the relations between parents and children or between marriage partners without reference to the concept of a right. The institutions around which my arguments will center are those concerned with the resolution of disputes, since I think it can be shown that any community must have some such institution,[3] and the workings of the institution cannot be explained without reference to rights.

It might be thought that my argument shows that every society must have rights, but not that every society must have the concept of a right. This is not so. Societies may be very unreflective at times, but not in a way that allows them to have rights without having the concept of a right. A society might have gold deposits on its land without having the concept of gold: they might, for example, use gold to make sinkers for fishing, whether or not they also use lead, and they might thereby show that they have the concept *dense metal* or the concept *what makes good sinkers*, but, if they do not bother to distinguish between gold and lead, then they do not show that they have the concept of gold. Having and using gold is not enough to show that one has the concept of gold. The case is different with money: a society could not have and use money without having the concept of money. Members of another society, while passing through the territory, might drop some gold coins that were later found and used as sinkers, but those pieces of gold would not be coins when found by the people who had no concept of money. Money is not simply the items one puts in one's pocket; it is what one can spend, save, loan, borrow, invest, and all the other activities one finds referred to in economists' definitions of money. Money is conventional in its nature in a way in which gold is not. That those little bits of gold are money is a matter of how people behave and of various ways in which people discriminate; for there to be money is for people to be aware of the fact and to operate in terms of it. Some people might not operate that way or have the concept of money, but, for anything conventional to exist, others must be aware of it and discriminate in terms of it. For a society to have money, it must have the concept of money, because to have the concept simply is to have the appropriate discriminatory abilities.

Rights, too, are conventional, and the same sort of point applies to them as to money. Rights involve certain sorts of behavior and distinguishing between certain sorts of behavior in the judgments we make of them. They involve the drawing of certain sorts of discrimination, and having the concept is having the relevant discriminatory abilities even if they are not exercised by the use of just one word. People who have the ideas of coins, checks, credit notes, and so on have the concept of money even if their language has no one word that can be translated accurately by the English word "money"; they have the concept of money because they discriminate in the ways we mark off by the use of the word "money." People who have such ideas as property, money, promising, office (as in "official duties"), and contract have the concept of a right even if their language lacks a single word that can be translated accurately by the English word "right." To have the concept "red" is to be able to discriminate between things in terms of redness; to have the concept "square" is to be able to discriminate between things in terms of squareness. In general, to have a concept is to have the relevant discriminatory ability; because of the conventional nature of rights, operating in terms of them means exercising the discriminatory ability. My argument that communities must operate (in part) in terms of rights is, therefore, also an argument that they must have the concept of a right.

In operating the concept of property, people operate the concept of a right (the idea that the owner has a right that nobody destroy or take away X, for example), and they cannot operate that concept unless they have it. Clearly, this is our concept of a right: it may not have all the applications that ours has, but that is simply to say that they have fewer rights than we have; it is not to show that the concept is different or that they have not the concept of a right. If redness occurred only in conjunction with squareness, though squareness occurred also in conjunction with other colors, a special word to discriminate red squares would show possession of a concept of red. Similarly, if people have the idea that pushing the switch makes the light come on and poisoning the weeds makes them die, then they have the concept of a cause even if their concept has not as wide a range of application as ours has and even if their language has no one word accurately translatable as "cause."

It should also be made clear that I am not claiming that everybody has lots of rights in every community. Rights might be very unequally, and even very unjustly, distributed. Some people, such as those held in various types of slavery, might even have no rights at all, though their having no rights would mean that they were treated as something other and less than people. I shall argue that every community must have and operate the concept of a right, but not that every community must have some special distribution of rights. Kant argued that without having and operating the concept of cause we could not have the concept of an object and hence could not have experience, but nothing followed from his argument about what particular things cause what. I shall argue that without the concept of a right we could not have community life, but nothing follows from that argument about the particular rights that people must have, or what particular people must have them.

There are many different sorts of rights,[4] so it should be made clear that the sort of right at issue here is the one that has a correlative obligation: A's having a right against B is exactly the same relation as B's being obligated to A. The standard example here is that of a promise: if B makes a promise to A, then, in the absence of special circumstances, A has a right against B that B shall do what he promised to do, and B is obligated to A to do what he promised to do. This does not mean that B must (even that B morally must or ought to) do what he promised to do, since A may release him from the promise or choose not to exercise his right. What it means is that A is in a position morally to determine that B shall do X (where X is what B promised to do).[5] It does not mean that A is in a position to determine *whether or not* B shall do X, since, *prima facie*, B is free to do X or not to do X once A has released him from the promise, or, having promised to do X, B could do it even if A never asked him to or asked him not to.

If B promises A that he will do X and willfully fails to do X though A requires it of him, he displays a vice that can be quite publicly noticed. Others need not ignore B's promise-breaking in deciding whether to trust him in future or whether they want to associate with him, and others may properly reason with B and point out to him the dastardly nature of his conduct; A is in no special position in any of those respects. But others may not interfere and enforce compliance on B without A's agreement. On the face of it that is because, in the circumstances, A has only to express his agreement to make it proper for others to interfere, and in the absence of that agreement we must take it that that is how he chooses to exercise his right—he may want to avoid the ill will that might follow from enforcement, he might want to leave B to feel guilty about his behavior, he might sympathize with B's circumstances, or there might be something else. He can enforce compliance with our help, but for one reason or another chooses not to. In those circumstances, by interfering to enforce compliance without his agreement we should infringe his rights as much as B does.

A's special position in the circumstances does not consist in the fact that it was him to whom B was nasty, because B's action or inaction might have been a matter of nastiness to somebody else. As in Hart's example,[6] B might have promised A that he would look after A's mother. B's failure to keep his promise might then be a matter of unfortunate consequences for, and deliberate nastiness to, A's mother rather than A. Nor is it a matter of any compensation paid as a result of the broken promise being paid to A, because it might be paid to A's mother, though the claim to compensation would depend on A's right and not on his mother's. The special position of the right-holder is simply that it is his right that is infringed and he is the one in a position to determine that X should be done. He is the one who can make the requirement of the special sort appropriate to rights. When B breaks his promise to A he does wrong, as all of us can see, but he does *a* wrong specifically to A. My claim is, then, that every community must have rights of this sort: Hohfeldian claim-rights.

If there were a community without rights, it would plainly be very different from ours. We should not imagine, though, that all moral and legal restraints had been removed, because morality and law involve a good deal more than rights. We might consider, for a start, the possibility that the community we are attempting to imagine has all the other parts of morality and law. That there are other parts of morality can be seen clearly if we consider that people who do only what they are obligated to do and no more are not remarkably pleasant people and would not be held up as moral paradigms. If I pay the grocer five bob for goods that I buy and turn up to give the lectures I am paid to give, then that is well and good. If my moral behavior is restricted to that kind of action, and the only reason I am prepared to accept as a good enough one to go out of my way to help somebody else is that the action is strictly owed, then I am not kind or generous, but I am cold, inhumane, and unfeeling. So we are to try to imagine a society in which the people are kind and generous, care about each other's interests and act so as to further them, show courage in the face of danger, and so on, even though they have no conception of rights. They have all the warmer feelings of humanity, even if no concern about justice.[7]

Nor, on the face of it, need the society lack prohibitions and requirements. I have not promised anybody that I will refrain from spitting in the street or smoking in a nonsmoking compartment, but I am nevertheless required to do so. Such rules do not appear to allocate rights (to whom, specifically, do I do a wrong if I smoke in a nonsmoking compartment of which I am the only occupant?), but they certainly impose requirements and prohibitions. One can, at least apparently, do wrong without doing a wrong to somebody. On a desert island, completely cut off from any contact ever again with anybody else, one could still, at least apparently, do wrong: one could not be unjust, but one could exhibit the vice of imprudence, or be cruel to animals, or be cowardly. Even if it had no rights, it appears that the society we are trying to imagine might be imagined as having prohibitions and requirements as well as having thoroughly nice people.

All of this seems fine so far, but a number of things not mentioned seem to me to make this imaginative exercise incoherent. Various aspects of the imaginary society have been described, but they make sense only because we assume a context of the rest of the society. Consideration of the other aspects of the society necessary to make sense of those already described does, I think, require reference to rights.

The society we have tried to imagine has laws imposing requirements and prohibitions. We may imagine that it allows for many instructions, not all of the same kind or importance: "Do not drive on the right"; "Answer four questions from this examination paper"; "First catch your hare"; "Put flap A into slot B"; and so on. If I do not want a personally assembled cellophane-paper ashtray, then the instruction to put flap A into slot B has no bearing on me. I may quite properly ignore it. The fact that, since I am young and stupid and seeking adventure, I have no wish to avoid the risk of traffic accidents, does not free me from the grip of the requirement that I refrain from driving on the wrong side of the road. Some of these requirements are binding and others are not. What is the difference between the two classes?

The requirement that flap A be put into slot B is aimed at the good of anyone who wants a personally assembled cellophane-paper ashtray, so we might think that the requirement that one refrain from driving on the wrong side was aimed at the good of the society as a whole. What makes it binding, we might think, is that obedience to it will achieve that good, and what makes it binding on everybody, despite what particular people might care about or not care about, is that obedience to it will achieve the good of the community as a whole. Such calculations would involve reference to people's interests, but not to their rights. But bindingness cannot adequately be explained simply in terms of intention to serve the good of the community as a whole or in terms of anything about the content of the law.

Suppose that it could somehow be demonstrated that the best system of property for any society to have was a system of private property properly respected, that is, a system of private property and a group of people who never took anything without the consent of the owner, due payment, and following all proper forms to avoid mistake. General obedience to the requirements of the private property system, like general obedience to the requirement that one refrain from driving on the right, would achieve the good of the community as a whole. Suppose, furthermore, that people simply do not behave in the required manner—they take anything they want without consulting anybody, or perhaps they take what they need and leave the rest for others. Alternatively, suppose that one economist, F, demonstrates that the private property system is the best, but that nobody else, no matter how honest, sincere, and caring they are, believes him, and they all go on ignoring the claims of private property. In those circumstances, is the requirement that private property be respected a binding one on F? We need not imagine that the general noncompliance makes F's obedience completely ineffective. His obedience to the requirements of the private property system might help a little to further the good of the community as a whole by slightly reducing the competition for goods elsewhere and by slightly increasing the security of those in possession of the goods, even though it leaves him at an alarming disadvantage with respect to everybody else.

What reason could be given to F in support of the claim that he ought to obey the requirements of the private property system? He would bear a huge burden to provide others with a slight benefit. A supremely self-sacrificing person might do that, but it can hardly be *required* of F: his obedience provides no more than would be provided by the obedience of any other member of the community, and obedience is not, in any reasonable sense, required of them. (Their obedience is required if the law is to be fully effective, but that gets us nowhere useful because it is just as true of laws requiring mass suicide or that everybody wear party hats. In no significant sense is their obedience required.) If the law does not bind the others, then it does not bind F; the bindingness of a law does not lie in its form or in its actual or possible consequences, but in the way it relates people to each other.

The issue here is one that we have touched on before: private and public judgment. F has made a private judgment. His private judgment might even be true. But as long as it remains a merely private judgment it will not be binding on anybody and will not serve to structure the relationships between people. To take on that significance it must become a public judgment through the use of a public decision-procedure.

The bindingness of a law cannot be explained simply in terms of the content of the law. The nature of the wrong of disobedience to a law does not lie simply in the fact that a law was broken, but in the facts that the law was broken and that it ought to have been obeyed, and to think that whether a law ought to be obeyed is *simply* a matter of its content is to confuse the significance of the distinction between private judgment and public judgment.

It is not always plain what a law should require, and it is not always plain what we should do. It is not clear, apart from the law, which side of the road we should drive on. There might be reasons of international efficiency for driving on one side, but our concern here is with what is morally binding, and there seems to be no special moral reason for choosing one side rather than the other. Australians drive on the left, lots of other countries drive on the right. There seems to be no moral mistake in either choice. Similarly, there is nothing morally magic about the number of witnesses required to make a will valid. Some jurisdictions might require two, others three. Again, no mistake seems to be made in either case. It is not that no mistake *could* be made in such matters. The law is, in those cases, serving a point, and a point that has moral import. Restricting drivers to one side of the road introduces some consistency in driving and thus helps to protect human lives and limbs; it does matter that we do that, even if it does not matter which side of the road we choose in order to do it. The requirements about witnesses for a will go some way toward protecting us against fraud and against having wills made by people of unsound mind, and, again, it matters that we have such protection even if it does not matter whether we decide on two witnesses or three. So mistakes can be made in such cases; they will be primarily mistakes of efficiency, but will have moral import because of their consequences. A mistake would have been made if a will were required to have 5,000 witnesses, because that would make wills largely inoperable. A mistake would also have been made if the Minister for Transport, unable to decide between contending arguments, compromised and required that everybody drive in the middle of the road.

In cases of this sort, the law takes something morally neutral, such as which side of the road we drive on, and determines it to a moral end, such as the saving of human lives. The law plays an intermediate role in the morality of the situation, and there is no *prima facie* problem about obligation: if one has an obligation to pursue the end, one has an obligation to obey the law. My obligation to drive on the left is simply a special case of my more general obligation, a moral obligation and not merely a legal one, to avoid unnecessarily endangering other people's lives. So a moral obligation to obey such laws, or a reason that such laws should be binding on me, seems unproblematic: the law merely determines in a particular way an already existing moral obligation. And it really is a matter of *obeying* the law, because the law creates the consistency that enables people to drive safely.

But not all cases are like that. Sometimes it is perfectly clear what we ought to do even apart from the law. Quite apart from any legal requirement, we ought to refrain from bashing babies with bricks simply because we need exercise and find jogging a boring activity. If a law is introduced requiring that we refrain from bashing babies with bricks simply because we need exercise and find jogging a boring activity, there seems to be no problem: we have a moral obligation to do what the law requires. It seems to be simply one more specific case of my more general moral obligation to avoid unnecessarily endangering the lives of other people.

Simple as this might seem, though, it goes no way toward solving the problem that faces us. It might give a reason, in one class of cases, for *conformity* with the law, but that is not the same thing as showing an obligation to *obey* the law or as showing that the law is binding. Having a moral obligation to do X is not the same as having a moral obligation to obey the law even if the law in question is one requiring that I do X. If somebody orders me to read the English works of Thomas Hobbes when I am in fact reading the English works of Thomas Hobbes, then I plainly disobey him if I put the book down and go for a beer. If I continue to read the book, it does not follow that I am obeying him. I might be obeying him, or I might be simply ignoring him and following my inclination. The test of whether I am obeying him is whether I did it *because he told me to*. Would I have done what he told me to do had my inclination led me elsewhere? My moral views stand to the content of the law, in the case that we are considering, much as my inclinations stand to the order to read Hobbes. To show that I have an obligation not to bash babies is not to show that I have an obligation to obey the law or that the law is binding: to show that, we should need to show that I have the obligation *because of the law,* whereas the point of the example is that I have an obligation to behave in the relevant way quite apart from any requirement of the law. The role of my moral convictions in such cases is a good deal more complicated than might appear on the surface.

Then there might be cases in which the law required us to do what was wrong. Faced with a report showing that jogging has deleterious effects on the cartilage in the knees, the minister for health might be successful in having passed into law a bill requiring that all joggers take up the bashing of babies instead. Where do we stand with respect to a moral obligation to obey such a law? This is a question that, for the moment, I want to bypass with but one comment: in this case it does matter that the example is absurd.

The final type of case I want to refer to is that in which the law deals with something the morality of which is in dispute. It declares that abortion at the mother's request is legal, for example, or it legalizes euthanasia or says that the smoking of marijuana is illegal. Each of these cases is, or has been, disputed. Some people think that marijuana-smoking is harmless and nobody's business but the smoker's; others believe it to be a terrible activity that weakens the moral fiber of society. Some believe that abortion is only the mother's business; others believe that it is also the father's business; some believe it is the fetus's business; still others believe that it is everybody's business. In such cases, no matter what the law says, a lot of people are going to think that the law is wrong. In such a case, it is plainly pointless to try to start the argument from the premise that the law is wrong or from the premise that the law is right. The argument between us will get somewhere only if we have common premises, so it is no good my putting up a premise that, *ex hypothesi*, the other side is bound to reject. We start, not from the premise that the law is wrong, but from the premises that I think it is wrong and that you think it is right; that is, we start from the premise that we disagree. And the point is not simply a political one about what is necessary to get people onside: even if I have all the guns and do not need to persuade you, it is obviously morally improper and unfair for me simply to force my views on you.

That is why I suggested earlier that the role of one's moral convictions in determining whether the law is binding is more complicated than it might appear. It is also why I bypassed the sort of case in which the law is clearly wrong and pointed out that in that case it mattered that the example I gave was absurd. Only an absurd example could do the job—if I gave an actual example of a case in which I think the law is wrong, I should find people disagreeing that it was an example at all. Except for some cases that are better classified a different way, that class of cases is null. Most of its apparent members turn out on inspection to be cases in which I think the law is clearly wrong, but other people, as honest and sincere as I, disagree. At least those who made the law disagree with me, and they are usually not the only ones. The remaining cases, those in which even the people who make the law also agree that it is wrong, are more importantly classified as cases of corruption, that is, in terms that reflect, not only on the content of the law, but also on how it came to be made. In those cases where the people at the top are not even trying to do their jobs, are not trying to serve their functions as legislators, judges, and so on, it is at least arguable (since institutions are usually explained in terms of their points or functions) that there is no legal system to obey or to disobey.

The central class of cases to which we must pay attention, then, is the class in which there is a disagreement about the propriety of the law. Why should I pay any attention to the law, let alone recognize it as binding on me, if I think that what the law requires is morally wrong?

Suppose that I believe the law to be wrong. I therefore make speeches, write letters to newspapers and politicians (or to the absolute monarch), and generally join in public debate on the matter, but I fail to persuade people. They respond to me with arguments that I recognize as invalid and with premises that I recognize as false, though they cannot see the faults in their arguments when I point them out. I have followed the legal means of persuading people, but without success. Where do I go from there? If the law is wrong and I have tried to explain that point, even though all these idiots still cannot see it, surely the law cannot be binding on me?

That is one sort of picture of the situation: the law is wrong, and these fools still cannot see it. Another picture, of course, is this: the law is right, and this crank keeps on boring people stiff with bad arguments against it. But as I explained earlier, we cannot start from the premise that the law is right or from the premise that the law is wrong; politically it is impractical, and morally it is improper. The premise we must start from is that there is disagreement. We do not start from the question: What am I to do with these idiots who cannot see reason? We start, instead, with a question such as: If I think it unfair that I be made to fit in with their views, which I believe to be mistaken, is it any more fair if they are made to fit in with my views, which they believe to be mistaken? This does, of course, invite the question: Is it any less fair? But a new picture is emerging, one in which each of us lives with other people and there are questions of fairness to be raised about the decision-making procedures between us. We no longer see the matter simply as one of the wrongness of my having to fit in with everybody else, but rather as one in which the alternative is that I claim the right to act as a dictator, and, when we disagree, everybody has to fit in with me. (This problem can be made more difficult if we imagine somebody with information not accessible to others. It is likely to be somebody working with secret material, such as, say, the scientists working on the Manhattan Project in World War II, and not at all likely to be simply somebody who has suddenly seen the truth about Russian imperialist ambitions or the nature of capitalism. The information that person has, and needs to back up his claim in argument, is likely to be public.)

The claim that everybody has to fit in with me if I break the law is, of course, too strong: I do not become dictator of Australia simply by exceeding the speed limit in my car. Nevertheless, the claim has a point to it. It is the same point as the Laws have in mind in Plato's *Crito* when Socrates imagines them accusing him of trying to destroy them by disobeying them. Had Socrates disobeyed the Laws by escaping, that would not have resulted in the immediate collapse of Athenian society any more than my speeding would make me dictator. The claim looks as though it is one about the consequences of Socrates' action, but in fact it is not. The Laws plainly are not concerned simply about the consequences of Socrates' not living in Athens, since his death will bring that about, or about the consequences of his living elsewhere, since he was offered exile as an alternative punishment. They have a different and somewhat more formal point in mind.

Had Socrates wanted to overthrow Athenian society, it would have been the sheerest egotism had he tried to achieve that aim simply by going to live elsewhere. It would have been egotism to the point of stupidity, and, while Socrates might have been hard to get along with, he was not stupid. He could surely have replied to the Laws that his act of disobedience would not have the consequence of destroying Athenian society, and it would have been difficult for the Laws to contest the claim. Plato does not bother to fill out the argument, and that gives it a misleading appearance.

The objection might be made that, though Socrates' breaking the law would not have the consequence of destroying Athens, that consequence would follow if everybody broke the law. To this objection, two replies might be made. The first is that Socrates quite clearly had a lot of opponents in Athens; not everybody would take him as an exemplar, so his breaking the law would be unlikely to have the consequence that everybody broke the law. In that case, what would happen if everybody broke the law is irrelevant to Socrates' act. When I go fishing and wind up to cast with a four-ounce star on the line, what matters is that I am standing alone in the middle of the beach; the consequences of my going through the same action in a crowded room would be irrelevant.

The other reply that might be made is that if everybody else broke the law, killing at random, stealing, and so on, then Socrates would be silly and would not live long if he remained as the only one who kept the law. The point is not simply one of prudence: if everybody else is simply after his cut, it is not unfair for me to go after mine. If others kill at random, then I may have to kill in self-defense, and their behavior licenses me to do so. People who try to kill me, steal my food, and so on, have no claim on me that I not respond in kind in order to defend myself. Again, the objection in terms of consequences does not show that the law is binding.

So not even speculating about what would happen if everybody did the same shows that Socrates would be destroying Athens if he escaped, and the same holds good of my becoming dictator by speeding. What it does show, though, is something at a different level: Athenian society cannot continue if everybody breaks the law, so Athenian society, if it is to defend itself, cannot allow everybody the right to break the law. Unless Socrates can show what is special about himself that justifies him in claiming a right that others lack, he must accept either that he has no right to break the law or that everybody has such a right. In escaping, he would then be acting wrongly in doing something that he had no right to do, or he would be allowing that everybody had the right to break the law, which means that he is willing to see the destruction of Athens. Either he is being unfair, or he is making a move toward the destruction of the Laws (even if the move will not, in fact, succeed). The argument is actually about rights, not about consequences.

That argument obviously has a lot of bite to it. It is plain that, in appropriate circumstances, it would give reasons for saying that the law was binding on somebody. Its strength is sufficiently clear for its limitations to be worth noting.

For one thing, the argument applies only if one has some commitment to the society. Somebody who believes that the whole society is rotten and all its laws absurd (a much stronger claim than that the wrong party won the most recent election) might cheerfully contemplate its destruction (and look forward to a restructuring without elections that could be won by the wrong party). Such a person might well say that everybody had a right to ignore the laws. This brings out the point that the argument is about consistency.

Another thing is that some laws deal with matters where common action is not necessary and breach of the law poses no threat to the continued existence of the community. In such a case, I could quite consistently say that everybody had a right to break *that* law and still refuse to contemplate the destruction of the community. Either we are at war or we are not, and a community might well need some definitive way of determining which is the case. Life would be, at best, very difficult if some Australians could be at war with New Zealand while others were not. On the other hand, it is not clear that either we all smoke pot or that none of us does, or that those who do smoke pot thereby make life harder for those who do not, or that those who do not thereby make life harder for those who do. Whether or not that is an example, there certainly are cases in which each can do his (or her) own thing without serious effects on others, and breach of a requirement of common action in such a case would not, in itself, threaten the security of the community. This does leave a serious question about who is to determine whether or not a law is of that type, which is a matter about which we can and do disagree.

And one more limitation: even in matters in which common action is necessary, the law can sometimes harmlessly leave loopholes. When there is conscription in time of war, for example, the status of conscientious objectors can still be recognized. In other words, there might be an answer to the question "What's special about you to give you a right that others lack?" I have, but my son lacks, a right to drive a car on public roads, because I have passed the relevant tests and hold a driving license.

We return now from these limitations to the main point. If I disagree with a law and therefore break it, I do not thereby become dictator. I do, though, subject to the limitations set out, seem to approach the position of one who claims the rights of a dictator. But if the alternative is that I be subject to the dictatorship of others, what is wrong with that? The question we came down to earlier was this: If I think it is unfair that I be made to fit in with the views of others when I think them mistaken, is it any more fair, or less fair, if they are made to fit in with my views when they believe that I am mistaken? Who actually should have what rights in the situation? And this leads us to look at the problem in another way. If the issue is one of the fairness of making one submit to another when each thinks that the other is mistaken, then we should concentrate on the fairness of the method by which it was determined who would submit to whom, rather than on the contending claims about mistakenness. The question ceases to be: Was the answer to the question about what to do the correct answer? and becomes: Was the dispute about what to do resolved fairly? If it was resolved fairly and I insisted on having my way nevertheless, then I am claiming the rights of a dictator. If it was not resolved fairly and the other side tries to force its views on me, then I am not claiming the rights of a dictator, but roughly those of a citizen in good standing, if I insist on going about my business as I see fit. If we freely agree to resolve the dispute by tossing a coin and I lose the toss, then I should submit, just as I expect the other person to submit if I win the toss. If the dispute is resolved by the other fellow pointing out that he has a bunch of goons who will beat me to a pulp unless I do as I am told, then there are no moral reasons, though there may be reasons of prudence, why I should submit.

The emphasis, then, shifts away from the content of the particular resolution of the dispute and comes to rest on the procedure by which the dispute is resolved. It is perfectly clear that I can easily reach a conclusion about what ought to be done if I start from the premise that the law is right or from the premise that the law is wrong. That method will not enable me to reach any useful conclusion starting from the premise that we disagree. But once we shift the emphasis and concentrate on the justice of the procedure by which the decision was reached, we *can* start from the premise that we disagree and hope to reach a worthwhile conclusion. Procedural points are important.

We have already seen that points about the content of the law can matter and need consideration in trying to determine whether a law is morally binding. If our decision-procedure produces a law prohibiting the smoking of marijuana, and if the smoking of marijuana by some or all citizens has no effect on the security of the community, not even indirectly by weakening family ties or causing more absenteeism among workers, then it seems to be nobody's business but mine if I smoke the stuff. My smoking it does no harm to anybody else, so it is not the state's business; the law cannot properly require me to refrain, so, if it does require me to refrain, the law will not be binding. But the matter is not nearly as simple as that, because those various claims are contested. Whether marijuana-smoking does any direct or indirect harm to anybody is contested, and, generally, whether marijuana-smoking is the business of the state is contested. We do not have a straightforward case; we have a dispute about whether the law is a proper one. That takes us right back to where we were: the dispute about whether the law is a proper one has to be resolved, and whether that resolution is binding (which, in this case, would mean that I should be bound to refrain from smoking marijuana) depends, at least apparently, on the justice of the procedure by which the resolution was reached. Once again, even in this sort of case, the content of the law falls into the background, and the main significance attaches to the procedures and their justice.

Whatever might be the requirements for a law to be binding, then, they are not likely to be about the content of the laws. That the law is right (or, more accurately, that I think it is right) is not a necessary condition of its being binding on me. For the same reasons, reinforced by the point about obedience and conformity, the law's being right is not a sufficient condition of its being binding on me. My personal views on the morality of particular laws are not at all central to the issue of whether or not those laws are binding. One should not expect that my personal views on such a public matter would be any more important than anybody else's. Let me stress again, though: the claim that the law is wrong, or that I think it is wrong, is one thing, and has very little significance with respect to whether I ought to obey; the claim that the government is corrupt and is not even trying to do its job or apply the procedures properly is a quite different thing that does, *prima facie*, have a good deal of significance with respect to whether I am obligated to obey. If the government is corrupt and is not trying to operate the decision-procedures fairly or properly, then the effective procedure by which the decisions are reached is not fair, so the obligations that follow from submission to a fair procedure do not follow in such a case. The government is then setting aside the procedures and merely using its power; the situation is essentially the same as that in which the person who disagrees with me simply tells me that he has a bunch of goons who will beat me up unless I fit in. To be a citizen in such a situation is simply to be a slave, and escape is no moral error. A different situation again is that in which I think the government is not trying to do its job properly because I have a different idea from everybody else's about what the job of a government is. That is simply one more disagreement to be resolved by reference to the appropriate fair procedure.

The stress, then, will be on procedure rather than on the content of the laws. The issue is one of reciprocity and of the fairness of the relationships set up between the contending parties by the decision-procedure. I should obey the law, not simply because it is a good law, but because, in fact, it governs my relationships with other people, setting up mutual limitations such that it is just that I be limited in the relevant ways, provided that other people are so limited. Since it is a matter of justice and reciprocity, others have rights against me that I obey the law, and I have the same right against them. Herein lies the law's bindingness. It is not enough that our imagined society has a set of rules; to impose requirements and prohibitions in the relevant sense it must have a set of binding rules, and that leads us back to rights.

Consider our economist F, who discovered the wonders of a private property system. Somebody might object that F's discovery and demonstration of the virtues of a private property system do not constitute a requirement or law in the appropriate sense because they are not promulgated or accepted. Appealing to it is like appealing to natural law on some accounts of natural law and has all the problems traditionally associated with that move; F's statement that private property is the best property system has status only as an expression of his private view, not as a publicly recognized law or requirement, and that is why it is not binding on anybody.

The same holds true of other less conventional issues, such as particular people's views about the rights and wrongs of abortion, euthanasia, and other morally contentious matters. The views on such matters of particular people are private views and, simply as such, not something that others are required to comply with. We could not sensibly speak of the community's having a requirement in such matters unless there were a publicly accepted way of determining which of contending views about such matters as the legalization of abortion should prevail. Again, a declarer of the law is needed. If natural law is to govern, then there must be a way of determining for everybody, no matter what their private views may be, what the natural law requires in these particular circumstances.

This is all rather like Hobbes's move on natural law. Private views are no doubt important; they give a point to the public requirement, argument in terms of them probably lies behind the public requirement, and some agreement in private views (at least about what counts as a just public procedure) may well be necessary if there is to be some procedure to determine the public requirement. Nevertheless, *merely* as private views or private interpretations of natural law, they serve no great public purpose because they do not act interpersonally and are not binding on the community. To achieve public purposes, to have a community and community requirements, there must be a declarer of the law who determines the community requirements, a person or body of people properly constituted to resolve the disputes.[8] This body may not have any special access to the truth, but that does not matter. It does not matter even if that body is required to try to find out the truth and to make its decisions in the light of its findings. The function of the body, even if it must try to find out the truth, is to make common action possible by determining what is to be done when conflicting private judgments cannot agree about the best course of action. Perhaps that body cannot provide a definitive account of the truth, but it can provide a definitive answer to the question "What is to be done?" and thus make common action possible.

The role of this declarer of the law is simply to deal with disputes among citizens, so it would be superfluous where there was agreement, and it could be overruled by agreement. It is not quite the same as Hobbes's declarer of the law, because a Hobbesian sovereign can intervene whenever he sees fit. There are several reasons for this. One is that Hobbes seems to make a number of empirical assumptions about which I differ with him: assumptions about the likely frequency of disputes, about the likelihood of people's being able to settle them by private discussion even if it is only a matter of muddling through, about the likelihood of people's constantly pressing their views even to the point of violence when faced with disagreement, and about the necessity of having a *guarantee* that any problem that could ever arise can be dealt with. I think that people are pretty good at muddling through by concentrating only on the problems that are practical problems. A constitution may be obscure in some possible circumstances, as appeared to be the case with the

Australian constitution in 1975,[9] but some possible problems never arise, and others do not arise for a long time. In the meantime, we can often get by.

It should also be noticed that what I have said does not suggest that it should always be the same body of people acting as declarer of the law. If there is a disagreement between the sovereign and a citizen, there is no reason why that disagreement should be settled by the sovereign. Indeed, there is reason why somebody impartial should be called on to handle the dispute: allowing one of the parties to the dispute to make the decision would not be binding, because that procedure fails to satisfy the condition of initial equality set out in Chapter 3. That condition means that the decision-procedure must be, in a special way, content-free,[10] not building in preference for any one party's view of justice. The job of the decision-procedure, among other things, is to decide between conflicting views of justice. If A and B differ about the justice of some arrangement, then, for the reasons given earlier, the procedure cannot properly decide between their views while starting from the premise that A is right and B is wrong.

We do sometimes distinguish between people in terms of the judgment they show in moral matters, and it could be that the person or people set up as the declarer of the law are chosen because they are regarded as being authorities on such matters. (It might, on the other hand, simply be that everyone has a vote and everyone is bound by the majority decision whatever his private views.) As long as it is simply a matter of these people's knowing more (or being commonly believed to know more) than the rest of us on such matters, their views are still merely some views among others and are not binding on those who disagree with them. The fact that experience has shown that C's private views are more likely to be right than anybody else's private views does not make them any less private views or any more binding on others. For one consideration, even those who know a great deal are sometimes wrong and always fallible; to remove dispute and produce a definitive community requirement we need, not somebody who describes as accurately as he can the truth of the matter as he sees it, but somebody who determines what the right thing to do is. The declarer of the law must be equivalent to the maker of the law. What we need is not a body that is *an* authority on abortion, but a body that is *in* authority on abortion. Only such a body can play the necessary role of making communal action possible despite disagreements in private judgments.

To recognize a body as being in authority in this sort of way involves recognizing that there are rights, because it involves recognizing that, if the decision is contrary to my private view, then I am obligated no longer to act in accordance with my private view. It is not simply a matter of its being wrong (unwise, inconsiderate, selfish) if I still go ahead and act in accordance with my private view. The argument for the impropriety of my doing so is not the sort of argument used to show that an act is selfish or lacks wisdom; the justification for requiring me to curb my action is a story that refers to and depends on our cooperation with respect to the decision-procedure, so it is an argument to show specifically that I am *obligated* no longer to act in accordance with my private view.

The English words "right" and "wrong" cover a wide variety of cases. Not only are there different ways in which an act can be wrong; there are different *sorts* of ways in which an act can be wrong. It might be wrong for me not to give alms to a beggar, but not in the same sort of way as that in which it is wrong for me not to repay a loan. Not giving alms to a beggar may be selfish or callous, but not repaying a loan is unjust. (My example assumes economic relations and distribution as they are, but the point I am after comes out in recognizing that people who disagree with the example will want to argue that the distribution is unjust, so that those who are well-off owe debts of justice to those who are not, that one's dealing with a beggar is not merely a matter of charity or kindness. But such people do not want to argue that there is no such thing as kindness; they want to presuppose the distinction I am calling on and to argue that the case of the beggar is misclassified as one of kindness but is really one of justice and obligation. They may be right. Nevertheless, I simply assume the current economic framework to help me make my point.) The rightness or wrongness of giving alms to a beggar is unaffected by whether he or anybody else tells me to, because the relationship is not one of authority, or of right and obligation, in which one person determines by fiat the propriety of another's course of action. If a beggar "releases" me from giving him alms, or declines my offer, I should look around for somebody else to whom to give the money: another beggar, or the Red Cross, or Amnesty International. The reasons for giving alms to the beggar are reasons for doing these other things, too, because they are not reasons concerned with the specific relationship between the beggar and me, but with the nature of the world and the suffering in it. My relationship with a creditor is quite different: the propriety of my action in repaying or in not repaying a debt depends specifically on my relationship with my creditor and on his decision. If he demands payment when it comes due, I must pay. If he releases me from my debt, there is no particular reason in that fact for me to look around for somebody else to give the money to (unless, of course, I have many creditors and am having trouble paying them all). The morality of my action depends, not on

118 Liberty, Community, and Justice

its "natural" content, but on the formal relationship between my creditor and me. It is a matter of obligation. So it is in a case of authority when the decisions of the authority do not accord with my private views. I may still believe my private view to be correct, and I may try to persuade others, including those in authority, that it is correct and that their decision should be changed, but to recognize that the declarer of the law is in authority and sets community requirements is to recognize that it has a right to decide what is to be done in those areas,[11] and that I have a correlative obligation to comply. Without that structure to the authority, the declarer of the law cannot serve its function. Even if we *think* of all the rights as lying with God,[12] people in this world must *function* as rights-bearers.

An attempt to evade this point by imagining that there might be no legislation where there was disagreement would fail. Requirement is requirement that one does something whether one wants to or not, and that notion is lost if we restrict ourselves to areas of agreement. There is no legislation and no community requirement if each simply works out for himself what he thinks is the right thing to do and acts as he, personally, sees fit.

This point, and the general point about bindingness, can be reinforced by considering what R. P. Wolff has to say about unanimous direct democracy,[13] which he regards as the only possibly justified form of authority on the ground that it does not require that anybody be subject to anybody else. But Wolff's account of the propriety of this form of government leaves questions to be answered for just the sort of reason that I have been suggesting. Why is my consent to the law enough to justify enforcement of the law on me without my consent to that particular use of force? Why does the fact that I voted for the law commit me to it if I later change my mind? (And if it doesn't, what sense is left to the notions of voting and law?) The only plausible reason is that this is a just procedure and binds me for that reason, but that leaves us with the question of whether there are other just procedures. Autonomy, on the significance of which Wolff rests his case, does not require that I be allowed to do injustice.

If any binding law is made by unanimous direct democracy, rather than each of us simply declaring that, at the moment, he happens to think that X is a good idea, then it is binding no matter what the individual wills; that is, it holds even if somebody changes his mind. Its being binding cannot, therefore, be a matter of nothing being imposed on any will from outside. It must be a matter of procedure. If binding law is made, then Wolff's problem arises, and, if it is solved in the case of unanimous democracy, then people can properly be subject to authority.

Community life without a public decision-procedure is impossible.

Wolff's claim appears to be, substantially, that participation in a decision-procedure by those subject to it is a necessary condition of its being just.

What is it for a person who has voted for compulsory arbitration procedures to "recognize the principles as his own"? It is not simply for him to recognize the principle as one he would follow independently of the voting, or arbitration would be out of place—one arbitrates about what each person's due is, because if the disagreement is about whether each person should get his due, one party will not be prepared to accept the decision of the procedure if it goes against him (that simply decides that his submission is due to the other person) and all that is left is fighting. An arbitration procedure can be, for example, submission to the decision of the oldest member, or tossing a coin, or the best two tosses out of three. His recognizing the principle is simply his being committed to it, and the voting is important because that is what commits him, not simply his independent views about its content. That is to say, Wolff recognizes that one can be committed to the outcome of a procedure without prior knowledge of the outcome of that procedure. The remaining problem is whether voting or consent is a necessary or sufficient condition of being so committed.

It is not a necessary condition, as is shown by the case of the nearly desert island:[14] if ten of us are shipwrecked on an island with enough food for only ten, nine agree to equal shares, and the tenth insists that he will take whatever he wants, we do not need his consent before we may restrict him to his share. Nor is it a sufficient condition: apart from my consent, we need a story about why I cannot withdraw the consent (some story such as that my consent placed me in a cooperative endeavor in which my continued submission can justly be required). Plainly, consent can often be withdrawn. If I say that you can decide what we shall do next weekend and you decide that we shall blow up the Sydney Harbour Bridge or hang by our thumbs or read Agatha Christie, I shall withdraw my consent and tell you to forget it. On what ground could you require that I do as you wish? The story would be more complicated if I had agreed that you could decide about next weekend in return for my being allowed to decide about the weekend after next or about last weekend.

Wolff writes: "I have an obligation to obey the laws which I myself enact . . . But on what grounds can it be claimed that I have an obligation to obey the laws which are made in my name by a man who has no obligation to vote as I would."[15] What emerged from Wolff's consideration of unanimous direct democracy is that I have an obligation to obey the laws that *we* enact, not laws that I enact (that would be an expression of my present preference, not the enactment of a law). *We* can enact them (i.e., act corporately) only if there is a decision-procedure determining what counts as the community's act (in this case, unanimity—but it is the community's act, and binding law, only if it is more than merely the summing of a lot of individual people's decisions). The procedure determining the community's act might equally well be voting among representatives. We might then want to argue about the justice of different representative systems.

The point arises out of consideration of disagreement, but it will not suffice to say that we can imagine that there might be no such disagreement. To imagine a case in which we could rule out having to consider all these disagreements, to imagine a situation in which everybody's judgment was infallible or, even more implausible, where everybody spontaneously made exactly the same mistakes as everybody else, where nobody's judgment was ever distorted by his own interest, would be to imagine not a community of people with no rights, but a group of angels with no need of a morality. If the point depended in that sort of way on everybody's agreement, so that change of mind was enough to free one from the requirement, then, though each person might make requirements of himself, we could not sensibly speak of a community requirement.

In any community of people there will be disagreements: disagreements arising from clashes of interests, disagreements about the facts, and disagreement about the interpretation of the law. These disagreements are often not noticed because we simply build into our perception of the world our everyday ways of resolving them. Where there is a clash of interests we might defer to the older person, one person might not even consider pushing his own interests because they are very slight and the other person's are very great, one person might give way because he does not think that whatever is in dispute is worth the trouble of an argument, or, most frequently, one person will not even consider pushing his interests because he recognizes that the other person has rights in the matter and he has not. Where there is disagreement about the facts, we might resort to empirical tests where they are practicable (actually count the Hollywood stars to see if nine out of ten of them do chew their fingernails), we might simply trust the other person's judgment and defer to it, we might refer to somebody whom both disputants agree to be an authority on such matters, or we might call all possible witnesses to consider what they have to say about whether somebody really did fall asleep while the vice-chancellor was speaking. If we cannot agree about what the law requires (Are *funny* Irish jokes contrary to the Race Relations Act? Is a seaplane an airplane or a ship for purpose of insurance?) or about the interpretation of a term in a dispute (is so-and-so really a Hollywood *star*?), then the standard move, if the issue is sufficiently important, is to refer to an arbitrator or to take the matter to court.

One thing is clear: when such disputes arise and endure, a change in procedure is necessary if they are to be resolved effectively. More of the same might make for lively conversation at parties, but it will not solve the problem. Where 362 witnesses have given their views about whether Jeremy fell asleep during the vice-chancellor's address, we do not resolve the disagreement simply by calling one more. If my neighbor and I are in some dispute about who is liable for damage to our common fence, the addition of his wife's view may put him in a majority, but it does not settle the issue. Faced with contending private views about what happened or about the interpretation of the law, we cannot resolve the problem in favor of truth simply by adding one more private view.

Resolution of the dispute is not always necessary: if you think that carrots should be planted in gravel and I think the best way to grow them is to plant dahlia bulbs and utter incantations, then, in the normal run of things, each of us can go to hell in his own way. The situation is somewhat different if we are responsible for producing the community's food, because that places our carrot-growing in a wider cooperative endeavor. Where resolution of the dispute is made necessary by the necessity for common action, we must move beyond private views: if discussion does not result in agreement, then we need a public procedure that *determines* the right thing to do, that is, a public procedure that is not taken as offering one more private view or description of things, but as presenting binding decisions about what is to be done. Since it is deciding a matter that was in dispute, some people are going to think that the decision reached is the wrong one, but that disagreement is part of what gives point to the decision-procedure and cannot by itself be a serious objection. The role of the decision-procedure is not that of being infallible, though the decisions that it reaches should be reasoned as well as possible. The role of the decision-procedure is to be determinative; it must be a matter of authority, with the rights that authority involves. Without something playing that role, there could be no community for want of common action in crucial cases.

Similar points can be made about disputes arising from clashes of interest. One cannot resolve *clashes* of interest simply by setting out to further people's interests. That one increases satisfaction of interests is a matter of aggregation, but the problem of clashing interests is one of distribution; one must discriminate and choose between the interests. Nor is it clear that one could simply opt for the maximum satisfaction of interests, since it is not clear that interests are commensurable in the required way any more than pleasures are. Each person may (or, at some stages, may not) be able to rank his own interests, but how, in terms of aggregation, could one decide between the interests of somebody who wants beautiful scenery and the interests of somebody who wants air-conditioning when the only way to provide the air-conditioning is to tear down the scenery and build a factory? The effects on somebody's interests of tearing out his rose-bushes depends on how obsessive a rose grower he is, on the role that the roses play in his life, and that is not easily measured. Comparing it quantitatively with the role played in somebody else's life by stamp collecting is, at best, not an easy task. But, setting that problem aside, whatever distribution is finally decided upon will be effective only if it is accepted as authoritative, that is, as binding and as generating rights and obligations.

Feinberg gives a law requiring that one stop at a red traffic light as an example of something that is a requirement even though nobody has any rights in the matter: "there is no determinate person who can plausibly be said to claim our stopping as his due."[16] One reason why one might think that there is no particular person with a right against me that I stop at a red traffic light is that there is no particular person who can release me from my obligation to stop at a red traffic light, as there *is* a particular person who can release me from my obligation to do what I promised him I would do. Promising seems to be the most common model for obligation, but in this sort of respect it can be misleading. Obligations can arise, not only from particular transactions between two people, but from wider cooperation among larger groups of people. People at large have an interest in the activities of drivers arriving at an intersection and, on the face of it, we protect those interests (not only those of our fellow motorists, but of pedestrians, those who sit at home wondering about the safety of venturing outside, and those who might have a heart attack and need an ambulance to get them to hospital) by cooperating in terms of a set of conventional signs determining who has right of way when. If that is the case, then everybody has a right against me that I stop when I come to a red traffic light. The reason why no particular person can release me from my obligation to do so is that I am obligated to all the others as well; what one says to me does not affect my obligations to the rest or mean that I would not do them a wrong if I run a red. Even if the only person I hit when I run the light is the one who "released" me from my obligation to him, I have infringed the rights of others, and the rights I have infringed are important because they affect the security of those people in making any plans that involve crossing roads. Because this sort of problem could arise, it could be that each person is obligated, not only to stop at red traffic lights, but also to refrain from "releasing" anybody else from his obligation to stop.

It is fairly common to distinguish between duties and obligations, duties coming with one's role and obligations as a result of a particular transaction. If one is a father, one has duties. If one makes a promise, one has obligations. It has also not been uncommon to take it that obligations have correlative rights, but that duties have not. This, I think, is false, and arises from a misunderstanding. There may, sometimes, be differences that matter between duties and obligations as so distinguished, but they are certainly not far apart. One has the duties of a policeman as a consequence of the particular transaction of joining the police force and swearing an oath. Both duties and obligations place one in a social institution, and they derive their force in the same way, in terms of what is required if one is to play the part in which one has been cast. The clear difference between them is that, in the case of a promise, there is one clearly identifiable person who has the right against the particular person who made the promise. There is no clearly identifiable person who, in the same way, especially has a right that a particular policeman shall act in certain ways. That is not because nobody has such a right, though; all of us have rights (or Hohfeldian powers that we exercise when we call for help) against policemen, even though we may not have a right to decide which particular policeman shall answer the call. And there are certainly specifiable people who especially have rights against a father.

Another point is relevant to the argument about rights in the case of the traffic light. If I run a red light, I am likely (though not very likely in Western Australia) to be charged, convicted, and punished. If I fail to meet the requirement of the law, I can be called to account. If somebody suggests that I stop at a red traffic light, I can ignore his suggestion. If somebody requests that I stop, I can refuse to accede to his request. In neither case would one think that there had been no suggestion or request. But if nobody has the right to call me to account for running a red light, and if there is nobody to whose calling of me to account I have a duty to respond, one cannot make sense of the claim that there is a law *requiring* that I stop rather than merely a general suggestion or request that I do so. The police and the courts, through their part in enforcement, play a role in giving sense to our notion of law. More generally, we can say that, even if a requirement does not generate rights, unless somebody has a right to interfere with the malefactor there can be no way of making sense of the idea of requirement as opposed to suggestion or request.

The claim might be made that the difference lies in the fact that one is regarded as having done wrong if one runs a red light. This defense is unsatisfactory for two reasons. One is that it will hardly serve to draw the distinction required, since one can plainly be regarded as doing wrong in ignoring suggestions and requests. The other is that it overlooks the ways in which some things are wrong. The mere fact that one regards what somebody did as naughty is not enough to show that one regards him as having failed to meet a requirement: there is more to morality than requirement proper. Justice can be required of me in a strong sense; kindness cannot. Again, there are two reasons why kindness cannot be so required of me. One is that the fact that I was forced to do X is sufficient to show that, in doing X, I did not display the warm and immediate concern for another's welfare that is characteristic of kindness, whereas the fact that I was forced to pay my debts means that I have paid them unwillingly, not that I have not paid them. Justice has been done, even if not willingly. Kindness is much more a matter of the agent, and justice a matter of the outcome. Justice must be, in an important way, a matter of outcome, because it is concerned with what must be insisted on if people are to be able to live together. The other reason is that somebody who does only what can be required of him (somebody who literally is no better than he ought to be) is not kind; kindness involves going beyond what can be required or demanded, being charitable rather than merely paying taxes. If somebody suggests to me, correctly, that it would be kind of me to spend my day off visiting my aged aunt, then it would be unkind (and thus wrong) for me not to comply with his suggestion. Nevertheless, there is no strong *requirement* that I visit my aged aunt. Nobody could properly force me to do so. The situation and the wrong are quite different if the suggestion with which I fail to comply is that I fit in with the standard requirements about satisfying the needs of my infant son. In the latter case, I can properly be dragooned. Not all of morality is concerned with requirement, and not all wrongs are the same wrong. The mere fact that somebody is regarded as having done wrong is not sufficient to show that he is regarded as having failed to meet a requirement. Some wrongs justify interference, others do not. Wrongs consisting of breach of requirement justify interference.

There can be requirements that do not allocate rights, and there is more to morality than simply rights. Because of these facts, it looks at first glance as though it would be possible to imagine a society with no rights. It looks that way, though, only if we ignore the context required to make sense of those parts of morality imagined to be present in the society without rights. Investigation of what is required to make sense of them shows that we cannot do so except in a context of rights, and shows, in fact, the impossibility of having a community of people without rights.

Notes

1. See H. L. A. Hart, "Are There Any Natural Rights?," *Philosophical Review* 64 (1955), reprinted in A. Quinton, ed., *Political Philosophy* (Oxford: Oxford University Press, 1967); and Joel Feinberg, "The Nature and Value of Rights," in *Rights, Justice, and the Bounds of Liberty* (Princeton: Princeton University Press, 1980).
2. See also Alan Gewirth, *Reason and Morality* (Chicago: University of Chicago Press, 1978), pp. 98–102.
3. One point that I should want to make, for example, is that it is not enough that the citizens of Feinberg's Nowheresville ("Nature and Value," p. 144) have respect for the law. They must also have a common interpretation of it in all of its detailed applications.
4. See, e.g., Wesley Hohfeld, *Fundamental Legal Conceptions* (New Haven: Yale University Press, 1964). The relevant ideas are summarized above in Chapter 2.
5. I am ignoring as not to the immediate point here issues such as what follows if it turns out that keeping the promise will involve B in doing something reprehensible because he was ignorant of certain circumstances when he made the promise, or because circumstances have changed since he made the promise, and so on. My concern is simply to make clear what sort of right is at issue, not to deal in any detail with the morality of promising.
6. Hart, "Are There Any Natural Rights?," pp. 57–58.
7. See also Chapter 4, n.2, above.
8. On ways of resolving disputes and maintaining order without a state, see Michael Taylor, *Community, Anarchy and Liberty* (Cambridge: Cambridge University Press, 1982). It should be noted that Taylor uses the word "community" in a somewhat more restricted sense than I do. I mean simply a group of people who can speak and act as one, so that a group of people could become a community by being organized as a state.
9. The Australian Labour Party, though in government and having a majority in the House of Representatives, did not control the Senate. The Senate refused to pass the Budget, and thus denied the Government funds, unless an election were called. The Government refused to call an election. The deadlock was broken by the controversial intervention of the Governor-General, who fired the Labour leader as Prime Minister and appointed the Liberal leader, after being given an undertaking that the Budget would be passed and an election called.
10. See Chapter 6, below.
11. Such authority might be better understood as a Hohfeldian power than as a Hohfeldian right, but the argument here is that the power must be exercised, that is, that rights must be generated.
12. Cf. Feinberg, "Nature and Value," p. 148.

13. R. P. Wolff, *In Defence of Anarchism* (New York: Harper Torchbook, 1970) pp. 22ff.
14. To be discussed at greater length in Chapter 6.
15. Wolff, *Defence of Anarchism*, p. 29.
16. Feinberg, "Nature and Value," p. 144.

6

The Public Procedure

IN THIS CHAPTER I shall raise a number of related problems about what I have called the public procedure. We have already seen the need for such a procedure, but questions remain about what is required if a public procedure is to be binding and what effect the public procedure has on rights. I shall examine the role of a public procedure with respect to rights in a community, and, along with that, shall examine the relationship between rights and agreement about them: if all (or most) of us agree that somebody has a certain right, does it follow that that person actually has that right? Or, in the form in which that problem more usually comes up: if all (or most) of us agree that somebody lacks a certain right, does it follow that that person actually lacks the right? What sorts of arguments could be presented in the face of such agreement to show that the agreement was mistaken and the right should be recognized?

Whether we think that somebody has a right affects the way we cooperate, because cooperation is marked by such recognition of rights: that is what marks off cooperation from invisible hand cases, other cases in which people's activities simply so fit together that each benefits from the activities of the others, and so on.[1] If cooperation is also what generates rights, then it seems that agreement would produce rights: if we all agreed that Australian aborigines had no right to vote, then they *would* have no right to vote. In a sense, that seems true: if we all agree that Australian aborigines have no right to vote, they will not get to vote. But we also want to say that excluding aborigines from political life infringes their rights, and I think sense can be made of that. It excludes them from rights that they should have, and the reason we should recognize those rights in aborigines is not merely that it would be kind or beneficent for us to do so, or anything of that sort, but a reason to do with justice. I shall try to explain how that can be. In the face of agreement that a certain person lacks a certain right, there are still various questions that we can raise: Is that agreement necessary to the cooperation? Is it consistent with the rest of the way we cooperate? And the question

127

on which I shall concentrate: Does such cooperation satisfy the conditions that allow cooperation to generate binding rules or that mark off cooperation from other activities such as exploitation?

This problem will crop up in a number of forms during the course of this chapter. It will crop up in the form of a question about what objections can be raised against a public procedure if it is the public procedure that determines rights. In dealing with that form of the question we shall need to bear in mind that a community need not be restricted to only one public procedure. Government is one very common form of public procedure, but most communities will have others as well, including tradition and, more vaguely, simply the way things are done. There is no doubt that legislation can change the rights of parents and children as such, but it is a point of not merely political significance that a government can legislate about such matters only within limits. There is another public procedure operating in that area, one that comes out as community expectations about family organization. That procedure, too, generates rights, and the two procedures could come into conflict. One procedure might then infringe rights generated in terms of the other.

And the problem will also come up as a question about the conditions a public procedure must satisfy if being subject to it is not to infringe one's proper liberty. This, I think, is the same as a question about what is required if such a procedure is to be binding. R. P. Wolff has argued that no such procedure can ever be morally binding and that subjection to such a procedure will always infringe one's proper liberty.[2] I shall show that he is wrong.

People's interests clash, and, if that is all there is to it, then nothing can be done: irreconcilable interests cannot be reconciled. We usually manage to deal with irreconcilable interests by determining fairly easily which takes precedence: I may realize that it would be unfair to press my interests, you may be kind enough to put your friend's interests ahead of your own, and so on. But sometimes people's judgments differ, too. We might disagree about whether it would be unjust for me to press my interests, and we could disagree about that either because we disagree about what the situation is (who actually did what, and why?) or because we disagree about what would be just in a situation about which we otherwise agree. Good-willed people will usually find a way; if there is to be common action and if conflict is to be avoided in these circumstances, then we need to appeal to a public procedure, and the assumption of equality dealt with in Chapter 3 has important implications for the nature of that decision-procedure. If that decision-procedure is to do its job and bring people together peacefully, then it must make it possible for them to settle their disagreements on common ground rather than by appeal to force. To do this, it must treat the contestants on equal terms and not prejudge the issue in favor of either of them. Insofar as it fails in this respect, the likelihood of conflict and violence remains. In a fairly clear sense, if the decision-procedure is to do its job and to satisfy the presupposition of equality, it must be content-free with respect to the matter in dispute: it cannot *simply* amount to requiring that one submit and concede that the other's reasons are right, because that stage of the discussion has already been passed; to stick at that point and to require submission would amount to mere coercion in the face of disagreement. It would not, therefore, have any serious claims as a peaceful resolution of the dispute, not even if the loser took it lying down. If a public procedure is to have any serious claims to bindingness when it is called on to resolve a dispute, one particular resolution of that dispute cannot be built in at the start as part of the procedure.

Whether forcing somebody to submit causes disruption, it might be pointed out, is a straightforward matter of fact, and, if the loser in the dispute lay down in the face of threats, the dispute was resolved peacefully. How can I make my claim in the face of these undoubted truths? For a start, the making of threats is a use of violence and a departure from peacefulness (let alone peaceableness) even if nobody is hit, but there is a deeper point to be made when we consider the problem in the context of community life. The point is one about qualities of character. Claims about human nature may be ridiculous if they are taken as claims that everybody is the same, but there must be general truths about people: if people were not, by and large, certain sorts of beings, they could not live together in communities any more than tiger snakes can. This is a point that Hobbes made in his argument about the laws of nature, which he said are "qualities that dispose men to peace";[3] the laws of nature are Hobbes's list of virtues, entry onto the list being determined by the role of the quality of character in making communal life possible. It is a condition of communal life that people recognize these qualities of character as virtues and encourage their development, no matter whether the explanation of their doing so be a matter of genetics, upbringing, something else, or a combination. The first requirement is that people be peaceable; willingness to settle disputes by recourse to violence when other means are available is a vice and, if sufficiently widespread, would make communal life impossible.

It is worth noting that the quality required for community life is willingness to resolve disputes peacefully, *not* merely willingness to resolve disputes peacefully so that communal life can go on. Somebody with the latter quality of character might well realize that the continuation of communal life does not often depend on the resolution of any one particular dispute, and he would be prepared to resort to violence in any other case. His quality of character, if common, would make communal life impossible. Some things can be achieved only by *not* taking them as the aim of one's endeavor and making them the yardstick of what is done. Peaceableness-for-its-own-sake is the virtue, not peaceableness-to-get-the-benefits, even though it is a virtue because those who have it are therefore able to live with the benefits.

People differ, in their judgments as in their wants. There are plenty of differences to be worked out, and if people's first and last response to a disagreement with somebody were to resort to violence, then life would be solitary, poor, nasty, brutish, and short. Communal life would be impossible. Somebody who resolves his disagreements by resort to threats, even if the victim takes it lying down so that, in the end, no fisticuffs ensue, shows the vice of one who is not prepared to seek peace and follow it. The method he has chosen is not a peaceful one in that it is not one that would recommend itself to peaceful people. Simply forcing somebody to submit is clearly possible when we have community life; by then we have escaped the problem of our natural condition and can have unequal forces. Sometimes it will be proper to force people to submit; it will be proper if, for example, they refuse to discuss anything and insist on resolving their disputes with weaker people by violent means. But sometimes it will not be proper. It will not be proper when it expresses the vice of somebody who is unwilling to seek peace and follow it.

If they are prepared to seek peace and follow it, honest and intelligent people who still disagree about something after exhaustive discussion must be prepared to consider other peaceful means of resolving their dispute. They must turn to some sort of conventional decision-procedure which, if it is not to be a resort to mere coercion, cannot have built into it at the start some particular resolution of the dispute. If I disagree with somebody, and if the decision-procedure to which we had to submit did have built into it something that prejudged the issue against me, then it could not provide me with a new reason that I could give myself for submitting; yet a binding decision-procedure can give me new points to consider and a reason to behave in a way other than I was going to do, despite the fact that I have not changed my original opinions. If we disagree about a matter in which there must be concerted action if we are to achieve anything, even if all that we aim to achieve is for at least one of us to be able to go his own way without interference, and if that disagreement is resolved by reference to a procedure that I can see to be fair, then I can present to myself, as reasons for submitting, the necessity that one give way and the justice of the method by which it was determined who should do so. If, however, I think that X is unjust, and built into the procedure is the idea that X is just, then, in my view, the procedure itself will be unjust and I should not be able to regard it as fully binding. Since it would be, as I saw the situation, the unjust part of the procedure that produced the decision against me in the dispute about X, I could not regard that decision as being binding at all. I might fit in with it for all sorts of reasons, especially if jail were the alternative, but I could not regard the decision as binding or as providing me with a reason for fitting in other than coercion.

The bindingness of the decision-procedure, if it is binding, cannot depend on its having got the decision right, because the one most chafed by the bonds, the one whose recognition of them is most necessary, is the one against whom the decision went. If that person was honest in his protestations before the procedure, then he is sure to think that the decision is mistaken: it does not accord with the decision that he argued would be the right one. But the decision-procedure can do its job only if it is recognized as binding despite this, so its bindingness cannot arise simply from the content of its decisions. The argument, before it went to the decision-procedure, was a substantive one about the content of the prospective decision, which content it would be best for the decision to have, but the operation of the decision-procedure adds a new consideration, and a new sort of consideration. It adds a formal consideration: the person in favor of whom the decision went has a right that the other abide by that decision, and the person against whom the decision went has an obligation to abide by it. These rights and obligations are new considerations that were absent before the decision-procedure came into play, and they take precedence over considerations about the content of the decision, otherwise the decision-procedure could not be effective and we could not resolve our disputes peacefully. These considerations of rights and obligations are the new sort of reason with which the decision-procedure can provide me. If I am to object that I am not bound, my objection must be to the procedure itself, and not merely to the decision that emerged from it.

If I do accept that the procedure is binding, then I cannot object that it is *mere* coercion if my compliance is enforced. Such enforcement does not infringe my rights; it prevents my infringing somebody else's. Those who enforce compliance on me do not show the vice of people who are unwilling to seek peace; they took the chance of having the decision go against them when they went before the procedure, giving my views equal hearing with theirs, and there is now no further step that they could take to seek peace except for submitting to *my* refusal to fit in with peaceful means. Sometimes that sort of thing is done, and sometimes it has to be done, but what is wrong with that sort of situation is that it is a submission to vice.

So the decision-procedure can give me a new reason for acting. It is a formal reason, whereas the reasons we presented to each other in our dispute before going to the decision-procedure were substantive, but that does not mean that the two sorts of reasons must be completely different. The formal reasons are reasons of justice, concerned with rights and obligations. Our original dispute might have been about the justice of some possible act. There is no clash here: there is merely the recognition that I can believe *both* that it is unjust to do X *and* that it is unjust to respond to disagreement by simply forcing my views on others. That the reasons can, in this way, be of the same sort explains why one can sometimes feel so torn in deciding what to do despite the arguments to show that the result of a binding decision-procedure takes precedence over private judgment.

It is not that I must accept the decision-procedure before its decisions can properly be enforced on me. In some cases, it might provide a proper reason that I could give myself for submitting, but, blinded by self-interest or fanatical about the truth of my cause, I might not put that reason to myself, or, if I do, I might reject it. I might insist that any just decision-procedure would have to favor my case. But if the only reason I can give in support of my claim that the decision-procedure is unjust is that its decision went against me, then I am being unfair to others. I am insisting that the decision-procedure provide the right answer, the true answer, as I see it, and the truth, as I have already argued, is not the main consideration in such cases: insisting on the truth when we differ (after proper discussion) about what is true makes common action impossible, is intolerant, and denies the presupposition of equality. I should be treating the decision-procedure as though its point were no more than the enforcement of my own private views. A decision-procedure can be binding without my recognizing the fact, and part of our problem is what makes a decision-procedure binding.

My agreement that the decision-procedure is just will certainly be enough for the argument to work on me, and that is probably the best set of circumstances, but, as we shall see in more detail later,[4] it is not necessary that I agree. If my objection to the procedure is the very blunt one that it should, but does not, exclude black people on the ground of the color of their skins, then it will be proper to force me to comply with various decisions despite my rejection of the procedure. To some extent, though, this point depends on my being the odd one out. The numbers can be important. If people cannot agree in sufficient numbers on a fair way to resolve disputes, then they cannot live together peacefully in communities. When there are just a few who disagree, though, the rest can form a community and make the few conform. That is usually what happens. But we shall have to return to this problem and consider the propriety of making them fit in. We shall have to consider in particular whether their rights are infringed, especially if the rights that they claim are based on no more than judgments of private conscience.

I have said that the appropriate sort of objection to raise if one is to show that a decision does not bind one is an objection to the decision-procedure itself, and not merely to the decision. That is simply a claim about what sort of reason is appropriate; there is no guarantee that one's reasons, even if true, will effect any change in the situation. Again, the numbers are important: it matters whether one's beliefs are eccentric, whether or not they are true. Life with other people can be a fragile thing that breaks easily into violence. There is no guarantee that a group of people will be able to live together peacefully forever, especially if they have fundamental disagreements.

The public procedure may be called on to deal with disagreements at different levels. If we are agreed on a project, such as the building of a town hall, then it is obvious that common action is necessary and disputes about details of the project must be resolved. Sometimes, though, we might differ about whether common action is necessary. Some might think that marijuana smoking affects nobody but the smoker, so that each can do his own thing and no common policy is required. Others might think that marijuana smoking has social effects that make a common policy necessary. The two groups of people would be disagreeing about whether marijuana smoking is the sort of thing that must be taken to the public procedure for determination of a common policy. This is a second-order dispute between them about whether a particular first-order dispute should go before the decision-procedure. Such disputes must be resolved if community life is to be possible, so such second-order disputes are always proper subject-matter for the public procedure. The public procedure might produce the decision that the first-order dispute about whether Fred should smoke marijuana is none of its business, and that would be a resolution of the second-order dispute. But, in an important sense, the public procedure must ultimately decide its own sphere of authority; disputes about its sphere of authority must be referred to a public procedure. The highest court in the land must determine for itself whether or not a given case comes under its jurisdiction.

Through all of this, if the public procedure is to be binding, it must, in the required sense, be content-free. If it were not impartial between those who came before it, but had already built into it one particular resolution to the dispute, then it would fail to satisfy the presupposition of equality. If the dispute were about justice, and one particular resolution had been built into the procedure, then the person against whom the decision went would have to regard, not only the decision, but the procedure as unjust, so he would not see the decision as providing him with a new reason for acting. He would have to regard any attempts to enforce conformity on his part as mere coercion. That the decision-procedure must be content-free in this way might appear to mean that it cannot have anything about justice or rights built into it, since that is what the relevant disputes are about, and then it might seem that the rights it determines must emerge from people's clashing wants and must be simply the determination of which want takes precedence, so that liberty would be, at base, a matter concerned with people's wants rather than with their rights.

The claim that the public procedure must be content-free is a puzzling one in some respects and stands in need of further explanation. It seems perfectly clear that a decision-procedure requiring that the rich get whatever they want would be ineffective if the dispute were about whether or not to have an egalitarian society, but problems nevertheless remain. If the decision-procedure is content-free, must it decide arbitrarily? We might be happy to see the dispute resolved by the toss of a coin if coin-tossing were the decision-procedure we had agreed upon, but we should be a good deal less happy after employing the best and wisest judges in the land to see them go out for a cup of tea while arguments were presented and then come back to decide the issue by tossing a coin. We should expect them, not only to know what was in dispute, but to acquaint themselves with the reasons for deciding either way and then to come to a reasoned decision. Complete lack of content seems out of place in that decision-procedure. And since a content-free decision-procedure cannot be guaranteed to produce any particular decision, we must ask: what if the decision-procedure keeps on getting things wrong? If it consistently favored Negro slavery and the persecution and execution of Jews, could it serve the function that such a decision-procedure is supposed to serve, and would its decisions be binding? Could one recognize the injustice of such decisions without regarding the decision-procedure itself as unjust? The only way to guarantee that such decisions will not be made is to build into the decision-procedure some content excluding them. Perhaps such content should be built in. But if it is not an open question at any stage whether being a Negro or a Jew makes special treatment appropriate, what are we to do with those who regard high birth or wealth as making special treatment appropriate and want that built into the decision-procedure? There are *reasons* why people should not be persecuted simply for being Jewish or Negro.

Tossing a coin is sometimes as good a way as any other of making a decision, but it is certainly not the case that any decision-procedure is as good as any other no matter what the circumstances. Tossing a coin would be likely to result in a decision in favor of Negro slavery half the time, and that fact suggests that coin-tossing is an inappropriate way of making decisions about such matters.

If we cannot agree about where to go for our picnic, we might agree to settle the matter by tossing a coin. In that case, tossing a coin seems as good a method as any other. Not all cases are the same in that respect. One might feel inclined to say that, if honest and intelligent people still disagree after exhaustive discussion of the justice of some policy, then the matter might as well be decided by the toss of a coin, since it seems that the matter cannot by decided by reason. But honest and intelligent people, recognizing their own fallibility and the importance of the matter in dispute, might prefer to resolve the dispute in terms of reason insofar as that is possible by arguing their cases before an arbitrator who, to serve the function of arbitrator, would have to be recognized as reasonable and impartial. That the authority of a public procedure does not depend on its having given the right answer does not mean that there are no right answers or correct decisions; if there were none, or if nothing hung on them, disputes would probably not be taken so seriously in the first place. Where there are right answers to be found, and where they matter, a decision-procedure that is more likely to find them is clearly a better choice to make. (But in these terms: a committee of doctors is more likely to diagnose a disease correctly than a committee of moral philosophers. Not: the right answer is X, so what we need is a decision-procedure that will produce that answer.) Tossing a coin is, in its nature, no more likely to produce the right answer than the wrong answer. Trial by jury may be imperfect and may sometimes seem to be something of a lottery, but it is not of its essence that it will make a decision at random rather than try to come to the correct one. The point of trial by jury is to come to the correct decision in terms of criteria that are agreed. The point of a national government is different from the point of a hospital;[5] what is efficient in one will not be efficient in the other, so the procedure appropriate for determining who makes decisions in one will not be appropriate in the other. The issue may often be one of efficiency, but not *merely* one of efficiency, because unnecessary inefficiency is unjust to those who suffer it. It is unjust because it imposes burdens that need not be borne for the enterprise to achieve its point, and burdens imposed in an enterprise, even a just enterprise, must be justified in terms of its point. Tossing a coin would be appropriate when there is nothing to choose between the alternatives and when the point of using the public procedure is simply to resolve the dispute with no further aim in view.

Hobbes really had two points to make about equality.[6] One is about vulnerability, and the other is about the political aspect of moral relations between people. The first point is clear: anybody can be killed. No matter how strong he may be, anybody can be killed by stealth or weight of numbers, so there is no significant difference between people in their vulnerability. Each of us is equally dependent on the restraint of others for his continued existence, since each of us is vulnerable and can be killed or injured, so any debt arising from this dependence is a debt that each of us has to all of the others. The second point is less straightforward, and perhaps less clear as Hobbes waxes sarcastic:

> such is the nature of men, that however they may acknowledge many others to be more witty, or more eloquent, or more learned; Yet they will hardly believe there be many so wise as themselves: For they see their own wit at hand, and other mens at a distance. But this proveth rather that men are in that point equall, than unequall. For there is not ordinarily a greater signe of the equall distribution of any thing, than that every man is contented with his share.[7]

One thing that emerges with great clarity from Hobbes's vituperative dispute with Wallis is that Hobbes did not believe that all people are equally intelligent or make equally good decisions. His point here is, rather, a different one: each person must be taken at least fairly close to his own estimate of himself in the first instance if there are to be peaceful relations. Somebody who finds that his dispute with another is to be resolved starting from the premise that he is an idiot, or even from the weaker premise that he is wrong, will not regard the matter as properly and peacefully settled and is unlikely to regard himself as bound by the decision. In the absence of enforcement, he will see no reason why he should submit. From this equality arises equality of hope in attaining ends, and from that arises war. If war is to be avoided, there must be some peaceful way of recognizing the equality that leads to it. Any method not working on the assumption that I am at least the equal of others will not be adequate to the task. The argument is, in effect, about the necessity of toleration.

What makes people *feel* bound together as a community is important to their being a community because of the presupposition of equality. Once a community exists, it can have a binding decision-procedure in terms of which we can see the point of saying that a particular person is part of the community and is bound by that procedure even if he does not feel bound, but that decision-procedure does not just come down from the skies; it arises from human convention and presupposes that a community already exists. The origins of community, the logically basic way of somebody's being or becoming a member of a community, cannot lie in such enforcement of obligations on people who do not feel obligated. The presupposition of equality shows that there could not be such general enforcement on particular people except by groups of people who had already increased their strength and security by forming communities; isolated people set down in a completely hostile world could not exercise such power over each other. The growth of communities depends on people's social inclinations, on their recognizing and feeling certain ties with each other. How people regard the decision-procedure is, in this sort of way, just as important a matter as how the decision-procedure actually is, as is to be expected since it is a question of how a convention works. I do not suggest, though, that there is no connection between how the decision-procedure is and the attitudes that people take to it, or that people can take any old attitude to any old decision-procedure. Certain conventions work in this world and others do not. It would plainly be unreasonable to take a favorable attitude to one that did not work. And it should be remembered that a particular decision-procedure's working might be a matter of its determining and protecting rights, establishing justice, and so on.

This point comes up in different guises at several stages of Hobbes's argument. One way it comes up is in the point that there is no natural authority: authority, the right for one person to determine what another shall do, arises from convention. If two people, especially after reasoned discussion, hold differing views, then, in the absence of convention, there is nothing to pick out which view should prevail. If I decide in the light of past experience that you are more likely to be right than I am even though I cannot see what mistake I have made, then I may accede to your views. If I am not persuaded, though, only force can make me submit. I cannot be required to submit on the ground that you are right and I am wrong, because that is what is in dispute; if I do not accept your views in the first place, then I shall hardly accept their correctness as a premise from which to resolve the argument. The intermediate step required is a political one: political relations can introduce authority and change the situation. The establishing of conventions, giving people roles and, in some cases, giving some the right to determine what others shall do, can provide a separate reason for submitting: even though I think my views are correct, and even though I have not been subject to coercion, a procedure binding on me has determined that the other view shall prevail. "I think that X is the right thing for you to do, therefore you must do X" is not a good argument. Movement from that premise to that conclusion requires a relation of authority, and that relation of authority is created by the political relationships between people.

The moral importance of this political move, or the importance of the political element in morality, is sometimes missed, and objections to all authority relations result. What is at issue is the moral importance of formal points in relationships between people who can differ at a substantive level but have enough humanity to value peaceful settlement of disputes when that is possible. R. P. Wolff, for example, writes: "The autonomous man, insofar as he is autonomous, is not subject to the will of another. He may do what another tells him, but not *because* he has been told to do it. He is therefore, in the political sense of the word, *free*."[8] That is to say, Wolff takes autonomy to be a matter of decision-making isolation, not of fitting in properly with other people in communal action, and he takes complete autonomy to be something for which each person should strive. Given Wolff's use of the term "autonomy," this means that he thinks that nobody could ever properly subject himself to authority. He does not mean only that one is responsible for one's action in subjecting oneself to authority; he means that one should never do something because one has been told to do it or because some body other than oneself decided that it would be the best thing to do. The only proper reason for going along with authority, on Wolff's account, is that the authority has ordered one to do X and one has decided, quite apart from the order, that X is the best thing to do. One may act in accordance with authority, but may never subject oneself to it; to subject oneself to authority, on Wolff's account, gives up autonomy, which is something like a loss of self-respect or integrity.

A sensible and decent person might subject himself to authority. He might do it because he decided that, whether or not what was commanded was good or wise, it was good or wise to do what was commanded as such because common action was required and there was no special reason why his views should be given precedence over everybody else's. That is to say, there is a *variety* of sorts of point that a reasonable person might consider, not only the immediate substantive ones about whether what was decided accords with his private views. Wolff overlooks the point that politics is about making it possible for people to live together and undertake corporate action despite disagreement, and treats it as though it were a matter of isolation. The point is not just about politics, but about the political element of morality; Wolff writes as though one cannot have moral integrity unless one regards oneself as infallible and forces one's views on those who disagree. The whole context of *corporate* action is overlooked (Wolff's thesis is not simply that governments sometimes intrude unnecessarily, or he would have no opponent), and hence the problem of fairly resolving disputes is overlooked. This does not require the total submission that Wolff fears, as the importance of assessing the public procedure shows.

Consider an example drawing a relevant distinction: it has been common in Australian universities for professors, appointed (largely) on academic grounds, automatically to become administrative heads of their departments. There is some reason for this, since, as official intellectual leaders of their departments, they are officially best at what the department is for and, presumably, they are devoted to its intellectual ends. Apart from personal vagaries, however, there are other aspects to the job of administering a department, and the professor is not especially likely to be the best administrator. The procedure for choosing the best head of department, therefore, will not be to give the job to the professor automatically. Other procedures, though, may cause other problems: people may seek the job because they see it as a path to promotion, or may have the good of the department at heart and be tired of living with their own infallibility and the incompetence of their colleagues (forgetting that that is simply the human condition), or whatever, and the department may become spiteful and ill-willed over the appointment and consequently suffer much more than it would from the occasional incompetence of an automatic appointment that ruled out those problems. The best procedure for appointing a head may not be the procedure for appointing the best head (or, if you like, the procedure chosen can partly determine the context in which it works and the quality of its own outcome). The best procedure for deciding on corporate action need not be the procedure for deciding on the best corporate action, and that point should be borne in mind when a Wolffean insists on having his own way. Formal points can be as significant for the outcome as can any others.

Imagine an outing on the Titanic for ships' captains. When the ship starts to sink, there are six different courses of action each of which will save everybody. Each of these courses of action is advocated by one of the captains. The person to obey is the captain of the Titanic, not because he is giving good advice (the other five are doing that, too), but because he is the captain of that ship. Public office has functions.

Quite plainly, it is not enough that there be a convention setting up positions of authority or procedures for resolving disputes. The convention can serve its function only if it is binding on the parties to the dispute, and one way of considering our problem is as that of determining what such conventions must be like if they are to be binding.

One answer to this, suggested by Hobbes among others, is that consent makes a convention binding. On this account, a convention governs me if and only if I have consented to it, so consent is primary among political relations. Such an account would certainly require that people be taken by the procedure at something very close to their own estimates of themselves, because each person would decide for himself, in terms of his own estimate of himself, whether or not to consent. The idea that consent plays this sort of role seems to be very common among contemporary theorists of democracy.[9]

It is not at all clear that nothing can properly be forced on a person without his consent. This can be brought out at an intuitive level, which is all that is required at the moment, by considering the imaginary case of the almost desert island, a case not too far removed from some causes of war. Imagine that ten people are shipwrecked and are eventually washed up on an island far from the shipping routes or any chance of rescue. The island, they discover, can provide just enough food to keep ten people alive. Yams and coconuts grow in just sufficient numbers, and killing more of the wild animals than necessary for ten people to subsist will result in decline of numbers of stock so that everybody will starve. Nine of the ten people immediately agree to make the obvious move: they agree to ration the food and, since no one of the ten has any special needs, to share it equally. The tenth, an undergraduate who has been reading Robert Nozick and far too many free enterprise economists, refuses to go along with this. The food was simply there when they arrived, he points out; no one of them has any special right to it, so each can simply take as much as he sees fit. He, for his part, feels hungry after the long swim and plans to make substantial inroads into the population of wild goats.[10]

Now, it simply is not obviously improper for the others to enforce rationing on this fellow even without his consent. His estimate of his place in the situation is not the crucial point. Even though each must be taken at somewhere near his own estimate of himself, and even if the other nine were to take the tenth at his own estimate of himself, in these circumstances it is impossible for them to live in community with him. Community is impossible because it is impossible for all of them to live, given the behavior that he intends. I am not at all sure how some of the contemporary consent theorists would handle such a case, but it is clear how Hobbes would accommodate it: the fellow who refuses to consent to the convention remains in his natural condition with respect to the others. Perhaps he retains, as he asserts, his right to all things, but he has no Hohfeldian rights against the others and they have no obligations to him. No matter how they treat him, he can have no proper complaint of rights being violated. They might be merciless, ruthless, or even cruel in their treatment of him, but they could not violate his rights because he has no rights against them. If they respond to his irresponsibility by restricting him to the same share as each of the others, the appropriate response from him would be one of gratitude: on a Hobbesian account, they are quite entitled to kill him to give themselves security against his taking the food they need, and are even entitled to add him to the common store. If they refrain from doing so, that is an act of grace. This is one theory explaining the propriety of enforcing a convention on somebody without his consent, and thus effectively gives an account of how a convention can be binding without the consent of all those concerned.

The line that I have been running fairly clearly leads to a similar conclusion: if rights are socially determined and this fellow keeps himself outside the community, then he has no rights that the others are bound to recognize even when they disagree with him. If you think that X is yours and I think that X is mine, then we can go to our shared public procedure to resolve the matter. If it rules in favor of you, then you have a right that I am bound to recognize even if I think that both you and the ruling of the public procedure are mistaken. Our renegade, though, lacks that relationship with the other nine islanders, so they are not bound to submit when they disagree with his judgment. It may not be proper for them to kill him and eat him simply on that ground,[11] but it is certainly not improper for them to restrict him to no more food than each of them has. And if his constant attempts to take extra food pose a serious threat to them and can be controlled in no other way, they might well be justified in killing him. They might be justified because they should infringe none of his rights in killing him, and the killing, far from being wanton, would be necessary to self-defense. They would be attacking him rather than properly defending themselves if they prevented his taking only what he had a right to. If he wants to be in a position in which he can assert rights against them, he must also be prepared to accept a position in which they can assert rights against him. And he cannot insist that he be the sole judge: he has (in the absence of a very special story) no right to that position that cannot be claimed equally well by anybody else. This is Hobbes's second point about equality coming up again: the renegade must be prepared to give proper consideration to the estimates others have of themselves. One requirement made of anybody if he is to be a member of the community and have rights is that he respect the rights of others. This is the bare minimum of toleration.

If somebody is not party to the conventional procedure that generates rights, then, in the absence of a superior convention, he will have no rights to assert against the decisions of the decision-procedure. Nor will those who are party to it have rights to assert against him. The two will simply be in competition, which is to say that it will be proper for the one to make the other fit in with its rules if it can.

There are qualifications to be made to that last claim, though; there are various virtues and vices that can be displayed in such situations. One important point about the nearly desert island case is that the renegade does affect the rights of the others: if he is allowed free rein in his planned activities, then survival for the group is impossible; that means that cooperation and the rights that it generates are impossible for them. He affects the rights of the others by making it impossible for them to have those rights. They can, therefore, quite properly be regarded as defending their rights in making him conform to the rationing system. They are not merely coercing him and showing the vice of those unwilling to seek peace; they have already taken every possible peaceful step toward solving the problem that faces them all, and what makes a peaceful resolution impossible in this case is the intransigence of the renegade. The group is, clearly, morally justified in requiring conformity of him. Whether he is morally bound to fit in *might* be a different question, though it is not at all clear how it is significantly different: they are not merely in a state of competition in which they are at liberty to try to win; they are defending a number of claim-rights that are attacked by his activities. That makes the situation different from a standard case of competition. That the renegade is taking away their claim-rights is at least very like his infringing them, and that would be equivalent to his failing to fulfill his obligations; if he is failing to fulfill obligations, then he is bound. But in practice the two will certainly come to the same: the group will be able to enforce rationing on the renegade and will be quite right to do so; he will have no legitimate complaint to make about it.

The cooperation that the renegade makes impossible is cooperation without which the group cannot get by. He makes cooperation and the generation of rights in general impossible for them, not merely some specific piece of cooperation and the generation of some specific rights. If it were merely that they wanted to form a choir and needed his bass voice, then the same conclusions would not follow. Leaving him alone is a possible resolution of that dispute within a general context of cooperation. Ignoring that possibility and forcing him to sing is putting coercion before peaceful resolution.

It is the base character of the renegade that causes the problem, or is the problem, on the nearly desert island. The others have done all the right things: they have been prepared to try to solve the problem of food shortage cooperatively, they have satisfied the presupposition of equality in their suggestions about how to do it and, in general, they have done all those things that will create genuine rights. The renegade has refused to cooperate; he has done nothing to generate rights, so he has no rights to assert against the others until he comes under the umbrella of their cooperation.

The rationing system is, in effect, binding on the renegade even though he does not consent to, or even accept, the decision-procedure that gave rise to it. And if there is a sense in which he is not bound, even though he is rightfully forced to comply, that sense will be no joy to him in moral arguments about what he ought to be allowed to do without interference.

So there are a number of points to be made and of questions to be raised if somebody claims rights against others on the ground that no decision-procedure binds him. Such claims that it is improper to enforce the rules on a renegade are not as simple as they might look. One does not gain rights against others simply by saying that one has them, and putting oneself in a Hobbesian state of nature with respect to the others will not generate rights, either. But claims of this sort usually come up in cases more like the choir example than like the nearly desert island and are usually, in import if not in expression, less extreme. The complaint is usually that there is too much unnecessary interference: not that others have no rights against one, but that they lack some of the specific rights they think they have. The point of the objection is that the form of cooperation into which those specific rights fit is not necessary for us, because we can get by with other forms of cooperation that are a lot less restrictive. In these looser forms of cooperation, each of us will have rights against the others, but not the rights against which objection is being made. In the face of this sort of objection, one does need to justify forcing the person into the specific form of cooperation. Coercion without appropriate justification will be mere coercion, the display of a vice.

At a very basic level, that justification will be given by showing that we cannot get by without the cooperation and rights that are being questioned. That is the nearly desert island case. At less basic levels, we can also call on wider areas of cooperation to show a straightforward obligation to join in a specific cooperative enterprise. This is common in the wider context of cooperative endeavors. Why should I pay taxes that will be used to build drains in your area? Because, under the same system, you have paid taxes that were used to build a hospital in my area. Why should I be compelled to pay a Medicare levy when I rarely see the doctor? Because of a complex set of relationships that I have with medical care: I have security in the knowledge that doctors are already trained and hospitals already built, so I can reasonably do things that might be too risky otherwise; because I benefit from others' doing dangerous things that would be too risky or too expensive otherwise; because I get a better mail service if the mailman is not always off sick; and so on. Such considerations can tie a particular case of compulsion into a wider cooperative enterprise generating rights and obligations that mean that it is not mere coercion when I am forced to join in.

The nearly desert island case shows that consent is not a necessary condition of a procedure's being binding on somebody. Nor is it a sufficient condition. For one thing, I can change my mind and withdraw my consent: having decided to sell my house and having put it in the hands of a real-estate agent, I can fire him and withdraw my house from the market or turn it over to another agent. Having done so, I am no longer bound to the first agent and committed to his actions: whatever he does will not count as selling my house. If I am to be bound whether or not I want to be, which is to say, if I am really to be bound, there must be something in the story to show that it would be improper for me to withdraw my consent. I might have received some sort of payment for my consent, for example. Plainly, there can be unjust contracts. My consent will not bind me if the person who gains it does so only by keeping me in ignorance of relevant facts that would have led me to withhold consent, or only by threatening to beat the bejabbers out of me if I do not agree.

It might be objected that these are not cases of free consent, but that move is a lot more complicated than it looks. When I give my consent only because I am in ignorance of relevant facts, the way the situation seems to me and how I feel about it might be exactly the same when the other fellow is deliberately withholding the facts as it is when he is ignorant of them, too. Nevertheless, a contract made in mutual ignorance will be binding. The difference between the two situations does not lie in me or in what went through my mind before I gave my consent; it lies in whether the other person was taking unfair advantage of me. The issue is not simply one of consent, but one of justice. This is no more than might be expected: in the absence of magic, there must be some further story to explain why uttering the sounds "OK" will commit me to some specified course of action.

Somebody who deliberately misleads another person or who uses propaganda or brainwashing to persuade another to give up some of his rights by contracting, promising, or whatever, acts improperly. The impropriety of his action is explained by my point about the political element in morals and the presupposition of equality. Manipulating somebody in this way is not treating him as an equal. I may be manipulating him for my own ends, in which case I am straightforwardly being unjust, but there is also a *prima facie* case of injustice if I manipulate him for his own good (as I see it). I am conducting the discussion by starting from the premise that he is wrong, which is contrary to the presupposition of equality, and, by withholding information and thus limiting the field of eligible actions that he sees before him, I make the situation less cooperative and more exploitative so that I am, *prima facie*, treating him unjustly. If I mislead the other person because I myself have been misled or am otherwise (not culpably) ignorant, then I have not exploited him and he has not been badly done by. The motivation of the misleader is crucial to the morality of the situation. That is because the presupposition of equality imposes some strong limitations on what a decision-procedure must be like if it is to be binding.

Justice seems to keep on raising its head. In the case of the nearly desert island, it matters that the proposal put forward by the nine was a just one. If the proposal had been that each of them, being of high caste, have a larger share at the expense of the tenth, or that he be chopped up and used as fish bait to improve their diet, then, fairly clearly, we should not feel that it was unreasonable or unfair for him to refuse to fit in. On the face of it, justice explains the bindingness of the procedures. On the other hand, it seems that we cannot require of the decision-procedure that it be just when justice is one of the things about which there is likely to be dispute. So how can there be a binding decision-procedure that is content-free?

The problem comes up in Milton Friedman's discussion of discrimination. He says:

> It is often taken for granted that the person who discriminates against others because of their race, religion, color, or whatever, incurs no costs by doing so but simply imposes costs on others. This view is on a par with the very similar fallacy that a country does not hurt itself by imposing tariffs on the products of other countries. Both are equally wrong. The man who objects to buying from or working alongside a Negro, for example, thereby limits his range of choice. He will generally have to pay a higher price for what he buys or receive a lower return for his work. Or, put the other way, those of us who regard color of skin or religion as irrelevant can buy some things more cheaply as a result.
>
> As these comments perhaps suggest, there are real problems in defining and interpreting discrimination. The man who exercises discrimination pays a price for doing so. He is, as it were, "buying" what

he regards as a "product." It is hard to see that discrimination can have any meaning other than a "taste" of others that one does not share. We do not regard it as "discrimination"—or at least not in the same invidious sense—if an individual is willing to pay a higher price to listen to one singer than to another, although we do if he is willing to pay a higher price to have services rendered to him by a person of one color than by a person of another. The difference between the two cases is that in the one case we share the taste, and in the other case we do not. Is there any difference in principle between the taste that leads a house-holder to prefer an attractive servant to an ugly one and the taste that leads another to prefer a Negro to a white or a white to a Negro, except that we sympathize and agree with the one taste and may not with the other? I do not mean to say that all tastes are equally good. On the contrary, I believe strongly that the color of a man's skin or the religion of his parents is, by itself, no reason to treat him differently; that a man should be judged by what he is and what he does and not by these external characteristics. I deplore what seem to me the prejudice and narrowness of outlook of those whose tastes differ from mine in this respect and I think the less of them for it. But in a society based on free discussion, the appropriate recourse is for me to seek to persuade them that their tastes are bad and that they should change their views and their behavior, not to use coercive power to enforce my tastes and my attitudes on others.[12]

This is the sort of claim that is likely to set one back on one's heels, though Friedman's statements that some tastes are better than others and that some tastes really provide no reasons for discriminatory treatment suggest that he is not really taking seriously the idea that racial discrimination is simply a matter of taste. The cases that he presents are not comparable: the point of some activities lies in the satisfaction of tastes, but the point of other activities does not. A singer who appeals to no tastes provides no service and has no claim to payment, but a Negro who folds cardboard into boxes correctly or does his actuarial work accurately does provide a service even if people do not like having that sort of work done by Negroes. The point of the activity determines what is relevant to carrying it out. In provision of entertainment, it is relevant whether the audience likes what it is given and the way it is given. In other cases it is not. And the point of the activity will determine whether race is relevant. This does not mean that there will always be one clear point to an activity: a housekeeper, perhaps, has a more general job of keeping his employer happy as well as the specific job of producing porridge for breakfast, so if the employer's taste lies toward employing Scots, it may be proper for him to exclude the Welsh. On the other hand, refraining from drinking Coca-Cola on the ground that it tastes horrible is quite different from refusing Negroes the right to vote on the ground that I don't like black skins. One is a matter of taste, and the other a matter of moral concern. The point of Coca-Cola is that it satisfies some tastes, but the point of voting is not simply to please me.

If an enterprise has a point or points, then what is relevant to that point or those points clearly provides reason for action within the enterprise. A right fielder's ability to bat .400 at the highest level is a reason to sign him up. The decision still need not be easy: his inclination to ignore fly balls and his long record of causing dissension among his teammates are also relevant. Such facts are clearly reasons for acting, for choosing to sign him up or to find somebody else. But to exclude somebody on grounds that are irrelevant to the activity goes against the presupposition of equality and shows at least the raw form of injustice. It displays a vice; slave-holding is wrong even when there is no price to pay. Questions about what I like or do not like will be relevant when the point of the activity is simply the provision of pleasure.

Friedman, in the passage I quoted, is concerned with commercial discrimination, but his point spreads somewhat wider than that: "there are real problems in defining and interpreting discrimination . . . It is hard to see that discrimination can have any meaning other than a 'taste' of others that one does not share." This is not really so, and, where it is important, the discrimination is not simply a matter of taste. Somebody who shows discrimination in choice of music is a person of taste, and that is an excellent thing to be. What is at issue here, though, is not discrimination as such: it is unjust discrimination. The discrimination that matters, in this context, is injustice. Values are given, forced upon us by the world in which we live; they are not created by anybody's fiat, and injustice is not simply a matter of taste. What affects cooperation is a question of fact, and the answer does not depend on whether or not I like it.

The point might be made that skin color can affect cooperation: if somebody is black, the whites might refuse to cooperate with him, and cooperation would then be impossible. But to conclude that skin color has made the cooperation impossible would be to allow bias to rule in its own favor. What the example shows is that possession of vices such as the raw form of injustice can make cooperation impossible, as it does in cases of unjust discrimination.

The point of voting is not simply to please me. We do, in fact, rule out some from voting: lunatics, criminals currently serving sentence, aliens, anybody under the age of eighteen, and so on. There is discrimination, even if most of us would agree with that discrimination. What is to be done, then, when somebody wants to add people with black skins to the list of those excluded? The decision-procedure for resolving the dispute must give that view as fair a hearing as any other and cannot properly start from the premise that it is wrong. Until the decision-procedure has resolved the issue of who has which rights and what is to be considered, all is like a matter of taste when we disagree. And here again we can see some pull toward the idea that what an account of liberty must start from is not rights, but simply consideration of what people want.

This problem cannot reasonably be dealt with simply by requiring that no class be excluded without its consent. Apart from the problems raised earlier about consent, there is the fact that we do not require, and rightly do not require, the consent of lunatics before excluding them from various activities. The weaker position that a voice must be given to any group that might be excluded is too weak, because it means that the decision simply rests with weight of numbers or with a dictator's whim.

The idea that Negroes should be discriminated against is abhorrent, and the idea that a decision-procedure might produce such a decision is worrying because of that. That the decision-procedure allows such a decision, we might be inclined to say, shows that it is faulty and that its decisions cannot properly be taken as binding. Suppose, then, that we consider a different example, one that created some argument just a few years ago: the registration of women for conscription into the armed forces in the United States. This proposal raised heated voices on both sides, whereas proposals to discriminate against Negroes usually have to be dressed up very carefully these days. In such a case, where there is genuine disagreement, where a decision must be reached, and where we can recognize that our opponents are reasoning properly and considering the right sorts of things even if we disagree with their assessment and their conclusion, and that they are good-willed and not merely trying to force their views on us, we might be more willing to accept the decision of an impartial decision-procedure. The decision-procedure might be as impartial as coin-tossing, but if it consists of appeal to a committee of wise people, we should not require that they ignore the arguments as long as they are unbiased and have no ax to grind in this particular dispute.

Problems of this sort arise in a community. In cases of disagreement, members of the community argue the matter out, in the first instance, in terms of their primary decision-procedures, which are their shared moral concepts. If they cannot resolve the matter that way and a decision must reached, then a choice must be made between the views. We cannot reasonably insist that the right view prevail, because what is at issue is which view is the right one, so we refer to a public procedure that we can agree is not unjust. If we cannot agree about that, then our disputes cannot be resolved peacefully and we cannot live as a community. And there is no guarantee that any group of people with fundamental disagreements can live as a community. The public procedure does not play its role by being plonked down into a mess of complete disagreement: it deals with particular disagreements coming up against a background of agreement. Against a background of agreement that there should be no discrimination against Negroes, the public procedure simply would not come into play. Examples of possible decisions from the procedure will meet with universal execration only if they are matters with which the procedure would not be called upon to deal.

And yet there are racists. If one of them chooses to run the racist line it seems inconceivable that a just decision-procedure could allow the possibility of deciding in favor of him, but how could it give him less than a 50/50 chance and still be content-free or impartial in the required way? If that person is to live in a community with us and have a shared decision-procedure, then we must be able to agree at some point. Not simply anything counts as a reason or as making something just. Skin color might be an appropriate property to consider in working out a just distribution of sun tan oil, but it has nothing at all to do with a just distribution of political power. If the racist wants to be recognized as reasoning, and as having a claim to put forward as a candidate for recognition as a right rather than simply as expressing his wants, he will need to refer to something other than skin color: all Negroes are lazy and irresponsible, he might say, and the lazy and irresponsible should be excluded. We might agree that laziness and irresponsibility are relevant to the question of exclusion. The impartiality required of the decision-procedure then is simply that of ascertaining the facts: are all Negroes, and nobody else, lazy and irresponsible? The decision-procedure then gives the racist his fair chance and leaves him with no reasonable complaint about its operation, but it does not follow that the procedure is as likely to produce one decision as the other.

If we disagree to the point at which somebody simply sticks with the claim that skin color, as such, is relevant to whether somebody ought to be excluded from political power, then we shall have to argue out with him an account of justice. This would be a complicated job. We shall have to argue out with him what sorts of facts are relevant to questions of justice and why they are, all in the context of why what is so accounted for is a virtue and why it matters. Only if what is so accounted for is a virtue and is important in human life as such can it have the significance that it has in the dispute. Nobody will be able to sit there and say "What I mean by 'just' is 'keeping the black races down,' and that is all there is to it." He has to explain why

conclusions about justice are important if we are to place any importance on his conclusions about justice, so he cannot simply stop at
that point. If he does simply stop at that point, then he is not
somebody with whom we can live a common life in terms of justice.

Without some basic agreement, there can be no life as a community. Renegades who do not agree at this basic level can be accommo-
dated within social life only if they are so few in numbers as to make it
clear that their life outside the agreement, in the Hobbesian state of
nature, is unworkable. They must be so few that those who agree can
prevent effective disruption by those who do not, as on the almost
desert island.

If people are to be able to live together and resolve their disputes
peacefully, they must have a public procedure that they regard as
just, and therefore regard as binding. This means that, at some level,
they must agree about justice. A pluralistic society is possible. People
in the same community can have moral views that differ in all sorts of
ways. But if those differences are to be resolved peacefully, there
must be a level of agreement such that we can at least agree about
decision-procedures. What is required is that people have respect for
each other's views of justice: that is required by the presupposition of
equality and the toleration that that presupposition demands of
members of a community. But if each of us is to respect the others'
views of justice, those views of justice must be such that they can be
respected. They cannot simply be mad views. If I think that justice is
distribution according to need and you think that justice is distribution according to work, we can probably get by. Given that justice is
concerned with the distribution of goods, one can see how somebody
might think that need for those goods or work done to produce them
must be relevant. Either view is comprehensible, and there is a point
to discussion between the parties. (It would be a philosophical
discussion, an attempt to give an analysis of justice. This is one way
in which moral philosophy comes into practical arguments and is,
indeed, where moral philosophy comes from.) If, on the other hand,
somebody says that justice is the distribution of goods in accordance
with skin color, I am at a loss. If he believes that people of a certain
skin color are indolent and irresponsible and therefore contribute
little, so that distribution in accordance with work will match distribution in accordance with skin color, then I can understand: a claim that
justice is distribution in accordance with work is comprehensible
even if his claim as to who does the work is false. But if he sticks to
the view that skin color is itself the determining factor, then his view
is incomprehensible. If asked why need is important, I can say that
there would be no point to producing goods if nobody needed them.
If asked why work is important, I can say that no goods would be

produced if no work were done. Each answer shows the relevance of the suggested criterion to the point of being bothered about justice. No such answer can be given by a person who claims that skin color is a criterion.

If we disagree in that sort of way, then our dispute could not be resolved without recourse to a public procedure. Nor could our differences be resolved with recourse to a public procedure, because our differences about justice are such that we should not be able to agree on what a just procedure would be. Nor could we resolve the matter by tossing a coin. The loser would be faced with the prospect of a decision-procedure operating on grounds he regarded as completely irrelevant to justice, and therefore with a procedure that he could not regard as binding. For people who have not even basic agreement about justice, there can be no peaceful common life. Even if we cannot agree whether it is true that p, we must be able to agree on whether p is an appropriate sort of remark to make in the discussion. We must be able to agree on what sort of thing could be a reason.

In the end, all of this depends on our being able to agree at a basic level. If we could not agree, we could not produce an effective and binding decision-procedure that would resolve our disputes peacefully. We would be reduced to mere coercion: war, terrorism, and the use of violent means in general would become widespread, even if the disagreement came only from people's insisting on agreement at too high a level if they were to accept the procedure. The prospects for peace depend on people's being willing to go back to more basic levels in the search for agreement that will enable them to set up a proper decision-procedure, and that involves a lot of toleration. In the end, each must work out for himself or herself what is a reason showing something to be just, or whether a decision-procedure is binding. One should be wary about drawing from this point any conclusion that is too extreme. Certainly the fact that each must, in the end, judge for himself or herself does not mean that nobody is ever mistaken in such matters or that anybody is as good a judge as anybody else. One's position is like that of an umpire in a game of cricket. The laws of cricket say that the umpire is the sole judge of matters of fact. He, in the end, decides whether or not the ball did touch the batsman's pad or his bat. What he says goes, but nobody is under the misapprehension that umpires cannot be mistaken or that some people are not better umpires than others. To be in such a position is not to be left to act at whim, but to be given great responsibility.

When I go before the public procedure claiming to have a right to X, the decision-procedure determines whether I have that right. In what way, then, is the right that I claim to have interpersonally or publicly determined? The thesis I defend before the decision-procedure is that it *ought* to favor me, not that it *will* favor me. The right that I claim to have is interpersonally or publicly determined in that it depends on community standards and the way in which the community does things. I must defend my claim on publicly recognizable grounds. I can argue "It's mine because I made it," but "It's mine because it's purple" is not an argument at all no matter how much I may want it to be and no matter how much I may like purple things. The *criteria* for rights are public and interpersonal; I cannot set them for myself.

The formal public procedure plays its role against the background of this basic way of establishing rights. It is necessary because people can notice different facts, fail to notice different facts, give different weights to the same facts, and reason to different conclusions. A binding public procedure affects what is just by its intervention in cases of dispute, but that it cannot be the explanation of the nature of justice is clear from the fact that it must be a *binding* procedure. There must be an independent notion of justice: only against that background can the operations of the public procedure be understood. In terms of that independent notion we can argue that we have rights that the public procedure should recognize. Because people can disagree in their conclusions, and because common action is necessary, the public procedure comes to play its role of substantively determining justice and rights, but it does not determine them analytically. The terms "justice" and "rights" have their meanings apart from the public procedure, and there can be justice and rights apart from the public procedure.

This point shows that what the decision-procedure deals with can be claims rather than wants, and that many claims need not go to arbitration before being recognized as, and being, rights. The public or interpersonal recognition required if they are to be rights can come from general agreement without need for recourse to a public procedure. Because of that, the way in which the decision-procedure must be content-free does not imply that the primary material of liberty must be wants or what people are able to do rather than rights.

But what happens if the vast majority of a community agrees on the propriety of discriminating against the very few Jews or Negroes among them simply on the grounds of their religion or their skin color? One can imagine that there might be so few Jews or Negroes as to make clear the impossibility of their effectively disrupting the operation of the discriminating system. Given the role of convention and agreement in the existence of rights, how could it be that people have rights that they should not have or lack rights that they should have? Does it follow from what I have said that, where people agree to discriminate against Jews or Negroes, we must recognize the justice of the discrimination?

Agreement is not definitive. There are proper arguments that can be presented in the face of it. Any particular characteristic of people is not made relevant to justice simply by people's deciding or agreeing that it is relevant; we cannot make something a reason simply by wanting it to be one. What is relevant to justice is something to be argued out in an analysis of justice, not determined by a show of hands. The public procedure determines what is to be done and affects the justice of doing it, but being endorsed by the public procedure does not make a claim true. It might follow from agreement that that is how the rights are, but it does not follow that that is a just distribution of rights. We should need to argue about the point of the concept of justice, as we need to argue about the point of the public procedure to see what limitations are properly to be placed on it. When the decision-procedure determines the justice of a course of action, it does so in a special way. If there is widespread disagreement in the community about the justice of X, and I think that justice requires X, I do not have to change my mind when the decision-procedure resolves the matter in favor of not-X. The point of the decision-procedure is, and must be, that it resolves disputes rather than that it gives the right answer. A requirement that the decision-procedure give the right answer would make it pointless as a way of resolving disputes. In this case, I think that it has given the wrong answer: justice requires X; it does not require not-X. But I also recognize the injustice of forcing my own private views on others when the dispute between us has been submitted to a binding decision-procedure that came down on their side. That is the way in which the decision-procedure affects the justice of a course of action. Nevertheless, I can go before that decision-procedure to defend my claim that I have a right, not merely to assert my wants. I may point out that, despite widespread agreement to the contrary, public recognition of such a right is implied by our conventions and by our ways of doing things,[13] so that the widespread public agreement is unreasonable. I may win or lose my case, but I shall have presented an appropriate type of argument.

If rights depend on agreement, it is not just on any old agreement; it is on agreement on certain sorts of grounds. Argument about whether those grounds obtain will, therefore, be appropriate even in the face of agreement.

In the same way, we can argue that a decision-procedure that consistently discriminates against Negroes or Jews, simply because they are Negroes or Jews, that cannot connect being Negro or Jewish with the criteria used in other cases, and that reflects common agreement in doing so, is mistaken.[14] But in this case we can go further: we can argue that the procedure is not binding because it is not just, and it is not just because it is considering the wrong sort of things and is infringing the presupposition of equality. Skin color and religion, as is shown by an analysis of justice and its relationship to cooperation, are simply not relevant to justice in the normal run of things. So we are not committed to accepting the propriety of such discrimination. What I have said is consistent with argument against such a system. That public recognition is necessary for justice to be effective does not mean that it is sufficient. That I disagree with these people at so basic a level that I cannot live with them,[15] and that they outnumber me, does not mean that I am wrong: the public procedure determines what is to be done, but not what is true. It does mean that I am unlikely to prevail over them unless I can persuade them by my reasoning, and that will be a hopeless task if we cannot agree on basic criteria for reasoning about justice. If there is no common point, there can be no effective argument. I manage to live with some injustice; submission to a public procedure that sometimes goes against me means that I must see myself as doing so sometimes. Whether I can live with the discrimination against Negroes and Jews (which might not mean ignoring it, but, perhaps, remaining a member of the community to fight it from within) will depend on the form that the discrimination takes. If it is so serious that I cannot remain a member of the community and submit to its public procedure, my objection is not simply to the particular decisions, but to the injustice of a public procedure that operates on those criteria. It is not simply insistence that all decisions go my way. The objection is not that the public procedure made a mistake, but that it is not binding; that is, the objection is formal, not merely about the content of decisions.

What is at issue here is discrimination against Negroes and Jews as such. That is to say, the issue is what follows if the public procedure takes the fact that somebody is a Negro or a Jew as a criterion for allocation, not merely what happens if it keeps on picking out Negroes and Jews because they, and only they, park illegally. Discriminating against Negroes and Jews in this way means that they are excluded from the start, not merely excluded by particular decisions that the procedure reaches, so the procedure would be infringing the presupposition of equality, which is a basic requirement of cooperation and is one of the points in terms of which we can distinguish between cooperation and exploitation; the procedure would therefore display the raw form of injustice. It would, therefore, be denying moral rights that Negroes and Jews should have as members of the community.

We saw earlier how the point of an enterprise is relevant to determining what sort of decision-procedure is appropriate to it and how it shows the unreasonableness of using such a decision-procedure as tossing a coin when the enterprise is, say, that of a group of doctors deciding how to treat a certain illness. Tossing a coin is demonstrably not the best way of doing that job, so it is unreasonable to adopt that method of making decisions. The same point comes up here: the point of the enterprise determines who should be in the game and who should be out. That is to say, the point of the enterprise determines the reasonableness of including or excluding certain people or groups of people. The sort of reason that is appropriate will vary enormously as the point of the enterprise varies. Mere numbers may matter if the enterprise is one that can support only a limited number. If the golf club has as many members as it can handle without ruining the fairways and greens, then that is a reason for rejecting any more applications for membership. If both Jim and Fred apply for membership when there is only one vacancy, then the fact that Jim applied first or called "Heads" when Fred tossed the coin might be a reason for accepting his application and rejecting Fred's. That somebody has no idea how to defend himself, let alone anybody else, is a reason to exclude him from a company of bodyguards, but not a reason to exclude him from a medical insurance scheme. That somebody is a Negro is a reason for excluding him from membership in the Ku Klux Klan; it provides a reason for that in exactly the same way as the aims of the Ku Klux Klan provide a reason for excluding it from any community the point of which is the protection of the legitimate interests of all. And this is not *merely* a matter of efficiency. What can justly be required in a cooperative enterprise is what is necessary if the enterprise is to achieve its goal, so requiring more of people, or excluding or including them on other grounds, is not only unreasonable but unjust. If reasons of the appropriate sort cannot be given for discriminating against Negroes and Jews, then discrimination against Negroes and Jews is unjust.

Nothing that I have written suggests a way of guaranteeing that public procedures will not suffer from these faults, will not discriminate unjustly against Jews, Negroes, Australian aborigines, Catholics, Communists, women, and so on. Nor, as I shall explain in Chapter 8, do I think that there can be such an institutional guarantee. I have not been trying to show that there must be a way of guaranteeing avoidance of these faults, but that they are faults, and that I am not committed to the view that they are not faults simply because they occur in public procedures or in forms of cooperation. It is in terms of these faults that we can distinguish between proper cooperation and exploitation and can argue that a decision-procedure is not binding. I have been concerned to show, not that all decision-procedures are binding or anything of that sort, but what forms of argument about them are appropriate, and that a decision-procedure that satisfied the conditions for bindingness would not infringe my liberty, but would create liberty for all in the community by creating rights.

Notes

1. See my *Cooperation and Human Values* (Brighton: Harvester, and New York: St. Martin's Press, 1981), chapter 3.
2. R. P. Wolff, *In Defence of Anarchism* (New York: Harper Torchbook, 1970).
3. Thomas Hobbes, *Leviathan*, chapter 26.
4. Especially with the discussion of the nearly desert island later in this chapter.
5. See Stanley Benn, "Regulative Ideals and University Government," *Vestes* 14, no.2 (1971).
6. Hobbes, *Leviathan*, chapter 13.
7. *Ibid.*, chapter 13, p. 184).
8. R. P. Wolff, *In Defence of Anarchism*, p. 14.
9. See, for example, Carol Pateman, *The Problem of Political Obligation* (Brisbane: John Wiley & Sons, 1979) and *Participation and Democratic Theory* (Cambridge: Cambridge University Press, 1970), though she emphasizes the idea of promising.
10. The stronger the arguments for saying that living a normal life and accepting benefits cannot be construed as tacit consent to obey the law because we have no choice about living in a community, no choice about being subject to government, and so on, the stronger the case for saying that life in a community these days is, in relevant respects, like life on the nearly desert island.
11. They may kill him if that is necessary to their defending themselves, but, in other circumstances, it is not, on my account, merely an act of grace if they refrain from killing him. As the argument about the presupposition against killing people shows, they would display the raw form of injustice if they killed him unnecessarily.
12. Milton Friedman, *Capitalism and Freedom* (Chicago: University of Chicago Press, 1962), pp. 110–11.
13. Compare the argument about unemployment in Chapter 4.
14. It is, I think, only in the context of this sort of argument that a distinction between legal and moral rights is of any great significance.
15. We should bear in mind here a Hobbesian point about security. People who reason in an unrecognizable way are a threat to my security. If the dispute is one about whether justice is to be explained in terms of needs or works, a dispute in which I can see why the other fellow holds his position, then I can work out what is likely to happen next and how he is likely to behave. If he simply nominates Jewishness as a criterion for just distribution, not showing how it is connected to the production of goods or any other criterion for justice, then I am at a loss. If he picks

Jewishness out of the blue, he might next pick on being left-handed, atheist, or Catholic (and all of these have suffered at one time or another). If he does not reason in a recognizable way, showing how the criteria he picks out fit into the overall scheme of things, how can I reasonably feel safe against being picked on next?

7

The Value of Liberty

I̲F SOMEBODY SHOULD ASK what the value of liberty is, there seem to be two sorts of answers that could be given, and each of them seems to be unsatisfactory in its own way. We could say that liberty is good in itself, quite apart from any consequences that might flow from it, or we could say that liberty is good instrumentally, because of the consequences it has.

The idea that liberty is valuable in itself seems to have been an important one. It is an idea that seems to have played an important part in explaining people's behavior at various stages of history. If liberty were thought to be valuable only because of its consequences, one could see why one person might give up his life for another's liberty, but the possibility that whole communities would fight to the death rather than give up their liberty seems incomprehensible. When one person gives up his life for another, good consequences can follow for his fellow, but if all of us give up our lives, then any consequences that flow therefrom do not flow to us. One can imagine circumstances in which suicide might be the best course because of the terrors it avoided, but, unless liberty itself is believed to be valuable, simple bondage (perhaps as a well-cared-for slave or as a normal member of a colonized community) seems not to be in that class.

On the other hand, saying that liberty is valuable in itself *seems* importantly similar to saying that scratching one's armpits is valuable in itself. The point of saying that either is good *in itself* seems to be to rule out any argument about the matter, and if we really do rule out all argument (rather than simply pretending to ignore considerations of which we are all well aware), then the claim can equally plausibly be made about anything of which it would not be self-contradictory. It comes down to a claim of simple intuition and can be denied as easily as any other simple intuition. If it is simply a matter of intuition, then we lack criteria for the application of the concept. It is not merely that we sometimes fail to work out the proper limitations of the concept in difficult cases; if it is a matter of simple intuition, there is no such activity as *working out* the limitations of the concept. Judgments about liberty in difficult cases would be, for all practical purposes, equivalent to expressions of taste, and that suggests that judgments about liberty in easy cases are really no more significant than expressions of taste in which we agree. Liberty would no more be worth dying for than is strawberry ice cream. All of this seems to follow if liberty is regarded as good in itself, but I shall try to show that the situation is more complicated. The value of liberty might lie in its place in the scheme of things rather than in its consequences.

Different problems seem to follow if one says that liberty is a value instrumentally. There is a general problem of reduction here: the value of whatever is being justified in such a way seems to disappear, leaving only the value of the consequences. This can, in the end, result in an argument against what one set out to justify.[1] Suppose one says that liberty is a good thing because it promotes personal moral development and independence, that freedom of speech and information are good because they promote the discovery of truth, and so on. Liberty is then a good thing as a means to these ends and insofar as it promotes these ends. Suppose, then, that insistence on freedom of speech and information leads to an easy toleration that allows unusual views to be laughed off without serious consideration as the work of cranks, whereas in an atmosphere of repression and censorship people consider new ideas when they come across them simply because they have been judged sufficiently important to justify censorship. Suppose, also, that people with guaranteed personal liberty respond by becoming blasé, whereas those subject to repression and the closely detailed authority of others respond resentfully and fight for their independence, thus promoting their independence and moral development. In such circumstances repression would be valuable and liberty would not. It does not take much reflection to realize that those suppositions are not wildly implausible.

Perhaps, then, liberty is a good thing only in some circumstances: it is a good thing only when people will not respond better to repression. Liberty, given this instrumental justification, would not be an independent value like justice or courage. It would be more like the old virtue of being industrious. When a living had to be won from the earth and was not easily come by, it was important, in terms of both prudence and consideration for others, that people be industrious. Industry was valuable because of its consequences. With developments in technology, it could become much less important that people be industrious than that they be capable of passing their leisure time without resort to nastiness. Changing circumstances can change what is valuable. In this respect, liberty might be like industry. Liberty might be like a medicine: a good thing to give people in some circumstances but something that must be withheld if those who make the decisions do not like the consequences. And it must be somebody else who makes the decisions: if I do not like the consequences of my liberty and decide to restrict it, then I have the liberty and am exercising it in one way rather than another. There can be good reasons why others make the decisions, because I am not always in the best position to know my own interests. If I, ailing under chicken pox or some other foul disease, were in the best position to know whether a particular medicine would cure me and thus whether it would be in my interest to take that medicine, then I should not waste money on doctors' fees.

But, even accepting that sort of limitation, there seems to be a paradox in taking this sort of line in trying to justify liberty. The line quite clearly does allow, as at least a theoretical possibility, that liberty might be bad for people and repression might be good. The apparent paradox comes up when we remember that repression must be done *by* people when it is done to people. A situation of repression is one in which some are repressed by others, not one in which all are repressed by none. (If people's activities are limited by their physical circumstances, such as volcanoes or disease, we should not speak of repression. Objection is proper only to circumstances that can be controlled by people. We need to distinguish between simple lack of ability or opportunity and lack of liberty.) This point applies even if the community makes the decisions corporately. If unanimity is required then nobody is repressed, since each person is subject only to his own will; if it is a case of rule by some given proportion, even if the alignment of voters varies from case to case, in each case those overruled are repressed by those overruling. (This applies *if* the case is one of repression. It does not imply that all such decision-procedures lead to repression.) *Ultimately*, at any given time, those who repress cannot be repressed. Those who repress cannot, in the same respect and at the same time, be repressed, though they may be links in a chain of repression. A chain of people, each subject to the will of the next in line, must end somewhere if any decisions are ever made. If liberty is corrupting, then, this way of guarding against corruption simply makes sure that there is corruption among those who make the decisions. That surely is paradoxical. This sort of point is surprisingly often overlooked, though it has sometimes formed an important part of a political theory. John C. Calhoun, for example, argued that the state would not be necessary were it not that people have some nasty tendencies,[2] so that we must remember that the state officials are people who have those nasty tendencies and who will use their extra power to exercise them if they are not stopped by a constitution or in some other way.

One more problem seems to arise with this sort of justification of liberty, and it seems to arise apart from any possibility of change in circumstances. Liberty is never simply liberty to do something. There may be an overlying duty requiring that I exercise my liberty in one way rather than another, but liberty, as such, is, at worst, liberty to do or not to do something. That, indeed, is the main constituent of liberty. I have liberty in those areas in which the decisions about what is to be done are to be made by me. That being so, there can be no guarantee of what the consequences of liberty will be, and one might go so far as to say that the point of liberty is to rule out the possibility of any such guarantee. If there can be no such guarantee, then it seems clear that there could be no general justification of liberty in terms of its consequences.

We can often predict how particular people will exercise their liberty, but we can make no sensible very general claims about how liberty will be exercised. Different people will exercise it in different ways at different times when they are in different moods and in different circumstances. They might even exercise their liberty nastily:[3] one can do nothing one has no right to do, avoiding all injustice, and still be inconsiderate of others, spiteful, and exhibit a whole variety of vices. Perhaps the last cake on the plate is mine by rights, but one look at the expression on my infant son's face ought to be enough to make me give up my claim. Perhaps Sophie was nasty to me yesterday, and she might, anyway, have no right that I help her with her gardening today, but my refusal in exercising my right not to help might still be spiteful. One of the things about having somebody in a position in which the decision about what is to be done is to be made by him is that his decision will show something of his character and the extent to which and direction in which he is nice or nasty. Letting somebody make the decision does not guarantee that the consequences of his decision will be pleasant, honorable, or decent. There can be no guarantee even of what the moral consequences of somebody's liberty will be.

So perhaps we should start from a different question: instead of asking why liberty is valuable, perhaps we should ask whether it is valuable. Is it a good thing that people be free? This is a strange question, far too amorphous to allow of any straightforward answer. The immediate response must be to ask: is it a good thing that people be free to do what? Certainly there are some things that people should not be free to do: they should not be free to kill others so as to gain an inheritance earlier or so as to expedite promotion, they should not be free to take what another owns and needs, they should not be free in a nuclear family to ignore the needs of their infant offspring, and so on. In general, and unsurprisingly, they should not be free to do any of those things that they can properly be required not to do, which is to say that they should not be free to do injustice.

The relevant limitations on people's behavior are, once again, not simply limitations imposed by the physical world in which they live, such as the limitations imposed by a flooded river. Such limitations affect what people can do, but do not infringe their liberties, and they give rise to no serious objection because simply persuading some-body will not change the situation. The limitations in question are those within the control of other people, as when somebody plans to blow up a bridge across the river or has it in his power to decide whether or not a levee will be built, and these can give rise to serious objections. The relevant limitations are those within the control of people because there is no point to worrying about what cannot be changed by human endeavor. Moral and political concepts are practi-cal concepts concerned with action; they are not simply items to be used in a game of passing the time by fulminating about the intracta-bility of the universe in some of its aspects. There is a sense in which somebody alone on a tropical island has a very extensive freedom, but it is not a sense that is of concern to us. His freedom cannot be infringed or give rise to objection; it is simply a matter of his ability, not of his rights or of the liberty that matters in morals and politics. Since the limitations in question concern relations between people, it is not surprising that the answer is that people should not be free to do what others can properly require that they not do or what it would be unjust for them to do. It is less clear that it is a good thing that people be free to try to do all those things it would not be unjust for them to do and that they be free to do all those things it would be unjust to stop them from doing. This point is less clear because people free to do these things are free to be inconsiderate, selfish, cowardly, and generally nasty. Without failing to fulfill obligations, they can be extremely unpleasant people. "Good" and "bad" and "right" and "wrong" operate in different ways. One can avoid doing what is wrong while still doing something bad, and there might be nothing particularly good displayed in merely doing what is right. Our problem is: how can liberty be a good thing if it allows such bad actions?

The first thing we need then, in dealing with the value of liberty, is a distinction between liberty and license. People have liberty when they are able to exercise all their just rights, and they take license when they go beyond that to infringe the rights of others. License will plainly be a bad thing. Liberty, on a first glance at its consequences, will be a good thing or a bad thing depending on how it is exercised by those who have it. Certain things are ruled out of liberty, such as a right to kill somebody simply so as to gain an inheritance earlier, so that at least the minimum standard of behavior required if people are to live as a community is met. That some wrongdoing is ruled out, though, does not mean that all wrongdoing is ruled out; duty may require that people meet at least the minimum standard, that they avoid doing what they have no right to do, but beyond that their rights may be exercised for good or for bad. It is because of this, and the moral exercise thus given to the possessor of the rights, that possession of rights has been thought to promote moral development.

All of this has the consequence that specifiable liberties may vary from one community to another in the same way as what is required by justice may vary from one community to another, because different conventions in the different communities will generate different rights, and, as there is no reason to suppose that there is only one just set of conventions, so there is no reason to suppose that there is only one proper set of liberties. Different property systems, for example, may be equally just and will give rise to quite different sets of rights and thus to different liberties. The proper liberty that is distinguished from both license and repression need not have the same content in all communities.

This connection between liberty and justice does not mean that the two are the same. Justice covers a much wider range than liberty, because justice is concerned with the distribution of anything about which there might be dispute. Liberty is concerned with decision-making and the just distribution of power. The point may be brought out by means of an example. Property is constituted by sets of rights and may itself constitute part of our liberty, but it can also play a different role. Possession of great amounts of property may give one person great power over others and give him the opportunity to exploit them: those he employs and can fire at will when jobs are hard to come by, those who have no source of information but the newspapers he controls, and so on. A just distribution of property may be, in this way, a causally necessary condition of a just distribution of power, but the two are not the same thing. If everybody has a surplus of food, so that nobody is threatened with insecurity in that respect, then a just distribution of food does not seem to be necessary for a just distribution of power. Questions of the just distribution of other goods, therefore, are conceptually (and often practically) separable from questions of the just distribution of power. Where the two are connected, it is by matters of fact.

An example of the way in which property and power can be

connected, and of the ramifications of such a connection, is Robert Nozick's example of Wilt Chamberlain.[4] Watching basketball is a taste widely shared among those who like watching basketball, and Nozick imagines that the taste might be sufficiently strong for fans to pay an extra 25 cents to watch Chamberlain play and that Chamberlain might have a clause in his contract requiring that they do so and that the extra money go to him. If a million people pay the surcharge over the season, Chamberlain will have an extra $250,000. Nozick's question is whether this distribution could be unjust. His answer is that, given that each fan is entitled to the 25 cents he pays (it was earned by honest toil, not robbed from banks or poor boxes), and given that each freely chose to spend it on watching the basketball, there can be no injustice involved. Each fan gives up only what is his own to give, and one can do no injustice to oneself.

But people in a community are not really so independent of each other. No problem is caused if one person pays an extra 25 cents to see Wilt Chamberlain play basketball, and that one person would give up nothing that was not his to give, but when one million people do the same thing they give up something of mine. Moneyed people have consequence, and the possession of money has consequences. In this world, those with money have power and, notably, have extra political influence. Putting somebody in that position changes the distribution of power and makes me worse off, since it is in the nature of power that it is impossible for one to have more without others having less; there must be those over whom the powerful have power. No doubt one would not respond to this new and unjust distribution of power by stopping people from watching basketball if that is what they want to do, but one might give some thought to the sorts of tax structures that ought to be in force.

So our question becomes whether liberty, in the restricted sense in which liberty is distinct from license, is a good thing given that it can be exercised for good or ill. There might seem to be a very quick way to deal with this: I have already argued that the idea of a community without rights is incoherent, and, if people must have rights, it is clearly better that they have liberty than that they have rights that would constitute license. This would be too quick, though, because there was nothing in the earlier argument to show that a community must have anything like an even spread of rights—and just as well, too, since there plainly are societies that lack any such distribution of rights. All or most of the rights might go to rulers or members of some particular class, with the rest of the populace being unfairly repressed. That argument clearly leaves to be sorted out the question of the proper distribution of rights. There is still the problem that I associated earlier with Calhoun: if possession of rights is a bad thing, then it would be poor policy to put all power in the hands of the few who could be guaranteed to be corrupt.

Liberty in a community has two aspects: toleration and autonomy. The two aspects are related as two sides of a coin; a person's autonomy is his being tolerated by others in the community. What I propose to do now is to examine the roles of toleration and autonomy in a community to see what conclusions that leads to about the value of liberty. I shall consider first the role of toleration, because most of the relevant points have come up before and can be made very briefly.

Life in a community has its ups and downs and its moments of excited altercation, but nevertheless requires peace among the citizens as the norm. This requirement is imposed by the fact that they are a community rather than simply a group of people who happen to live near each other: if they are to be capable of taking corporate action, acting as one, there must be some peaceful way of determining what their action is. If they resort to fighting each other whenever a question of joint action comes up, each person might act in some way, but there is nothing that counts as a corporate action to which all are committed. The most obvious case is that in which they consider whether to declare war on a neighboring nation. If the members of the group fall to fighting among themselves when they disagree about the proposal, those who oppose it are not committed to it and are not at war with the neighboring nation; effectively, in fact, they are fighting for the neighboring nation.

Force may effectively resolve a dispute, but it does not bind people in such a way as to create a community. (In fact, force works best when there is already a community forcing its will on, say, a criminal. That there is a community means that there is a preponderance of force on one side, which avoids one of the problematic features of the Hobbesian natural condition, *viz.*, that in a war of each against all, no party to the conflict can have reasonable expectations of victory, let alone guarantee it.) Force may even kill off opposition in particular cases, and certainly people who have taken a battering may cease to oppose. What force will not do is bind the loser (unless, in order to break off the conflict, he has to make some undertaking to the victor). If I break a promise then I break it, even if I do so undetectably, but possession of Gyges's ring has more significance if my only reason for submitting was fear of force. If my only reason for submitting was fear of force, I have no reason to refrain from opposition if I can oppose without being hit. Force does not bind. Nor do intellectual displays. If somebody sets about blinding me with a lot of science or philosophy that I do not understand, then I may eventually shut up and stop arguing. Merely talking me down, however, does not bind me. What will bind people will be a procedure in which each gets a fair go. The decision-procedure, if it is to be effective, must be such that, after it has done its work, one can regard it as having made the wrong decision but nevertheless regard it as having given one a fair go. Such a decision will be binding. My views got a fair hearing, and a fair procedure decided against them; I can see, therefore, that it is not unfair that I be made to submit. Thus is community possible.

A necessary condition of this is that one thinks that those involved acted with a sense of justice. If those operating the decision-procedure were doing so simply to protect their own interests or to express their personal dislike of me, then my views did not get a fair hearing and I am not bound by the decision. There would be no explanation in terms of justice of why I should submit. In resolving our disputes, the decision-procedure must operate within those criteria of justice on which we can agree. If it does not do so, it becomes no more than a formal attempt merely to talk somebody down or to gain compliance by coercion, and we are back into the state of nature in which one gets what one grabs by whatever means, giving due consideration to who will hit one when one grabs what. One can still be nasty in this situation; one can be spiteful and cruel, and one can even display the vice of injustice by doing what one regards as infringing the rights of others even if one is mistaken in so regarding it. But the idea that there are rights in that situation that must be respected no matter what one's private judgment is an idea that no longer applies. Nobody else's judgment has a natural claim over me. Authority requires conventions of a binding sort.

Thus, there are limits on what is to be tolerated. An act that is to be tolerated must at least be one that could be countenanced by something recognizable as a sense of justice. Within that limitation, though, there must be toleration if community life is to be possible. I must treat each person as my equal with respect to his sense of justice, and give to the judgments of his sense of justice the same hearing as to mine. If I did not, his sense of justice could not reasonably require that he submit if the decision goes against him. I, of course, am always right, but that is a merit of no great importance when I must live among people who do not believe that I have it.

It should be noted that this is a logical claim, not causal. It is not a claim about the consequences of having liberty, as is the claim that possession of liberty promotes the growth of personal independence. It is a logical claim that people who disgree can live together only with toleration.

As toleration is required for life in a community, so is autonomy, the other side of the coin. The connection in this case can be seen through the notion of agency. Autonomy, as I pointed out in Chapter

3, is a political notion concerned with the possession of rights. Philosophers of mind often use the term "autonomy" to mean what I mean by "agency." They use it to refer to a set of capacities to weigh alternatives, decide what to do, and so on. In general, agency is a capacity to exercise rights, but a capacity to exercise rights is not the same as possession of rights. The two are, however, clearly closely related. Within a community, possession of agency makes recognition of rights appropriate given appropriate behavior on the agent's part. To see that somebody has agency and is therefore capable of cooperating, but nevertheless to refuse to cooperate with him when he shows willingness to cooperate, shows the raw form of injustice. It is not the full form of injustice, because it is not structured by social relations, but it shows a lack of willingness to cooperate with others that would make one unfit for social life and which takes the form of injustice once social relations are established. In the absence of an explanatory story, such as that about refusing an applicant membership in the golf club because the golf club already has as many members as it can handle, refusing to get along with people when one could get along with them is vicious. It is a form of injustice.

It is certainly true that we could give an account in mechanistic terms of what there is that would be, in *one* sense, a complete account of what there is. If everything listed in the account were put in a pile, for example, there might be nothing left out of the pile for someone to go and fetch. This would be one sense in which we could give, in mechanistic or purely physical terms, a complete account of what there is. But there is a more important sense in which an account in mechanistic terms cannot be allowed to be complete, because it could not include language *qua* language or any particular occasion of the use of language *qua* language, such as the giving of that account itself. This claim means that we cannot drop the concept of person, and that any Determinist or Physicalist who tries to make such a move is in a self-stultifying position. If we are to have any concepts at all, we must have the concept of purposive action and thus the concepts of agent and person. The statement that there are instances of the concept of action will be contingent in that things could have been otherwise, but it will be not merely contingent in that the fact that the statement is made is sufficient to show that it is true.

When someone says something we could, of course, describe what goes on then, too, in purely mechanistic terms: air being forced over taut fibers and producing sounds of a certain description, or whatever it is that happens. We may be able to explain, furthermore, why someone else reacts as he does when he hears those sounds, or, to put it another way, why certain movements follow when the sound waves reach another machine of a similar sort: we might be able to do this in terms of brain states set up previously and the effects on them of the relevant neural impulses. That we can describe what goes on in this way is part of what is meant by saying that we could give a description of the world in mechanistic, material object terms such that the description would be, in some sense, complete. But in describing what went on in this way we should not be describing language *qua* language or a particular use of it.

Use of language is a form of behavior, though it holds a quite special place among sorts of behavior. Use of language fits into the patterns of behavior with which we react to many different sorts of situations, playing parts ranging from an involuntary shout to an abstruse discussion of the psi-function. But the important thing about language, or the important thing so far as this discussion goes, is that language is for the most part used; that is, we do things with it, attempt to carry out some tasks, and succeed in carrying out others. Thus, we use language to give or request information, to enter bonds, to warn, and so on. This helps to explain why we do not regard a tape recorder, or a parrot for that matter, as using or having the language, even though it may produce the relevant sounds: tape recorders and parrots do not use language for these purposes and do not know what they are doing with the words. To use a language is to do more than produce sounds or other signs, whether or not we do this with some sort of consistency: a parrot would not be using the language even if it said "Polly wants a cracker" when and only when its owner entered the room with a cracker, for example. To use a language I must utter or otherwise publish the words and be capable of knowing what I am doing with them, whether it be giving information, requesting information, or doing anything else. I must use the words according to the conventions established for their use, and I must believe, above all else, that I am using the words correctly. If I can say to someone "R. B. Simpson's first Test century was scored at Manchester" and am not capable of realizing that these words are appropriate if my purpose is to inform somebody on the subject, then I do not have the language or, anyway, that part of it. Similarly, I could regard someone else as giving me information in a straightforward sense only if I thought that he was capable of realizing that he had given me information: this is the sense in which I should say that a parrot or tape recorder cannot give me information, though I may learn something from listening to them. I say it with consciousness of a joke if I say "The parrot informs me that . . ." The sense in which a parrot might inform me of something is similar to that in which a certain cloud formation might inform me of the imminence of rain. We might compare with this the case of a folk singer singing in a language he does not understand, or a person speaking *when we regard him as a machine.* I can regard something as a description only if I regard whatever gives the description as capable of realizing that it is giving a description.

The claim involved here is simply this: in using a language one is performing an action, and if one is to be regarded as using a language, one must be regarded as performing an action and thus as an agent. Insofar as people are reasoning and language-using beings, they must be regarded as agents. Taking away somebody's agency, therefore, is, strictly, taking away his personhood. He will still be a human being as a matter of biological classification, but not recognized as a person. Without agents, we could not have people to be in the community.

Autonomy is the recognition of agency. It is the recognition that, in this area, the person's actions are to be explained by reference to him and his purposes. Putting him in a position in which his behavior can be explained only by reference to the purposes and decisions of others takes away his agency and his personhood. Allowing somebody rights and thus making him responsible for his own actions recognizes his agency and his personhood by making it the case that his behavior must be explained by reference to his purposes. Taking away all his rights, so that he is completely subject to the dictates of others, refuses to recognize his personhood.

The same sort of point can be made more briefly. Those beings that cooperate, making claims and meeting claims, are, in doing those things, agents. Cooperation requires reciprocity. In giving somebody a place in a cooperative endeavor, we necessarily give him the rights and duties that constitute his role. In requiring that somebody be given rights in being brought into the endeavor, cooperation requires that members of the enterprise have autonomy even if, in less than perfect cooperation, their autonomy might not be as extensive as it should be.

We can see, then, that liberty is valuable, and why it is. We see it, not simply by intuition or by considering what consequences follow, but by seeing that it is necessary to the life of people in a community. On one meaning, this claim is clearly false: not everybody in every community has proper liberty. But that is not my claim. One's place in the community is marked out by one's rights (and by their attendant responsibilites) even if one has not all the rights one should have, or even if one has more rights than one should have. If one has a place in the community one has one's liberty, even if not one's proper liberty. If one has no rights at all, then one is not recognized as a person or as a member of the community.

One will have one's proper liberty, I have argued, under just social arrangements. This will be proper recognition of one's status as a person or member of the community, and is a separate matter from the consequences of liberty. To try to make the point in more detail, I shall proceed to a discussion of George Fitzhugh's defense of slavery.

Slaveholders differed markedly in their attitudes toward and treatment of their slaves. The life of a slave could be poor, nasty, brutish, and short, but a slave could also lead a relatively pleasant and carefree life, in some cases not even very hard-working. There is no real question that the life of a slave could be in many respects, preferable to that of a free laborer.[5] This point applied especially in comparison with the free Negro laborers of the northern states,[6] but extended well beyond that field. William Thomson, a Scottish weaver investigating North America as a place to which his fellows might emigrate to improve their lots, wrote:

> the planters in general treat their slaves with great humanity. Would to God the aristocracy or the government of this country would interest themselves half as much to improve the physical condition of the factory slave of England . . . I have seen children in factories, both in England and Scotland, under ten years of age, working twelve hours a-day, till their little hands were bleeding. I have seen these children whipped, when their emaciated limbs could no longer support them to their work; and I believe there is not a planter in America whose blood would not rise, and whose arm would not be lifted up to defend even the negroes from such cruelty; [in observing slavery] I have never witnessed one-fifth of the real suffering that I have seen in manufacturing establishments in Great Britain. [The slaves] have no responsibility, no fear that their children may be left to want, no provision to make for age, no fear of being neglected in sickness, or of being compelled, in their old age to beg their bread from door to door. Whereas the labouring men of this boasted country have all the care and responsibility of freemen, and none of their valued privileges.[7]

Given the truth of such accounts, one can see that slavery might appear as the best of a rather poor set of choices. As often as may be possible, I shall assume this view of slavery as benevolent so that the best case is made for it and against liberty. This fits with one of the main lines taken by Fitzhugh, who sets out to show "that the unrestricted exploitation of so-called free society is more oppressive to the laborer than domestic slavery."[8] We may properly assume the benevolent view because one of our questions is whether grounds of this type, no matter how strong they may be of their type, can be appropriate grounds on which to take away somebody else's liberty. The form of this question needs to be noted, though: faced with a choice between the hedonistic life of a slave and the hard work and responsibility of a free laborer, it might be proper, and even prudent, for me to choose the former. It does not follow that anybody else may properly make that choice for me. Perhaps, having carefully ascertained that I leave behind no dependents or debts, I may properly commit suicide to find whether there is an afterlife. It does not follow that somebody who has been trying to persuade me of the existence of an afterlife may, after carefully ascertaining that I leave behind no dependents or debts, murder me to further my knowledge.

One presupposition of the benevolence argument can be dealt with now in a fairly quick way. Writers such as Fitzhugh and Thomson describe the carefree life of a slave and the harried life of a free laborer as though we had only to compare those to determine which life was the better. This presupposes that there is nothing else to be weighed in the balance. In particular, it presupposes that liberty itself is not a good but depends completely for its value on whether it results in happiness or worry. We have already seen that liberty has a value apart from any tendency that it might have to produce such things as happiness or contentment.

Part of the point of Fitzhugh's argument is that it is not simply an argument about an inferior race, but an application to what he took to be an inferior race of much more general ideas about proper relations between people in a community. It was not only Negroes whom Fitzhugh took to be properly enslaved; he thought that many whites should be enslaved, too. We have already seen that autonomy, and its correlative toleration, play a crucial role in making life in a community possible. Cooperating with somebody requires recognizing rights and duties that he has, the rights and duties that make up his role in the cooperation. Exercising rights and carrying out duties require purposive action: accepting somebody's role in a cooperative endeavor involves conceding his agency and accepting his autonomy. His autonomy is not limitless, and his having it does not entail that he can do as he likes. It is made up of his rights, which determine the area within which he may decide what he does. Without the acceptance of roles and the recognition of autonomy which is part of that, cooperation is logically impossible. Enslavement cannot be a proper relationship between people in a community. Those whose autonomy is thus denied are no more parts of our community, even though they may contribute to its welfare and use some of its resources, than are the horses farmers used to pull their ploughs or the tractors that replaced them.

Cooperation and justice allow of degrees. Slaves, as a matter of fact, had some rights, even if it was very difficult for them to exercise those rights against a master who chose to oppose them. To a very limited extent, then, the relationship between slave and master might be regarded as cooperative. It is a very limited extent, though, because the relationship does not go anywhere near satisfying the presupposition of equality and is therefore what we should usually distinguish from proper cooperation and call, instead, exploitation. It exhibits, as I shall go on to show, the raw form of injustice.

It is sometimes said that slaves had certain rights (such as, perhaps, the right to vote, the right to be paid for their work, the right to decide where they would go) that were ignored, or that they had moral rights though not legal rights. One can, no doubt, make clear sense of this, and talking in those terms might sometimes serve a rhetorical purpose. Nevertheless, it seems less confusing in the long run to say that slaves lacked those rights and that that is what was wrong with the situation. Certainly this makes it easier to distinguish between a slave and somebody (say, a northern Negro who had been kidnapped) who is not a slave but is treated as though he is; such a person does have the relevant rights, and the person who holds him in that manner ignores them. Such rhetorical claims about unrecognized rights that people have usually pluck their rights from nowhere, and reference to rights is pointless without a grounding for them. In this case, the argument had to be carried on with slaveholders who denied that slaves had those rights. If there is to be reasoned argument in such a case, rather than simply abusive counterassertion, then it must go on to the question of how the rights are generated and determined. Mere intuition of who has what rights will not do the job in such cases of disagreement.

My derivation of rights from cooperation certainly implies that slaves lacked those rights in their relations with slaveholders. It does not follow from this, though, that there could be no moral objection to the holding of slaves. In fact, it does not even follow that there can be no objection of injustice to slaveholding, but infringing rights is not the only way of doing wrong; anybody who thinks that it is does not understand many of the subtlest ways of being nasty. For a start, refusing to grant those rights to slaves might be callous, arrogant, or inhumane.

In fact, I think that refusing to grant rights to people and making them slaves shows an even more serious vice: it shows a lack in the sense of justice of those who support the system of slavery. It shows the raw form of injustice. This might seem strange given what I have already said about justice and rights, but should seem less strange if we concentrate on virtues and vices. We need to consider the sense of justice at least as much as the notion of justice. I have argued elsewhere about the role of a sense of justice in making life in a community possible.[9] Part of this sense of justice is a willingness to cooperate, or a desire that, where we interact with others, we do so on a cooperative basis. (One can think of this problem in terms of what people would have to be like to get from a Hobbesian state of nature to civil society, or, more accurately, what they must be like not to have lapsed from civil society into a Hobbesian state of nature.) If they are to live together, people must, for the most part, be prepared to cooperate at least with respect to the basic decision-procedure governing the resolution of any clashes that they might have. This quality of character, a willingness to cooperate, shows itself first in a willingness to enter cooperative relations, and then in a recognition of the roles generating rights and obligations in that cooperative endeavor and thus determining justice. These are not merely two chronologically related steps; they bring out two aspects of what is involved in cooperating with people and show how a willingness to cooperate is the raw material of justice, a raw material that is given form by the specific terms of the cooperation. Lack of this quality of character stands to injustice as delight in wanton killing stands to infringing somebody's rights in murdering him.

The specific terms of the cooperation will explain how particular people can or must be omitted. Quadriplegics are ruled out of first-division soccer teams, not by prejudice, but by the nature of the cooperation and their inability to carry out the relevant tasks. They are not similarly ruled out of a chess club. Sometimes it will be a matter simply of numbers, rather than of the qualities and abilities of the people involved: if the enterprise will support only ten and there are nine already in it, Fred may be every bit as good a choice for the last place as Bill, but the inclusion of Bill itself gives a reason for the exclusion of Fred. The nature of cooperation as such explains why some are completely ruled out from cooperative endeavors: those who cannot or will not cooperate are thereby ruled out. Infants, snails, some lunatics, and generally those who suffer a lack of the reasoning capacities required to work out rights and duties cannot cooperate and hence cannot be taken into a cooperative endeavor. (This does not mean that others cannot cooperate to look after the well-being of those unfortunates.) Perhaps we could not cooperate with really determined criminals, those who exhibited an unwillingness to cooperate with the law-abiding. In general, the point of the enterprise explains the grounds on which somebody can properly be denied membership. (This also explains how a particular cooperative enterprise could be improper: it would be inconsistent with the point of another enterprise that it presupposed, as bank robbery is inconsistent with a community and its economic system that robbers require for their prey.)

Somebody might reply to this that it would be enough if each person were prepared to cooperate with some others, though not with all, and that I have no way of ruling out this possibility. Indeed, I have not. Quite plainly, there were enough slaveholders, and generally people not opposed to slavery, to form a community. It would be absurd for me to deny the possibility of what actually existed. I am not committed to the claim, however, that there cannot be injustice or that people cannot be partial in that way. If people cannot or will not cooperate, then they cannot be members of the same community, but that does not affect what constitutes proper relations within a community. A refusal to cooperate with Negroes does not generate rights over them. Caucasians and Negroes might be geographically mixed and the Caucasians might be able to bend the Negroes to their will, but the Negroes are no more obligated to do as they are told than is the victim of a mugger. They are not committed to the decisions, and are thus not part of the same community.

There were, in the southern states of 1850, enough slaveholders to form a community, but there are no slaveholders in the state of nature. How would distinctions be drawn there? The only distinction that matters in the state of nature is the distinction between those with the ability and willingness to cooperate and those without.

What would this willingness to cooperate with only some people be? It is worth noting that it would be a very strange quality of character. What is at issue is not a willingness to cooperate only with those who will do their share, or only with as many people as this land will support, beyond which part of our cooperation will be to keep out invaders, or any other distinction determined by the point of the enterprise. It is some sort of brute willingness to cooperate with some but not with all. It cannot be a case of my not really wanting to cooperate but of being forced by self-interest to do so to some extent; the Prisoners' Dilemma argument rules that out, at least as a general truth about people. We can see how those who already have social relations might be willing to cooperate with their friends but not with others, but the story here cannot be of that sort, either; that presupposes that the community has already got going so that one can distinguish between friends and others, so it cannot itself be presupposed in getting the community going. The same point applies to giving preference to one's family. A brute desire to cooperate with some but not all of those with whom we interact is a puzzling quality of character.

We need to bear in mind here just what sort of cooperation is at issue. It is not a matter of whether or not to form a car pool or a baby-sitting circle, but of whether or not clashes of interests and disagreements in judgment are to be resolved peacefully. A desire not to cooperate with some of those with whom I interact is a desire that my disputes with them be settled by resort to force. One might reasonably resort to force if the other party to the dispute were somebody who could not be trusted or who will not cooperate, but that is not what is at issue; the *brute* desire not to cooperate with some with whom we interact, not picking them out in terms determined by the point of the enterprise, is a preference for violence where there is no special reason to justify it. A person with that preference is not somebody who can be trusted and not somebody with whom one can safely cooperate. The quality of character he has is, in the nature of human communal life, a vice. Willingness to cooperate generally with those with whom we interact is a virtue, and its lack is a vice. Specifically, as I argued earlier, its lack is the raw form of the vice of injustice. Ruling Negroes out of the community at the start is distinguishing on grounds that have nothing to do with the point of the enterprise, and thus exhibits the vice of injustice.

Thus it matters that a justification in terms of fitness to cooperate be given if there is to be discrimination against Negroes or anybody else who is to be enslaved, and Fitzhugh, along with many others, did try to give such a justification. In 1841, the sixth census of the United States was released. It was the first census to enumerate the mentally diseased and defective, and claimed that these disorders were eleven times more common among free Negroes than among slaves. This was taken to show that Negroes were, by nature, particularly fitted for slavery, and that sort of justification was so important to the perception of slavery that the Department of State, headed by John C. Calhoun, stuck by the census figures even after Edward Jarvis pointed out that it listed insane Negroes in northern towns that had no Negro population.[10] Negro inferiority and inability to handle free cooperative relations were necessary to the justification of slavery.

"Man is naturally a social and gregarious animal, subject, not by contract or agreement, . . . but by birth and nature, to those restrictions of liberty which are expedient or necessary to secure the good of the human hive, to which he may belong."[11] Thus does Fitzhugh deny contract theory and any idea of initial equality, basing his account of society on human nature and the fitness of various types of people for various types of roles. "Social bodies, like human bodies, are the works of God, which man may dissect, and sometimes heal, but which he cannot create."[12] The inferior must be subject to control by their superiors:

> It is contrary to all human customs and legal analogies that those who are dependent, or are likely to become so, should not be controlled. The duty of protecting the weak involves the necessity of enslaving them— hence, in all countries, women and children, wards and apprentices, have been essentially slaves, controlled, not by law, but by the will of a superior . . . Many men become paupers from their own improvidence

or misconduct, and masters alone can prevent such misconduct and improvidence. Masters treat their sick, infant, and helpless slaves well, not only from feeling and affection, but from motives of self-interest. Good treatment renders them more valuable.[13]

Slavery is an indispensable police institution—especially so to check the cruelty and tyranny of vicious and depraved husbands and parents. Husbands and parents have, in theory and practice, a power over their subjects more despotic than kings; and the ignorant and vicious exercise their power more oppressively than kings. Every man is not fit to be a king, yet all must have wives and children. Put a master over them to check their power, and we need not resort to the unnatural remedies of woman's rights, limited marriages, voluntary divorces, and free love.[14]

(One of the problems about having different arguments for the one conclusion arises here. Is there any reason to believe that this class of masters will coincide with the class of geniuses on p. 63 of *Cannibals All!*? Can there be any guarantee that the genius will always be good-willed and concerned to look after the interests of others?) And one more passage: "All men are philanthropists, and would benefit their fellow men if they could. But we cannot be sure of benefiting those whom we cannot control. Hence, all actively good men are ambitious, and would be masters, in all save the name."[15]

The human race is such that paternalistic relationships are required, and Fitzhugh runs a lot of different relationships together. This blurring of differences helps to give an appearance of justification, as though the justification of one relationship will also justify another. We have already seen that the relationship between parent and child is different from that between master and slave in that it has the point that the child will grow to be an independent adult.

Given all that Fitzhugh says, there is still the question of who decides who is to be boss. Given that community is not a human creation and that this is, in fact, how things are, there remains the question of the legitimacy of these relations: what generates the authority? And what binding decision-procedure is there to deal with disputes when, for example, Negroes become abolitionists? In the absence of such a procedure, there is no community. Without the initial assumption of equality denied by Fitzhugh, there can be no community. This is the fallacy of the paternalism that sees itself as deciding or as overruling the rights of others.

One might query Fitzhugh's paternalist justification of slavery in another way, given that he offers a guarantee of it in terms of the slaveholder's interest.[16] The slaveholder might, indeed, provide the slave with security, but we need to know the point of his doing so. If the point is paternalistic, the good of the slave, then the master will provide for the slave what the slave cannot provide for himself and will try to develop the slave's independent ability to look after himself; that is how a father is expected to care for his son. In fact, all self-interest would lead the master to do is acts which might *accidentally* help the slave. That this is what it did lead to is suggested by the many laws prohibiting or limiting the manumission of slaves, because some masters were inclined to emancipate them when they were too old to work. Where paternalism might have come into play, masters would throw Negroes onto their own, no longer existing resources. Self-interest would lead a slaveholder to keep his slaves serviceable and away from rebellion; it would lead him to regard his slaves as replaceable by, and inferior to, machines, not to develop their autonomy. The only way to make sure that the slave's good was considered in its own right, and not merely accidentally, would be, to adapt Calhoun's point,[17] to put power in the hands of those who were subject. A paternalist justification of slavery could work only if the point of slavery were escape from that status, and could be acceptable only if some guarantee other than the slaveholder's interest could be given.

Much of Fitzhugh's defense of slavery consists of attacks on the free labor system of the North and assumes that the two exhaust all possibilities for types of social organization. This raises two related questions about what else there could be and about the relationship between slaveholding and other forms of authority.

That some people at least thought that there was another possibility is clear from the common Negro expectation that emancipation would bring a grant of land, and Fitzhugh himself certainly recognized the importance of land.[18] The emphasis on land suits the ethos of American independence, but, even in the United States of that time, it would be a good thing were we able to generalize in a way that covered industrial society as well. A person who has his own land and produces his own food and shelter is indeed independent and need enter no arrangements with anybody other than those he wants to enter; but the conclusion that liberty could be realized only in an agrarian society would be, at best, an unwelcome one, even though there have been people prepared to entertain it.

What is at issue here is the idea that working for wages must be wage slavery.[19] The notion of wage slavery can be taken quite literally, with the extreme being the peonage that replaced slavery in many cases,[20] but plainly does not apply to all working for wages. If somebody has a rare skill much in demand, so that he can pick and choose what jobs he takes and can more or less set his own rates of pay, then he cannot, by the furthest stretch of the imagination, be considered a slave. He has much the same sort of independence as the landholder; there is no particular person who can dictate to him.

Somebody whose only alternative to doing what the boss says and accepting what the boss chooses to pay him is unpaid unemployment is in a quite different situation; he is subject to the arbitrary will of another and can be exploited by him. Where the worker is faced with those alternatives, the boss can set rates of pay at the lowest level that will keep his workforce capable of working and can insist on all sorts of extra work that has nothing to do with the terms of employment. Such a worker is subject to the arbitrary will of another and, like the slave, has death as his only alternative. That situation can quite properly be described as wage slavery, and the situation of many northern workers in Fitzhugh's day was not too far removed from that. My need to support myself does not, as such, make me a slave. I become a slave when I am subject to the arbitrary will of another.

Plainly, there can be employment that is neither chattel slavery nor wage slavery. This is shown by the development of trades unions and legislation about working conditions that came with increased political liberty and the widening of the franchise. These developments gave workers their own power base and created a situation in which they and their employers were subject to law rather than the workers being subject to the arbitrary will of employers.[21] But when unemployment is high, these points can be escaped. Letters to newspapers recently have shown more opposition to unionism and more support for the use of scab labor, for example, and where jobs are hard to come by an employer can usually get away with insisting on something extra (if he needs to insist). It is difficult to see how there could be a *guarantee* that there would not be such exploitation. If each person knew that his needs would be met quite apart from any employment relationship he entered, such coercion would be impossible. Such a person could never be forced into subjection to the arbitrary will of another. Far from being a denial of liberty, some form of the welfare state might be a condition of it. That raises further problems about the extent of the franchise and control of government, since it allows the accumulation of enormous power in the hands of the governors, which in turn suggests that the central political liberties are the basic liberties, but we need not go into that. Enough has been done to deal with Fitzhugh's point.

It should, perhaps, be emphasized here that emancipation was not enough to give the slaves liberty. Liberty is not a merely legal status, but depends on actual cooperative relationships between people. Part of Fitzhugh's point is that northern free workers were also to some extent subject to an arbitrary alien will and thus lacked freedom as the slaves did, despite their different legal status. To make the point about mere legal status, one might also consider how voter-registration laws worked during Reconstruction and the years that followed.

Much the same points can be used to deal with Fitzhugh's running of all authority relationships into slavery.[22] He also distinguishes between slavery and other relationships, saying that slavery is marked by the possibility of resort to force rather than to litigation. His point is not that a slaveholder may resort to force as a mugger may simply steal my wallet rather than sue me with no hope of success; his point is that the slaveholder can properly resort to force because the situation is one in which the slave is subject to him, not one in which he and the slave are both subject to an impartial law. This is the distinction that must be drawn between proper employment and wage slavery, and between slavery and other authority relationships. Proper authority relationships other than slavery are mediated by an impartial decision-procedure reflecting shared assumptions about justice. And it matters in such situations that justice is *seen* to be done, because only then will those subject to the procedure *feel* bound and thus be part of the community. Conscription for national service, given its justification, is a far cry from slavery.

Thus the importance of Fitzhugh's implausible argument that slavery, apart from being natural and promoting benevolence, is just. It is just, he argues, because the decision-procedure is fair and so is the allocation of burdens and benefits. The decision-procedure is fair because all interests are represented, the master and the slave having identical interests.[23] What he has in mind (thinking of plantation slavery, though a similar point applies to industrial slavery) is that each depends on the produce of the land, so that it is in the interests of each that the land be worked productively. This is hardly sufficient to show identity of interests, however. The slave's interests might well be served by working as little as is consistent with producing a subsistence for himself, and that would hardly suit the master.[24] The allocation of burdens and benefits is fair, he thinks, because obligations between master and slave are mutual and equal,[25] and heaven only knows what he means by that. The obligations are certainly not the same in both directions. Presumably he has in mind that the slave is obligated to work for the master and the master to provide for the slave, but whether that is a fair division is a matter for separate argument rather than assumption. Fitzhugh's point is not that the decision-procedure is fair as I require it to be, reflecting shared ideas of justice in its structure and the criteria with which it works. His point is simply that it had produced a decision that was in accordance with his own private judgment of justice. That, as I have argued, has no special bearing on the bindingness of the procedure.

Now we come back to the issue of private judgment and the idea that society is infallible. Fitzhugh's statement of the point in terms of the infallibility of society is not something about which he is consistent, since he makes clear that he thought the North to be not only fallible but wrong, and that might make us doubt the argument against private judgment.[26] His argument about the matter revolves around a point that I have already argued to be insignificant: truth. What matters, as far as Fitzhugh is concerned, is that society is right and private judgment is likely to be wrong. When Fitzhugh refers to the judgment of society, he plainly means the judgment of the governing classes. Were it not so, there could be no judgment of society other than a concurrence or summation of private judgments, so that the judgment of society could hardly be used to oppose the formation and discussion of private judgments. The truth is to be forced on the people where there is disagreement; there is no need to resort to an impartial decision-procedure to resolve the dispute.

This is completely different from Hobbes on the evils of private judgment. Hobbes's point is that nobody is infallible; if we are to have a community, each of us must recognize his fallibility and the possibility that the other fellow is right. Disputes will not be settled by fighting, as they must be if each of us tried to enforce what he regards as the truth, but by an impartial decision-procedure operating within the limits of shared ideas about justice. Only in this way can people be bound by the judgment and thus form a community.

Notes

1. Cf. here the discussion of J. S. Mill's *On Liberty* in J. F. Stephen's *Liberty, Equality, Fraternity*, ed. R. J. White (Cambridge: Cambridge University Press, 1967).
2. John C. Calhoun, *A Disquisition on Government*, ed. Richard K. Cralle (New York: Peter Smith, 1943).
3. See also Jeremy Waldron, "A Right to Do Wrong," *Ethics*, October 1981.
4. Robert Nozick, *Anarchy, State, and Utopia* (Oxford: Basil Blackwell, 1974) pp. 160–63. Stephen Davies has drawn to my attention G. A. Cohen's paper "Robert Nozick and Wilt Chamberlain: How Patterns Preserve Liberty," *Erkenntnis* (1977), in which, among other points, a point very similar to mine is made.
5. See William Thomson, *A Tradesman's Travels, in the United States and Canada*, part of which appears in Willie Lee Rose's collection *A Documentary History of Slavery in North America* (Oxford: Oxford University Press, 1976), pp. 363–69.
6. See Leon Litwack, *North of Slavery* (Chicago: University of Chicago Press, 1961).
7. In Rose, *Documentary History*, pp. 367–68.
8. George Fitzhugh, *Cannibals All! or, Slaves Without Masters*, ed. C. Vann Woodward (Cambridge: Harvard University Press, 1960), p. 5.

9. In *Cooperation and Human Values* (Brighton: Harvester Press, and New York: St. Martin's Press, 1981).
10. See Litwack, *North of Slavery*, pp. 40–44.
11. Fitzhugh, *Cannibals All!*, p. 71. See also pp. 13, 22, 243ff.
12. Ibid., p. 22.
13. Ibid., p. 28.
14. Ibid., p. 66.
15. Ibid., p. 36.
16. Ibid., pp. 77–78.
17. See Chapter 8, below.
18. See *Cannibals All!*, pp. 19, 109.
19. Cf. the earlier quotation from Thomson and Fitzhugh's quotation from *The Edinburgh Review*, *Cannibals All!*, pp.162ff.
20. Cf. Pete Daniel, *The Shadow of Slavery* (Oxford: Oxford University Press, 1972).
21. Cf. the argument about whether New South Wales was a slave society in J. B. Hirst, *Convict Society and Its Enemies* (Sydney: George Allen & Unwin Australia, 1983), passim.
22. *Cannibals All!*, pp. 28, 77, 235–36.
23. Ibid., pp. 232, 243, 246.
24. Problems arose because of this in the Port Royal experiment. See Willie Lee Rose, *Rehearsal for Reconstruction* (Oxford: Oxford University Press, 1964).
25. *Cannibals All!*, pp. 84, 205.
26. Ibid., pp. 130–36.

8

The Role of Liberty in Democracy

IT IS SOMETIMES ARGUED that liberty is likely to be better defended in an absolute monarchy than in a democracy. The argument is a fairly straightforward one: a democratic government is responsible to us and elected by us; it is, in fact, the electorate governing itself through its representatives. Because it is seen in that way it seems to pose no threat and will not be watched too closely, so that it can get away with all sorts of things. The worst the electorate is likely to do when faced with another blunder or piece of mismanagement is to decide to vote the other way in the next election. So, memories being what they are, democratically elected governments can often get away with unpopular actions early in their terms of office and avoid paying any penalty, provided that they remember to produce a favorable budget before the next election. If such a government sets out to limit the liberty of its citizens, it is likely to succeed.

An absolute monarch, on the other hand, because of the all-embracing power that seems to pose such a threat to liberty, is immediately identified as *another* rather than *us*, an alien will ruling over us with separate interests of its own, and therefore as something we must watch carefully and against which we must be prepared to defend ourselves. If he makes an unpopular move, there is no question of the citizenry deciding that they will wait three years and then do something about it, thus giving the ruler a fair chance that they will forget when the time comes; the appropriate time for them to act is then and there. Because of this, there is a constant check on an absolute monarch who wants to keep his job, as there is not on a democratic government. The absolute monarch will have to be more responsive to public opinion and will not be able to get away so readily with intrusions into the liberty of the citizens.

The point is a simple one: whatever the form of government, the citizens are governed by a government, and the government is made up of people with interests of their own.[1] If one of the reasons that government is necessary is that people are imperfect and sometimes try to force their views and interests onto others, then it should be borne in mind that the governors are human and have not only those faults, but also a lot of power with which to exercise them. This is true of all forms of government, but it tends to be forgotten of democracy because that is thought of as self-rule rather than as rule by somebody else with independent interests. All governments have an interest in attracting power to themselves and limiting the liberty of citizens, but because we are less wary when we think we are ruling ourselves through governments representing our interests, and are then more inclined to fit in with decisions of which we disapprove, a democratic government is more likely to succeed in its nefarious aims.[2]

The government's aims need not be seen by the government as nefarious, and I do not mean to imply that all politicians are nasty, self-seeking people. Power tends to corrupt, and the need for power in order to do good can corrupt. Somebody who goes into politics and never does anything more than sit on the sidelines without power will achieve no public good no matter how strong his desire for the public good. To do good in politics one must enter into the hurly-burly, and once one has done so, when one's human frailties come into play they can do so to enormous effect. Quite apart from any question of personal advancement, one might find that a dirty trick is necessary to achieve some great good. If the good is plainly a great one, the dirty trick might be very tempting.[3] If one seeks the chance to do good in an imperfect world, one might have to work along with the world's imperfections. One would achieve more if the small-minded nit-pickers who get in the way could be stifled, so the temptation to limit people's liberty in order to do them good will always be there, increasing with the strength of one's desire to do good for the people. Whether one seeks personal or public good in politics, one needs power to achieve one's aims, and the need to gain and maintain power brings strong temptations.

A lot of the problem here depends on whether the insistence is on content or on procedure: whether one insists on achieving the good one thinks people should have, or insists on the maintenance of proper relations between people, including the relations between the person in power and those subject to the power. The temptation is to ignore procedural points in order to overcome opposition and to achieve the particular good, but those procedural points are what create the autonomy of citizens. A just procedure, it might be argued, is *the* good for a community even if it sometimes prevents the attainment of other particular goods. A just procedure determines the limits within which people who differ in their values or interests may pursue their own goods and, in a less pluralistic society, leaves the way open for the contemplation of change.

Argument about the content of particular laws will, of course, be proper, and so will attempts to have them changed by following the proper procedures if somebody disagrees with the content of a law. But the idea that whether a law is binding depends on its content is, as I argued earlier, false. Objections to the content of a law will reflect on its bindingness only if the content of the law affects procedure. Is the law more responsive to some than to others, say, because the rulers traditionally come from a particular class? Is it more responsive to people with money, either directly or by being more accessible to them? It could be more accessible to the rich in a number of ways: by depending on the employment of expensive lawyers, for example, or by imposing a tax on newsprint so that the rich can own newspapers and thereby spread their views while nobody else can afford to run even a broadsheet. Does the law allow and encourage free discussion of issues and the expression of all points of view? Outside of special circumstances, such as war, does it release all possible information to the public? Is the electoral system fair? All these questions deal with ways in which the content of laws might affect procedure and thus the bindingness of the law; each is really a question about the justice of a procedure, and they reflect the fact that procedures, too, are set out in laws. And the importance of general public debate and awareness in democracy comes out in the practical problems of dealing with any faults revealed in the answers to these questions by setting up a body with powers to police the procedure: in each case if there is a fault, can the system be changed without making it worse and throwing away liberty by, for example, putting enforcement powers in the hands of a small number of people who thus become immensely powerful?

The argument that I was setting out about liberty in different forms of government is typical of a whole range of arguments that I want to reject. What they have in common is the idea that, if there is a special connection of a favorable kind between democracy and liberty, it can only be that democracy produces more liberty and somehow guarantees that there will be more things that its citizens are allowed to do. Liberty is regarded as something that might or might not be a consequence of democracy, and as simply a matter of how much particular citizens can do of what they want to do, but, anyway, as something that is extrinsic to the form of government. I want to argue that liberty is intrinsic to democracy. Its role in democracy is not a matter of consequences nor of how much people are allowed to do.

The center of my argument here is my claim that democracy should be understood in terms of cooperation, and that only in terms of such an understanding can we fit together many of our intuitions about democracy and many of the ways we argue about, and within, democracy. The basic question is how a state can have the powers that a state must have without its citizens becoming no more than slaves of the state, and the answer is that, as the community becomes more cooperative, there is less repression or intrusion on liberty, and hence the citizens become less like slaves. In a fully cooperative community, they are not at all like slaves. The function of democracy is the preservation of the liberty of the citizens against both internal and external attack, so that they are not slaves.

The other question that interests me here is this: what institutions do we need to guarantee that government will be like this, or that a democracy will remain a democracy rather than be misused and corrupted into something else? The answer, I shall argue, is that no institutions can provide this guarantee. Whether we have a democracy and whether we keep it are very much matters of the temper of the citizens; democracy is not merely a form of government, but a form of community. A tradition of close watch on government and interest in public affairs by a citizenry concerned with the values of democracy and arguing about them in the right way might do the trick, but that cannot be institutionalized. It is dependence on the government in this area, rather than economically, that undermines democracy.

The core of the problem, if the issue is one of what is intrinsic and what is extrinsic to democracy, is that there is very common misunderstanding of what democracy is. There is a standard line on that matter these days,[4] and that line is quite wrong. The line in question, usually run as a species of realism in political science, is that democracy can be identified in terms of its institutions or mechanisms. The approach taken is that of ignoring all the claptrap about ideals and of simply looking at democracies to see what they really are, an approach leading to the unsurprising conclusion that, if the ideals are completely ignored, we do not find them playing an important part in democracy. Such an approach might appear to be scientific and realistic, but, in fact, it is inadequate and leads to a misunderstanding of democracy and what happens in democracies. The problem might be raised in terms of another example: if one tried to find out what witches are by setting aside all the claptrap and simply looking realistically at witches, one would conclude that witches were old women with broomsticks, cats, and black pointed hats. One has then been realistic at the expense of misunderstanding what a witch is and making it incomprehensible that witches should have been burned. Witches are evil women who traffic with the devil; that is why they were burned. It may be claptrap in the sense that there may be no witches and perhaps there could be no witches, but, nevertheless, it is that claptrap that explains what a witch is and makes comprehensible the treatment meted out to women believed to be witches. The same sort of thing is true of the relationship between democracy and ideals. Institutions are to be explained in terms of the points that they have. One cannot explain democracy in terms of its mechanisms; one must explain the mechanisms in terms of the ideals that they are intended to enshrine and achieve. One cannot explain what a university is by pointing to lecture rooms and libraries; one explains why there are such buildings by reference to what a university is for.

One popular line of this sort, though not actually the received line, may be dealt with fairly rapidly. That is the line that democracy can be identified with majority rule. In fact, it is very easy to imagine examples of majority rule that we should not dream of describing as democratic. Suppose an island is inhabited by two different races, the Greens and the Blues, and each of the two races is notable for its antagonism toward the other. If the Greens manage to become 51 percent of the population, take over the government, and rule the country completely in their own interests, refusing to allow the Blues a vote or to consider their interests, then the island is not governed democratically. Nor is the situation changed significantly if the Greens respond to international pressure by going through the tedious formality of giving the Blues a vote and then outvoting them on each issue, before going on to govern the island exactly as before. What is required is not simply a majority and a minority identified in that way, but a fair hearing for the views of each citizen. The point does not simply depend on numbers, because, if a neighboring island populated only by Puces happened to have 49 percent of their population under the age of six months, we should not regard it as undemocratic simply because they were excluded from the vote and the governing of the island was left in the hands of the 51 percent. The point depends on something about what the government is for and, in particular, on the citizens' being treated in accordance with the presupposition of equality.

Again, if everybody has the vote but the government keeps power by controlling what everyone is told by allowing no freedom of the press, no freedom of speech, and no freedom of information, we should not regard that as democratic government (unless, for instance, the moves could be defended as matters of national security in wartime) because of the role in which it casts the individual citizen.

And majorities are not always required for democracy: we do sometimes see the propriety of entrenched legislation recognizing special interests. Legislation requiring that the Blues not be placed under special disabilities not applicable to Greens without their own consent would not necessarily be undemocratic. Nor would legislation preventing that requirement from being removed without a 66 2/3 percent majority, which allows a 33 2/3 percent minority to determine what will happen. Such reasoning lies behind the decision that a minority of Australians should be able to determine whether the Australian constitution will be changed, provided that the minority represents the less populous states defending their rights against encroachment by the majority. Such legislation may reflect imperfections and show that this island is less democratic than others in which no such legislation is necessary, but democracy just does allow of degrees.

The point that lies behind these arguments, showing that democracy is not merely majoritarianism, shows also that a democrat is not committed to obedience-come-what-may simply because the government was elected. A democrat is committed to arguing in terms of certain sorts of values, not *simply* to going along with whatever the majority wants. As a democrat, he may be committed to disobeying laws requiring him to enslave heathen minorities, and even to trying to overthrow a government that would pass such laws. Authority is not necessarily unlimited: the university's parking officer may be able to make me move my car, but if he tells me to get a haircut I shall ignore him. In areas in which he would be exceeding his authority, he has none. Similarly, a government the point of which is democratic lacks authority when it goes beyond its bounds and acts in a way inconsistent with its point. Institutions are understood in terms of their points, and when a group of people acts without regard for the point of government, there is room for argument about whether it is (acting as) a government. Is a policeman acting as a policeman when he accepts a bribe or robs a bank? In the second case, he clearly is not, but in the first case he both is and is not: were he not a policeman no attempt would have been made to bribe him and he could not, therefore, have accepted the bribe, but the action is one prohibited in terms of the point of police and thus would be a ground for firing him from the force in a way in which my accepting money from my neighbor as payment for not objecting to the local council when he paints his house purple is not a ground for firing me from my status as neighbor or citizen. The same sort of point applies with respect to government actions. That I must ultimately work out for myself whether a government is exceeding its authority or whether it is corrupt, though, does not mean that I must deny its authority if it is neither.[5] If I am cooperating with others in terms of the laws, then I should recognize that the fact that this is the law, simply as such, affects the justice of my behavior even if it is not the only thing that does so. Recognizing it as a law and not merely as "a so-called law" means recognizing the authority of the state.

The primary objection to this simplistic majoritarian account of democracy emerges when we ask: a majority of whom? Perhaps all the people have votes and a majority of their votes determines what will happen, but the term "people" must not be taken here as a biological term. Australia, for example, excludes from the vote people born in Italy of Italian parents if they have never left Italy, three-month-old babies, anybody properly certified to be a hopeless luna-tic, and anybody currently serving sentence for treason. These may be human beings, but they are not, for the purposes of voting in Australia, people. In the nineteenth century, several courts in the United States (and even some judges of the Supreme Court in the Dred Scott case) determined that Negroes were not people.[6] That Australia excludes from the vote the classes of people listed does not show that Australia is not a democracy, but if the United States were again to exclude Negroes from the vote, that would show that the United States is not a democracy. One of the things determining whether a country is democratic is whom it counts as the people for these purposes, and that is something necessarily overlooked by accounts of democracy as government by the majority of the people or as sovereignty of the people or as government by those who have won a competition for the votes of the people. An adequate account of democracy must explain how to work out who should have the vote.

Schumpeter suggests that each *populus* must be left to define itself.[7] One can see his point: there might be differences about who should have the vote. Most of us, no doubt, would regard it as undemocratic to exclude Catholics or Communists from the vote, but we should be able to understand why others have, at times, disagreed. Both Catholics and Communists have, at times by some people, been regarded as holding their major allegiance outside the community governed by the decision-procedure in question and as aiming to turn our community into a minion of another. If those beliefs were true, then Catholics and Communists would be relevantly similar to trai-tors or, at least, to resident aliens whose outside allegiance, even if blameless, is still an *outside* allegiance. Somebody who wanted to exclude them on those grounds would not, necessarily, show an undemocratic frame of mind. Similarly, if Negroes really were as childlike and as inferior to Caucasians as they were sometimes believed to be in the nineteenth-century United States, their exclu-sion from the vote would be justified in the same way as the exclusion of infants. The people who held those beliefs were, recognizably, reasoning properly from their premises, but their sincerity about their premises does not guarantee the exclusion of mistake. Saying that those people determine for themselves whether or not they are a democracy is like saying that somebody who believes that God has told him to go forth and wreak vengeance on all sinners determines by himself the propriety of his doing his thing. I take it that Schumpeter would not suggest that excluding people from the vote *simply* because they are not of high birth or *simply* because they would vote against us is compatible with democracy.

A similar point emerges if we consider the variety of institutions that might be recognized as democratic: determination by simple majority, or (as in Australian Federal referenda) by majorities in a majority of states (which means that a minority of the whole electorate can determine what happens and thus protect the interests of the less populous states); first-past-the-post voting or transferrable preferential voting; direct representation or proportional representation; unicameral or bicameral legislatures; terms of office of different lengths; and so on. The problem is not just the obvious one of accounting for democracy in terms of its mechanisms when the mechanisms can vary so much, but that argument is possible about which sort of mechanism is more democratic. The standards by which the mechanisms are measured cannot themselves be simply a matter of the mechanism.

An example that may help to make the point can be found in Julius Nyerere's arguments about one-party democracy. While one might disagree with his claim that "a difference over policy is a difference over fundamentals—which inevitably involves disunity and potential revolution,"[8] and consequently with the implications of his strong claim that "where there is one party, and that party is identified with the nation as a whole, the foundations of democracy are firmer than they can ever be where you have two or more parties, each representing only a section of the community!,"[9] there can be no denying that his argument is to the point. What one must argue about is the truth of his premises, because those premises are clearly of the appropriate sort to support his conclusion. His suggestion is not that one should have a one-party state that is just like a multiparty state except that it has fewer parties: "if the only alternative to the two-party system were a one-party system which retained the rules and disciplines of the two-party system, it would be better to have even an artificial opposition party."[10] If democracy requires that Tanzania have only one party, Nyerere argues, then it also requires that that party have a new structure. In a multiparty state the parties impose, and must impose, their own discipline. They may have free discussion in the party room, but party loyalty and the Party Whip will require that the

party line be toed in parliament and other public places. Public
freedom of discussion is protected if there are several effective political parties that argue about these matters in public, but not all
countries have several effective political parties even if no party, is
deliberately repressed. To keep this sort of discipline and structure in
a state dominated in practice by one party, as Tanzania was dominated by TANU, Nyerere argues, places an unnecessary and undesir-
able limitation on freedom of speech; better to dispose of the party
system and its discipline so that free discussion can move from the
party room into the public arena. In the conditions of Tanzania,
Nyerere argues, freedom of speech and freedom of information
require a one-party state, so democracy requires a one-party state.
Whether or not the details of his argument work, the argument is
plainly of an appropriate kind.[11]

A further point of the same sort is that not only governments can
be democratic: particular laws or policies can be, too. The laws or
policies concerned need not be only those dealing with who is in the
electorate and who is not. Laws restricting freedom of speech or
freedom of information are not only bad laws, but are undemocratic
because of the low status they give to the citizens. That point holds
even if the laws are passed in the ordinary way by a properly elected
government, and that is a point which cannot be explained if democracy is taken to be simply a matter of mechanisms.[12] We speak also of
particular people as democratic, and not only because of their commitment to the political mechanisms. Somebody committed to adult
franchise only because he saw it as a way for him to achieve personal
power and enforce his views on others for his own good, or only
because he saw it as a way to make a personal fortune, would not be a
democrat. Somebody who was committed to toleration and a fair
distribution of power would be a democrat, and monarchs who ride
bicycles among their people as an indication that they regard those
citizens as their equals have been described as democratic. A true
democrat is one committed to political institutions because they
promote such values as toleration and a just distribution of power.
There is a fairly common idea that democracy is simply a peaceful
way of resolving disputes, that votes are simply replacements for
bullets and no more, preferable because they are less trouble rather
than because they act to produce a more just set of relationships
between the citizens. But somebody who thinks that, somebody who
would as willingly use brainwashing as a means of deciding social
policy if considerations of efficiency led that way, is not a democrat.

Schumpeter's account of democracy, the basis of the received
account, is that "the democratic method is that institutional arrangement for arriving at political decisions in which individuals acquire

the power to decide by means of a competitive struggle for the people's vote."[13] He wants to emphasize two points about democracy which, he says, his account reflects accurately and which more traditional accounts overlook or deny: power flows from the top to the bottom, and the range of choices is determined by the politicians. Some objections to Schumpeter's account have already been set out, but I want to take up now his two main points.

It may well be that the electorate's range of choices is determined by politicians but, insofar as that is all there is to the story, the country is not democratic.[14] Schumpeter's point actually has the restrictive implications that it seems to have (and that he intends it to have) only if the class of politicians is itself restricted. If I have the option of standing for election, my choice of what to vote for is not restricted to what others see fit to offer me. If I cannot persuade others to vote for me then I shall not get my way, but there is nothing about democracy to suggest that I should always get my way. This option undermines Schumpeter's point, and that it is available is necessary to democracy. If the class of politicians is restricted to, say, the aristocracy, with nobody else allowed to stand for office, then we are not faced with a democracy. Any improper limitation on the class of people allowed to stand for office detracts from democracy; the point is the same as that made earlier about the notion of a person in relation to the electorate, and the idea of propriety being employed is the same.

It might be that I am allowed to stand for election but that I cannot afford to pay for the necessary advertising, or that my opponents own all the newspapers and I cannot afford to start one. Candidature costs money, so it might be that only an economic elite could compete for power. That, as it stands, would be a fault in the organization of that state rather than a fault in, or point about, democracy. We need to distinguish two questions: "What is wrong with democracy?" and "What is wrong with democracies?" Confusing the two can lead either to quite ill-based attacks on democracy or to the pseudo-religious refusal to accept any attack, a refusal that is rightly rejected by Schumpeter. It must be possible to argue about the morality of Roman Catholicism, but Roman Catholicism is not shown to be immoral simply by reference to the activities of the Borgias. Faults that simply happen to crop up here or there, rectifiably, are simply faults in particular states and nothing to be held against democracy as such. Faults in democracy are faults that follow, logically or empirically, from the nature of democracy.[15] The problem of an economic elite is, at least on the face of it, a rectifiable one: democracy might require that there be a limitation on electoral spending, or it might even require a more or less egalitarian distribution of wealth.

This is certainly not meant to imply either that there are no empirical faults in democracies or that there could be no empirical faults in democracy as such. Democratic institutions lend themselves to all sorts of lapses, especially if the populace at large is not particularly democratic or concerned about the forms of argument used. Vote-buying is possible and is, to an extent, encouraged by the electoral system. I do not mean paying money to particular people to vote in a particular way, against which the secret ballot is a guard, but, for example, deciding to build a bridge in a marginal electorate rather than in one in which the election's outcome is quite certain, and deciding to do so simply because of the electoral consequences for the governing party. Democratic institutions as we have them sometimes encourage movement away from proper public debate because an election might be more likely to be won by employing an advertising agency's professional techniques of persuasion. Hence we get the emphasis on image, and the horrifying situation in which a decision as to who is to be president of the United States might depend on whether one man looks as though he needs a shave when he appears on television. A desire to keep power in order to do good might lead the governing party, so far as it can, to restrict the flow of information to citizens. The importance of the vote in democracies can be an encouragement to these abuses when there is normal human frailty.

Confusion among the citizens about what democracy is can lead to equally bad lapses. This is apparent nowadays in a common confusion between two notions of representation.[16] There is one sense in which a representative is typical of what is represented: a representative farmer, for example, is a typical farmer. When I am selling my house, my estate agent is my representative in that he can commit me by his actions; this does not require that he be typical of me or similar to me in any way. There is a widely held view nowadays, though, that, at least in politics, a representative of the second sort must also be a representative of the first sort: whoever represents women must be a woman, whoever represents university students must be a university student, and so on. This represents a view of what is going on; it both recognizes the way things are (at least to some extent) and encourages them to remain that way.

A political representative who will commit me by his actions and is concerned to do justice should know my interests, but not only mine. All of the representatives in the assembly ought to know everybody's interests and rights, at least by the end of the debate, so that they can work out what justice requires. But to insist on a representative who not only knows my interests but is committed to pushing them is to look for a resolution that favors me unjustly and is a move toward barrow-pushing politics. It is a move toward the replacement of democracy, a system concerned with values such as justice and liberty, by bargaining in terms of who has what power with which to bargain, government as an arrangement of the barons, though not the same barons as in days of yore. It turns the assembly into a clash of powers in which voting *is* simply a replacement for bullets. This is the domestic politics of confrontation, concerned with power rather than authority and with self-interest rather than justice. This confrontation over power does not fit the idea of democracy or the idea of community; the losers are simply losers unless the assembly is concerned to protect the rights of each, rather than for each representative simply to press the interests of those represented. But if that is what citizens look for, a representative who does not act that way will lose the next election. If citizens do not argue in the right sort of way, democracy disappears.

It is clear that one of the reasons for this shift is that there are (classes of) people whose interests have been, and are, overlooked unjustly. To some extent, the attitude is recognizing the way things are: they are by no means perfectly democratic. And that attitude is not an unfair one to take when others are doing the same thing. The difficulties of maintaining a democracy are not good reasons for letting others ride roughshod over one all the time, and, since democracy is a matter of relationships between people, one cannot maintain democracy by oneself when others will not. But if there is to be hope for democracy, such insistence that our representatives push our interests must be an interim measure that can properly be defended in terms of the claim that it is unjust to overrule the interests in this case. That is, the argument must still be one of justice. Simply to assume that the two sorts of representation must go together, necessarily and always, sets up a politics of confrontation over power, which fragments community and makes democracy impossible because it sets up a ruling group (even if the membership changes from time to time) that is clearly ruling over, rather than for, the citizens at large.

Problems can arise in democracies. They are not institutional problems, and it is by no means clear that institutional change can get around them. These problems, when they arise, arise in the citizens' attitudes to their community and government. Whether they are problems for democracy as such depends on the answers to a number of questions about people. Different social and economic structures, or different emphases in education, might change the attitudes that people are likely to take. These are matters for empirical investigations, and important matters.

Schumpeter's claim that power in a democracy resides at the top

need not be argued about. There is no question that the prime
minister would be given a table in restaurants that would throw me
out on my ear or that he can achieve many things that I cannot
achieve. The thesis that Schumpeter thinks he is denying at this
point, though, is not one about the location of power: it is a thesis
about authority and its legitimation. The thesis is that the authority of
the government is derived from the citizens, and this thesis is taken
to have implications about what the job of the government is. The
presupposition of equality means that, originally, nobody has natural
authority over anybody else, and the democratic thesis is that justified authority must be derived from that position without infringing
rights. Only if rights are not infringed will liberty be retained. One
person may gain authority over another: the other may wrong the
first and thus give up some of his rights, for example, or both may
submit to a fair decision-procedure when they come into dispute. In
either of those cases, the justification for the authority of the one over
the other starts from an assumption of equality, and the democratic
thesis is that any justification of authority must start from there.

The democratic thesis about the legitimacy of government authority is that it derives from the citizens. The point is often put in terms
of the authority's deriving from the citizens' consent, but it is plainly
false if put in that way. For one thing, most of us simply have not
consented, and that we go about living our lives in the normal way
cannot properly be construed as consent. For another, consent by
itself is neither necessary nor sufficient for the legitimation of authority.[17] That it is not necessary follows from the nearly desert island case
that I set out earlier: if ten of us are stranded on an island with just
enough food for ten, the presence of a free soul who refuses to agree
to the limitations of food rationing does not make it improper for the
other nine of us to introduce such rationing and to enforce it on him.
That it is not sufficient by itself follows from the fact that consent can
be withdrawn. Legitimate authority over me is something I should
obey whether or not I want to and whether or not I agree with its
particular decision, and that will not be the case as long as I can
escape the authority by simply withdrawing my consent. Consent by
itself, in this context, amounts to no more than my decision that I
shall follow this body's advice, and that is a decision I can change
whenever I feel so inclined. Before consent can do the job, something
would need to be added to show why it would be improper for me to
withdraw my consent: that, say, I sold my consent for a price
(perhaps the price might be somebody else's consent), so that the
reciprocity involved in the arrangement means that it would now be
unfair for me to withdraw my consent. This implies that showing that
I am obligated to obey the law requires more than showing that I have

consented. It requires evidence that the other party is keeping his side of the bargain, and that requires a fairly precise statement of what the bargain was, such as is not likely to emerge from the tacit consent that is sometimes taken to be constituted by living one's life in a normal way.

The problem is: under what conditions can somebody properly be required to do something that he would not do if left to himself? Under what conditions is such a requirement not an infringement of the person's liberty?

There will be an infringement of somebody's autonomy if he is subject to an alien, arbitrary will. This, we have seen, is the mark of slavery, and one of the problems about emancipating slaves is whether it can be done, and whether those who want to hold slaves can be restrained, without putting into the hands of the state such powers as to make all citizens slaves of the state. How can we have a state without the citizens being subject to an alien, arbitrary will?

The democratic answer to this is that all are made subject to the law. If we have the rule of law rather than the rule of people, then nobody is subject to the arbitrary will of another. The straightforward response to this is the Hobbesian one: laws do not make, interpret, or enforce themselves. Institutions have to be run, and they are run by people. If there must be rule at all, then there is no avoiding rule by people even if law is the means by which they rule. And there is certainly point to this reply, because there can be no guarantee that corruption will be avoided or that institutions will not be misused or that interpretations of constitutions will not change. (This point will be made clear with a brief discussion of Calhoun's theory of the concurrent majority later in this chapter.) But the point remains that, if the state is seen in the light of this theory, then using the law simply to impose the will of one on another or of some on others can be identified as a misuse of it. This need not be the case with all forms of government: the function of law in a monarchy might be simply to impose the will of the monarch on everybody else, and the monarch's end might be simply his own glorification.[18] But democracy has a different purpose, and because of that it makes such requirements as that nobody be a judge in his own case. People may have to interpret the law, but what *can* be done to see that the interpretation is impartial *must* be done. Democracy gives legal institutions a certain sort of function. There can be no guarantee that those institutions will not be misused, but insofar as they depart from their function the community becomes less of a democracy.

The idea that there can be institutional guarantees of liberty and justice, or generally of democracy, is a dangerous one; it leads the citizenry to sit back. The only guarantee is a lively citizenry that takes an interest in what is going on and argues properly about it, maintaining community and seeing to it that the public procedure operates in terms of what they share by way of an idea of justice. Constitutions and bills of rights can result in a false sense of security. With rights depending, as they do, on conventions, there is a common feeling that, once the appropriate conventions have been set up, our rights are guaranteed and we can just relax. That there can be no institutional guarantees is something I hope to be able to show by making a point in terms of arguments taken from Thomas Hobbes and John C. Calhoun.

Hobbes's arguments about sovereignty can be taken, at least in part, as arguments about whether constitutions can really guarantee people anything. His argument is intended to show that, ultimately, there can be no guarantee: the sovereign must be legally unlimited. This, Hobbes claims, must be true under any political system. Nevertheless, attempts are quite frequently made to disprove Hobbes's claim by citing political systems that seem not to fit in with it.

Hobbes's argument centers around the need for an arbitrator if people are to live together peacefully. People differ in their judgments and can have clashing desires; only if these problems can be settled peacefully is it possible for people to live together in communities. The problem does not depend simply on people's passions or on any claim that people are always selfish; even the best-willed of people whose greatest aim in life is to be perfectly just will sometimes differ about what justice allows or requires. This could fail to be the case only if each were infallible or, even more implausibly, if each were fallible but made exactly the same mistakes as all the others. What is required is a decision-procedure or a sovereign, and its (his) word must be final. There may be various steps along the way, a number of courts through which we may go, but, ultimately, there must be a decision-procedure from which there is no appeal. Without that the dispute would never be finally settled. The ultimate authority, as decider of all disputes, must be absolute, and because of that it must be legally unlimited. Were it legally limited, it would not be the ultimate authority; whoever had the power to decide whether or not it had overstepped the limits would be superior to it. There can be a community only if the members can settle disputes peacefully, and they can settle disputes peacefully only if there is a legally unlimited authority. Therefore, Hobbes concludes, we should not object to the presence of absolute authority as such, because it is present in any community. No constitution can guarantee the individual person's rights; all it can do is put those rights into the hands of whoever interprets the constitution.

The argument is not obviously a sound one, notably because of the empirical assumption that any dispute that can drag on will drag on. Hobbes's point might be that, without absolute authority, we might not be able to *guarantee* the resolution of disputes and therefore might not be able to guarantee that we could continue to live as a community. The appropriate reply is that, even without guarantees, we might be able to muddle through and handle in a piecemeal way those problems that come up. But this does not touch Hobbes's point about the possibility of guaranteeing the individual citizen's rights.

The point to come out of this can, perhaps, best be got at by setting out a political system of the sort often used to object to Hobbes's conclusion. The theory I shall set out is Calhoun's theory of the concurrent majority,[19] once a live contender to be the correct interpretation of the U.S. Constitution. It is an appealing theory that certainly looks as though it guarantees the individual citizen's rights and protects his liberty.

Calhoun starts with a description of human nature to explain why government is necessary and how it is possible. Man is a social being and enjoys life in a community; he is not naturally asocial and inclined to a solitary existence, nor has he the capacities required for such an existence. Because people have this much care for each other, social life is possible. Social life, though, requires government, because even though each man cares for others, he cares more for himself. That he should care for himself in this way is necessary for self-preservation, but having different people pushing their own interests leads to conflict and makes government necessary.

Unlike many who start in this way, Calhoun saw that the point carried on further: the same element in human nature that makes governments necessary makes them likely to abuse their powers. Government powers must be exercised by people, and, just like ordinary citizens, they will be people who care for others but care more for themselves. The powers they have will give them an advantage in their clashes with others, so a constitution is necessary to limit government powers and their use.

From the fact that a constitution is necessary we cannot immediately conclude that just any constitution is sufficient, so we must go on to ask how members of the government can be kept to the end of government. Setting a higher authority over them will not do the job, because that merely shifts the problem to the higher authority. Any attempt to limit the power of government is problematic, because if its powers are limited too much, the government cannot carry out its function of providing defense against internal and external attack. The powers necessary for a government to serve its function are always sufficient to allow abuse, so the constitution is crucial in preventing absolute government and protecting the rights of individual citizens.

Mere formalities are no more than mere formalities. Only power can resist power, so the ruled must be given the power to resist the rulers. That same tendency that leads rulers to abuse their authority also leads the ruled to resist, and what the constitution must do is to give them the means to resist systematically and peaceably. Universal suffrage is a necessary condition of this, but shifting the seat of authority to the community in that way merely shifts the problem and is not sufficient to deal with it. The community itself is made up of different interest groups, and the dominant majority would have the same tendency to abuse their powers over the minority as do irresponsible rulers.[20] Nor will this tendency be corrected by impending elections: the possibility of losing office will not lessen the tendency to abuse, but increase it as the rulers try to use their power to keep office.

The only way to rule out abuse is to allow that each interest group must have a concurrent voice in making the law, that is, it must have a veto on the execution of the law. This means that each person is in a position to stop any legislation or government act that is contrary to his interests; his rights cannot be taken away without his acquiescence. A mere written constitution will not prevent abuse of power by a numerical majority. Those protected by the constitution must be given the power to enforce it, and the theory of concurrent majority gives them that power.

Calhoun goes on to deal with a number of objections to the practicability of a concurrent majority, but we shall not concern ourselves with those. His theory, under which nobody's rights can be removed without his own consent, seems to be the complete guarantee of the rights of individual persons and the definitive refutation of Hobbes's claim. If Calhoun's concurrent majority will not guarantee the rights of individual people, nothing will. From this we should conclude that Hobbes was right: nothing will.

The point can be made bluntly, and probably persuasively, by pointing out that Calhoun's stirring defense of liberty was, in fact, written as a defense of slavery. Its point was to deny the right of the federal government to interfere in the southern states and the new Territories in any way that interfered with slave-holding. The rights Calhoun was primarily concerned with were the rights of the states and the slave-owners to reject legislation they did not like.

There might be an inclination to say that Calhoun misunderstood the implications of his own argument, and that, properly understood, it is an attack on slavery and a defense of liberty. To see why this is not so is to understand Hobbes's point about the power of the person who interprets the constitution. Calhoun took universal suffrage to be a matter of giving the vote to "every male citizen of mature age, with few ordinary exceptions,"[21] and this limitation of the universe aroused no outcry at the time. It expressed a very commonly held view. It should be remembered that in the Dred Scott case in 1859, Chief Justice Taney found that Negroes, be they slave or free, not only were not citizens of the United States, but were not people under U.S. law.[22] The word "person," as it occurs in constitutions, is a legal term that must be given interpretation. Whose rights it protects will depend on the interpretation it is given.

Again, there might be an inclination to say that Calhoun and his contemporaries simply got that term wrong and that the problem is solved now that we have got it right. But it needs to be remembered that it is not really very long since the voting age in Australia was dropped from 21 to 18, and it is even less time since the voting rights of British immigrants in Australia changed. Both of those involved changes in the interpretation of "person," and that reinforces the point that the relevant contrast is not between the false and the true, but between Calhoun's interpretation and ours. And even if we do have the right interpretation, we can have no guarantee that there will be no mistaken changes in interpretation in the future. Hobbes was right: constitutions cannot guarantee the rights of individual people, because the rights depend on the interpretation and on the people who give it.

The point here is not simply that thoroughly nasty people, once they achieve power, can deliberately misuse the law. Thoroughly decent people, once they achieve power, will try to see that justice is done, but views about what justice requires, and beliefs about the facts relevant to justice, vary. It is quite clear that malevolence and corruption do not always lie behind the Supreme Court's changing interpretations of the U.S. Constitution. With all the good will in the world, people can give differing interpretations of a constitution, and the more carefully one words a constitution so as to rule out varying interpretations, the more one entrenches whatever injustice there is and makes it harder to remove. A requirement that threats to national security be excluded from public office leaves itself open to many different interpretations; a requirement that Catholics be excluded from public office (at one time taken to be an implication of the more general requirement) does not lend itself to so many interpretations, but leaves us with other problems.

If we are to live with other people, then we must be tolerant. We must be prepared to recognize that the public decision-procedure will sometimes rule against us, so that other people will be given rights we think that they ought not to have. We must accept that that decision is binding if the procedure is of an appropriate sort. Nevertheless, the only guarantee of individual liberty is a persistent and combative insistence on it.[23] Insistence on simply getting what one wants is not the same thing and merely causes social disruption; the insistence must be on proper liberty, so argument about the nature of, and therefore the limits on, liberty is crucial. There can be no proper praxis without theory.

The citizens must argue and must insist on liberty, but that is not the same as simply insisting on getting what one wants. People must argue and must argue properly, but that people argue properly is something that must be inculcated rather than simply enforced by law. Philosophical debate must become a part of everyday life; it must be recognized that argument is more than the statements of clashing opinions.

The idea that opinion, as such, is important seems to come from several main sources. One is the straightforward majoritarian account of democracy, the idea that democracy is simply a matter of head-counting, with which I dealt earlier. If that is all that democracy amounts to, then what matters is what people think and not why they think it. Why they think it matters only if they have reasons that will persuade other people, and then it matters only because it changes the head-count; an offer of money to vote another way would be just as much to the point. From this we get the idea that public debate properly consists of people forming opinions and somebody carrying out a public opinion poll.

The other main source seems to be a false idea of toleration: the idea that one opinion is as good as another; that, in cases of disagreement, there is no answer to the question "Who is to be the judge?"; and that it follows from the lack of an answer to that question that nobody can be right or wrong. But opinions are not like tastes. If you like coffee and I like tea, we differ, but neither of us has made a mistake. If you hold the opinion that the world is round and I hold the opinion that it is flat, one of us is wrong. Treating opinions as though they were tastes is a way of evading responsibility for one's views instead of testing them in public debate.

Sometimes there is an answer to the question "Who is to be the judge?": the home-plate umpire is the judge of whether the ball touched the strike zone. That, though, is a matter of moving into the realm of public judgment. What interests us here is the debate of private judgments preceding (or about) the formation of a public judgment, and in matters of private judgment each is his own judge. It does not follow that debate is improper or impossible. To argue about every belief that somebody holds might well be boorish, and simply to preach to somebody on the assumption that one is right and they must meet one's standards is certainly boorish, but to argue properly with somebody about important matters is to take that person seriously in the way required by the presupposition of equality. Such argument is not ruled out by toleration; it is ruled out only by the assumption that the other person's views are not worth considering. And such argument is not ruled out by the fact that each is his own judge: all that rules out is the enforcement of the views of the one on the other. We are operating with quite public concepts in our opinions, so argument is possible: because we are using the same concepts and talking about the same world, there are things we can do to find out what shape the world is. Not all disputes will be easily resolved, and not all of them will even be resolvable in fact, but argument is possible and proper. If you think that a flat-rate income tax is better and I favor a sliding scale, the argument would probably take a long time and might never come to an end. We might have to sort out the various economic consequences of each system; we might have to argue out the nature and basis of the claim that each person has to his income; we might have to argue out a philosophical analysis of justice. Even if we cannot resolve any of these, we should advance in making our disagreements more precise, and that gives us a better opportunity to find a reasonable way to resolve them. Institutions might well come in at that stage of the game, but to hand over and leave the matter to institutions at an earlier stage is not to take other people, or ourselves, sufficiently seriously. It is an abdication of the responsibility that goes with liberty.

When the decision-procedure is called upon and decides in favor of my opponent, it puts him in the position of being able to decide what I shall do. Nevertheless, my autonomy has not been infringed by my being made subject to an alien, arbitrary will. Both my opponent and I were subject to a public decision-procedure. This procedure determines who has what rights in the dispute and, in doing so, determines (in that particular respect) my place in the community. That place in the community is my autonomy, so the procedure *determines* my autonomy and therefore, if it is a properly binding procedure, cannot infringe it. One of the claims that I want to make about the relationship between liberty and democracy is that proper autonomy is not a consequence of democracy, but is one of its constituents.

The question to be asked about the public decision-procedure is whether it gives to each person all the rights he ought to have. That is to say, the question is whether its decisions about rights are binding. If the procedure meets this test, then it is granting proper autonomy to its citizens. The procedure will meet that test insofar as it is a cooperative procedure, and that, I think, is how democracy is to be explained. The traditional reference to consent is, in fact, calling on a model for membership in a cooperative enterprise, and it is the reciprocity of the cooperation that explains why the "consent" cannot be withdrawn simply whenever one feels like withdrawing it.

At this stage, it is worth going over some points about cooperation. All of them have come up before, but a brief repetition will help to make the various points about democracy fall into place. How are we to tell whether the procedure is cooperative?

The first point is that there will be no official answer to this question. The problem will always be one for private judgment. As I argued earlier, the operation of a binding public procedure depends on shared notions of justice and, at least at the level of judging the procedure, on shared private judgments of justice. To have an offical body answer the question about whether an enterprise is cooperative would merely invite further questions about whether the findings of that body were binding or correct. Widespread disagreement in the private judgments of whether an enterprise is cooperative will mean that the enterprise is cooperative no more. Those who judge it to be noncooperative will not feel bound to conform; if there are enough of them, that means the collapse of the enterprise. They recognize no obligations in themselves and no rights in others, so no correlative obligations are generated in others, and the enterprise expires. That it is an issue for private judgment, though, does not mean that it is an issue to be determined at whim. Private judgments are made and defended in terms of public concepts and can be proper matters for interpersonal argument. What sort of point should be considered in reaching a judgment about whether an enterprise is cooperative?

Cooperation is not merely a matter of all of us doing the same thing. If each of us wants to improve his fitness and each institutes a regime of jogging on the beach at 4:00 A.M., swimming, and working out in the gymnasium, the fact that all of us are doing the same thing does not mean that we are cooperating. Each aims at his own good independently of the others. (We should begin to cooperate if we agreed that anybody who lagged behind would be encouraged by the others, or something of that sort.) If each of us is lazy and swiftly limits the regime so that, as it turns out, I jog, you swim, and Jane works out in the gymnasium, we are not cooperating. Each is still acting for his own good independently of the others, and there is no joint activity. We are not jointly producing a good; at best, I produce my health, you produce yours, and Jane produces hers. If there is some good that we produce jointly, such as a healthier nation with lower costs for medical care, our action is still not cooperative: we were not aiming at that joint good or recognizing it as a reason for our actions or as a ground on which others might require our actions of us.

Nor is cooperation merely a matter of our helping each other. One person might help another quite selflessly, with no idea that the help could be required of him or (especially in cases of anonymous help) that any return was to be expected or could be required. That is not cooperation. Nor is it cooperation if two people help each other in that way, though if that became a regular thing it would be likely to develop into cooperation as each came to expect help from the other and realized that the other relied on help from him. (It is worth noting that there need not be any selfish motivation here. In the case of simply helping each other or in the case of cooperation, we might be helping each other, not to promote our own interests, but to promote the interests of some third person.) We have cooperation when we have the idea that each has his share to do towards the production of some joint good and that that share can legitimately be required of him. That is, we have cooperation when the ideas of rights and duties or obligations come in. Since justice is fulfilling one's obligations and recognizing the rights of others, we have cooperation when questions of justice come in. The ideas of justice, rights, and cooperation all go together and are to be explained in terms of each other and in terms of the idea of requirement.[24] My argument about the need for a public procedure is an argument that we must have requirement, and thus cooperation, in human life.

This leads to a question about how the rights and obligations relate to each other within the cooperative enterprise: what limitations are placed on their distribution? The answer has two parts. The first is that the enterprise is open to judgment against the standard of the presupposition of equality.[25] Each of us is equal to each other in the need for social life and the recognition of mutal limitations; none of us could live long in the face of warlike behavior from everybody else. So none of us can properly claim any special position at the point of entry into social life. Each of us needs to enter cooperative enterprises in which obligations are generated, and each of us, therefore, can have claims made on him. At the foundations of communal life, people must treat on the basis of equality; the views of each must be given a fair hearing.

The second point is that equality at the foundations of communal life is compatible with difference at a later stage: equality in the Hobbesian state of nature is compatible with inequality in civil society. And here there can be no complaint if the different requirements made of people are necessary for the enterprise to achieve its point. Perhaps the ball-bearing factory cannot operate without somebody doing secretarial work, but it can operate without the secretary spending his lunch hour doing the supervisor's Christmas shopping for him. A supervisor who required that the secretary do his Christmas shopping or face the sack would be behaving unjustly, making the enterprise less cooperative and more exploitative.

It is worth stressing that enterprises can satisfy these requirements to a greater or lesser extent. Justice, cooperation, and democracy, therefore, allow of degrees. But this sets up the appropriate forms of argument for a democracy: matters of rights rather than simply of wants (though one can argue that, in certain circumstances, one has a right to do what one wants or to reject interference) and of what requirements are binding.

And the relationship between cooperation and autonomy is fairly straightforward.[26] One's autonomy is one's rights, and one's rights are created by the cooperation. One's proper autonomy is the rights one has in a fully cooperative enterprise. It might be a personal good for me that I can go beyond the bounds of proper liberty at the price of repressing others; it might give me more of what I want, but it is no virtue of a community that it gives me, specifically, what I want at the expense of others.

Institutions that are recognizably cooperative, at least to an extent, can nevertheless be unjust, but that is no problem for the sort of account that I have been setting out. There are two ways in which such institutions can be seen to be unjust, though the first is, ultimately, a special case of the second. The first way is if the institution is contrary to the point of another more wide-ranging institution on which it draws, as bank robbery is inconsistent with wider aspects of community life and the Ku Klux Klan is inconsistent with a community that has the purpose of providing just treatment for all its members. The second way is if the institution does not start from the presupposition of equality, in which case the institution is unjust and, specifically, is more exploitative and less fully cooperative. When a state is structured unjustly, the injustice will, at least usually, take the latter form. It is for this reason that the franchise is so important. Excluding people from the franchise on grounds of, say, religion or race or sex is improperly building into the public decision-procedure particular contentious views about justice that should come before the procedure instead of being built into it, and it is excluding from expression in the decision-procedure other views of justice. This is a denial of the proper presupposition that everybody's sense of justice starts off on equal terms with that of everybody else.

Individual autonomy is the area in which I legislate for myself, and, since people are not completely isolated from each other, I legislate as far as may be necessary for others. It is an authority notion. Liberty is one's own authority, and proper liberty is a just distribution of authority or political power. That is the connection between liberty and democracy.

The line that a decision-procedure is binding insofar as it is cooperative explains a number of intuitions that most of us have about democracy, and explains the appropriateness within a democracy of certain sorts of arguments. It explains why democracy can be a matter of degrees—why a country that is recognizably democratic can be improved and made more democratic. Enterprises can be more or less cooperative and more or less just, so states can be more or less democratic. It explains why particular laws or policies, as well as the organization of a state, can be described as democratic if they facilitate proper cooperation. It explains the peculiar appropriateness in a democracy of arguments about justice, and that is, in fact, how we argue out problems about the notion of "the people" or who gets the vote. Nobody is to be made subject to the rule of another without just cause, and just cause will be determined by the point of the enterprise. Criminals who have, by committing a serious crime, infringed the rights of others and thus given up rights of their own may justly be excluded. Lunatics who are incapable of exercising the rights may justly be excluded from their exercise. Noncitizens who will not take on all the responsibilities of citizenship may justly be excluded from some of its rights, such as voting. Apart from arguments of this sort, each person is to have the opportunity for as much say as any other person. And, to turn the last case around, if eighteen-year-olds are to be made to bear the burden of being conscripted and sent to war, they cannot justly be excluded from voting. The appropriateness of all this follows from the nature of democracy as the most cooperative (and thus the most just) form of government. Once we decide that, say, a different voting system would be more just than the one we have, as democrats we have no choice about whether to change. Justice and liberty are internal to democracy. Democracy is proper liberty, not something that creates it as a consequence.

Other things follow from the cooperative nature of democracy. It follows, for a start, that majority vote will not always be the determining factor even in governing the community. (It certainly need not be in other institutions such as hospitals or universities; a decision about whether surgery is necessary should be left to doctors, without the gardeners having a say.) Certain rights must be protected even against the majority's wishes: a democracy will, for example, protect the weak and minorities from persecution or other injustice even when it is attempted by the majority. This also explains how laws could be unjust or illiberal even if they applied equally to everybody—they would not be justified in terms of the necessity of having them if the enterprise is to continue serving its purpose.

It also follows that government will have two functions. One is the function of acting as a public decision-procedure. The other is the function of making sure, as far as possible, that citizens are in a position in which they can cooperate properly, and this[27] makes welfare, at least to a certain extent, a proper concern of government. Somebody who fits in only because all alternatives other than starving were unnecessarily ruled out is not fully cooperating or bound as strongly by the procedure's rules as he would be otherwise. Similarly, health and education will be the government's concern. So will the protection of those basic rights that should not depend on majority vote, such as freedom of speech, freedom of information, and freedom of the press. We speak of the liberating effects of various things: of increasing educational opportunity, of guaranteeing a minimum income, of taking drugs or ceasing to take drugs, of ignoring convention in relationships with other people. Government and other social intervention to promote such liberating activities will be proper, not simply as a response to wants, but if and only if the intervention will make relationships between people more cooperative and less blind or exploitative.

Freedom of speech is often defended on the grounds that it helps in the discovery of truth. As a defense, this seems quite weak: the activities and success of advertising agencies make clear that free speech can be used to persuade people to do all sorts of things without approaching the truth. Some popular songs seem to shape political attitudes without argument or serious consideration of the complexities of the situation. If the discovery of truth were the only defense of free speech, free speech would be under dangerous attack. The role of free speech in a democracy, though, is more fundamental than that: the role of the requirement that there be no limitations on free speech (and of the limitations in terms of national security, defamation, and so on, beyond which the speech is not considered free speech) is to go as far as possible toward seeing that each person's views get a proper hearing in the public debate. It is required by the presupposition of equality. The place of that presupposition in democracy is fundamental.

The presupposition of equality does not require that everybody be treated in the same way or be given the same rewards no matter what contribution he makes. That presupposition allows that, once people are in the enterprise, there will be differences between them that justify differences of treatment. But it does mean that there can be no presupposition against particular people at the point of entry into the enterprise. Given the nature of the enterprise and the characteristics of some particular person, it might be appropriate to place special burdens on him within the enterprise, but it is not appropriate to place special burdens on somebody so as to make it harder for him to enter the enterprise. The presupposition of equality does not require equal distribution of everything, but it does require that, insofar as possible, each person be provided with sufficient for him to cooperate freely rather than fit in at the behest of another or starve. One must have a certain amount of power in order to cooperate rather than be coerced, and herein lies a democratic justification for sliding scales of taxation. It is not simply that the money must come from those above the line if those below the line are to be brought up to it so that they can cooperate freely. Where the line is depends on how far some people are above it. As I argued in discussion of Nozick's example of Wilt Chamberlain, in our world the possession of money means power, and, power being essentially comparative, some people can accumulate power only at the expense of others, thus raising the line that marks the position at which one can cooperate freely rather than be coerced.

Democracy is, at least in theory, the form of state most like and most conducive to community. Modern industrial economic structures, the growth of bureaucracy, intellectual lassitude among the citizenry, and the growth of a class of professional politicians who have developed a new industry of electioneering manipulation of the voters, all detract from community and from the worth or possibility of democracy. With technological developments, production of goods is at such a level that we should be able to worry about the right things; it is no longer the case that economic pressure must force us to spend most of our time struggling just to get by. The state could be used to further community rather than to replace it. This could be done if the state concentrated on developing the conditions for cooperation by such moves as considering the introduction of a guaranteed minimum income.

It should be noted that there is nothing in my discussion of democracy about a common will or a common good. If there were a common will, there would be no need for a decision-procedure. What we have here, instead, is a fair procedure for resolving disputes between disparate wills. And there is no requirement that every act of a democratic government be for the greatest possible good of each individual citizen. There is no *a priori* reason to believe that any government could come up with any law that met that strong requirement. What is required here, instead, is that each citizen be given a fair hearing and get his fair share.

That democracy would be the best form of government does not

mean that it is always possible. Because it is not simply a matter of
having certain institutions, but of people thinking of government in a
certain way and accepting certain sorts of reasons and conventions,
the possibility of democracy depends strongly on the type of people
concerned. They must be both tolerant and prepared to recognize
their own fallibility, including their moral fallibility. For some reason,
people who are prepared to recognize their fallibility in all sorts of
other areas confuse moral integrity with moral infallibility, taking the
line that it would be immoral not to follow their own private judgment even if it means forcing their views on others. Oddly enough,
the best citizens for a democracy will be Hobbesian citizens prepared
to live as part of a community and to recognize that natural law in the
form of private judgments is ineffective in a community without
interpretation from a public decision-procedure. Absence of this
quality is shown in false ideas about liberty, including the holding of
a noncommunity idea of autonomy as something opposed to social
roles rather than as itself a social role.[28] Democracy does not sit
particularly well with the more common forms of individualism. Nor
does community life.

The conditions I have set out for democracy do not require that
everyone participate in government even to the extent of voting.
Actual participation is not a condition of political obligation. The
opportunity to stand for office or to join in debate may be necessary,
but actual participation is not.[29] Nevertheless, participation might be
important in a number of empirical ways. Participation in the community's decision-making might help to make somebody feel that he
is an autonomous part of the community, and, if it makes citizens feel
that way, it might aid genuine cooperation. Participation in any
cooperative enterprise, be it a business venture or a social club, is
likely to help to develop the qualities of character necessary to
cooperation and thus to help produce more democratic citizens.
Participation might affect the way people see themselves and the
world. Overwhelming stress on the powers of central government
means that people lose the feeling of community and cooperation,
and it seems a plausible speculation that that is part of the reason for
the recent growth of individualism of an invidious sort.

Democracy is a matter of the temper of the people rather than
merely of government machinery, so there are some ways in which
the citizens must participate. If the citizenry spend the time between
elections sitting back and waiting for the government to do everything, then, no matter how good-willed the government, the community will not be a democracy. Citizens need not participate in the
actual ruling or administration, though my argument implies that
they may not unjustly be excluded from an opportunity to do so, but

they must be active. They must consider and play their roles, they must be aware of points of institutions and watch for misuses of institutions, they must be argumentative, and they must keep themselves informed so that their argument is not merely squabbling or posturings. A properly democratic government would encourage these activities, but not all objections about lack of democracy should be aimed at governments. Technological education may be important, but emphasizing it at the expense of other sorts of education encourages subservience rather than proper autonomy. It encourages the idea that one has been trained for a job, that that job is one's role, and that one should restrict oneself to that role. It encourages a "pragmatic" insistence on argument only about means, so that ends play their roles in the argument unexamined and unnoticed. To have a democracy we need a citizenry which is also at home in such areas as history, politics, economics, and philosophy, and a democratic education system would encourage such studies much more than is now done. Citizens might then become, in some ways, much harder to govern as they argued out properly the extent of their proper autonomy.

Notes

1. Compare the writings of Max Nomad on this: *Dreamers, Dynamiters, and Demagogues* (New York: Waldon Press, 1964); *Aspects of Revolt* (New York: Bookman Associates, 1959); *Political Heretics* (Ann Arbor: University of Michigan Press, 1963); *Apostles of Revolution* (New York: Collier Books, 1961).
2. This argument is concerned with whether citizens in absolute monarchies are in fact touchier than citizens in democracies, but I shall not argue that point. My contention is that the argument misses the issue: it misconstrues the role of liberty in democracy.
3. Cf. Raymond Price's views on Watergate in *With Nixon* (New York: Viking Press, 1977).
4. It seems to come from J. A. Schumpeter, *Capitalism, Socialism, and Democracy* (London: Unwin University Books, 1947).
5. Pace R. P. Wolff, *In Defence of Anarchism* (New York: Harper Torchbook, 1970), p. 40.
6. See Leon F. Litwack, *North of Slavery* (Chicago: University of Chicago Press, 1961), especially chapter 2.
7. Schumpeter, *Capitalism, Socialism*, p. 245.
8. Julius Nyerere, *Freedom and Unity* (Dar Es Salaam: Oxford University Press, 1967), p. 197.
9. Ibid., p. 196.
10. Ibid., p. 200.
11. Nyerere's position could usefully be compared with the standard late-eighteenth century rejection of "faction."

12. Democratically elected governments can act undemocratically, but the same sort of point holds for other forms of government. In a country the constitution of which sets up a paternalist monarchy, a monarch who systematically failed to inform himself of what he needed to know, or who left the royal seals and conduct of public business in the hands of the cook so as to keep his own time free for hunting, would not be acting in a parternalistically monarchical way. If democracy is a morally superior form of government to monarchy (and that, along with whether it is a more efficient form of government, would depend, among other things, on whether democracy were possible for the particular group of people with their particular beliefs, traditions, attitudes to government, and so on), it is not simply because democracy has a point but because of what that point is.

13. Schumpeter, *Capitalism, Socialism*, p. 245.

14. R. P. Wolff seems to make this mistake, too. See *In Defence of Anarchism*, p. 33.

15. Robert Michels in *Political Parties* (New York: Free Press, 1962), and Gaetano Mosco in *The Ruling Class*, trans. H. D. Kahn, (New York: McGraw-Hill, 1939), for example, might be read as arguing that certain problems follow empirically from the nature of democracy.

16. Cf. A. Phillips Griffith, "Representation," *Proceedings of the Aristotelian Society*, Supplementary Volume, 1960.

17. See also E. D. Watt, *Authority* (London and Canberra: Croom Helm, 1982), chapter 6.

18. Or, of course, it might not. The constitution might impose all sorts of limitations and duties on a monarch. My point here is simply that a monarchy *can* be like that, and such a point to government is not possible for democracy.

19. See John C. Calhoun, *A Disquisition on Government*, ed.. Richard K. Cralle (New York: Peter Smith, 1943).

20. Cf. what J. S. Mill has to say about the tyranny of the majority in *On Liberty* (Totowa: Everyman, 1957), pp. 67ff.

21. Calhoun, *Disquisition on Government*, p. 45.

22. Taney's judgment can be found in Howard's *Reports*, Vol. 60. See also Don E. Fehrenbacher, *The Dred Scott Case* (New York: Oxford University Press, 1978), especially chapter 15.

23. See the writings of Max Nomad, especially his autobiography *Dreamers, Dynamiters, and Demogagues* (New York: Waldon Press, 1964).

24. See Chapter 4, above.

25. See Chapter 3, above.

26. See Chapter 7, above.

27. Pace Nozick, *Anarchy, State, and Utopia*, passim.

28. See, for example, Wolff, *In Defence of Anarchism*, passim.

29. Pace, for example, Carole Pateman, *Participation and Democratic Theory* (Cambridge: Cambridge University Press, 1970).

Conclusion

THIS INVESTIGATION OF LIBERTY and its relationship to community and justice has been concerned with a number of problems that are, I think, of current practical significance. Those problems are all closely related; they are, in effect, the same problem coming up in a number of different guises. The problems are not merely institutional, so no institutional change will solve them. They are problems about how people think of the social world in which they live and how they think about their own places in that world. What I have been trying to do is to argue out a view about the social world and the places of people in it, arguing that individual people are individual social beings and that various things follow from that. I have also tried to argue that those social beings can have and keep their liberty only if they argue in the right sort of way, arguing properly in terms of rights and not merely in terms of wants, and being prepared to argue about where those rights come from. Practical liberty is, in an important aspect, a conceptual problem and not merely a political problem. Part of my thesis has been that moral and political philosophy should not be restricted to the universities, but should be common among the populace at large; everybody needs to be a philosopher. Whether what I have written be true or false, if it provokes argument it will have achieved something worthwhile. Democracy is important because it is the form of government for free people. Problems about the possibility of democracy, and there are problems, are also problems about the possibility of liberty.

Throughout my argument I have raised a number of conceptual points, but I have also tried to show that such conceptual points are not entirely separate from practical problems. The invidious individualism that is at the root of a lot of the practical problems that have come up is itself a conceptual confusion. I have argued that liberty is to be understood in terms of rights, not simply in terms of getting what one wants, and I have argued that rights are to be understood in terms of community, not simply as some sort of emanation from private conscience. Confusion about these points, and an unwilling-

211

ness on the part of the general public to think about them, lies behind a lot of the problems of political life. I have also argued that rights can function only if the bindingness of a decision-procedure depends on the justice of the procedure rather than on what the particular decision is, and have argued out some of the limitations to be placed on a decision-procedure if it is to be properly binding, that is, the sorts of objections that can properly be brought against a decision-procedure even in the face of its general acceptance. And I have tried to show that a virtues-based moral theory, far from leaving no room for rights, embeds them in human, communal life.

The sort of invidious individualism that treats people as asocial beings cannot be the basis of a political philosophy. Asocial beings would not have rights, so any question about liberty for them would have to be one about how much they could do of what they wanted to do. Aspects of this invidious individualism can be seen in the irresponsible way in which rights are often claimed on no better basis than that the claimant wants something; the word "right" is used as though possession of a right followed simply from possession of a want, though with a lot of entailments that wants do not have. Liberty, I have argued, is properly a set of rights, and those rights are generated by life in a community and have to be argued out in terms of community; they will be the rights of communal beings, and liberty will be a virtue of the community.

The appropriate political relationships between free people, people not related to each other or to their government as slave to masters, are democratic relationships, but democratic relationships are a matter of people's thinking of themselves and of others in certain ways, not merely of having certain institutions. It is a matter of what *sorts* of facts people consider relevant to the sorting out of practical problems about what to do when there is disagreement. That is to say, it is a matter of how they argue or reason. The democracy that is worth worrying about is not merely the institutions and is not always a matter of going along with whatever the majority wants, because the majority might have considered simply its own inclinations and what it could get away with, rather than considering any of the sorts of facts that are relevant to who has what rights. There is no guarantee that the democrats will prevail: people who see politics as a matter of maneuvering to get their own way might outnumber them and have the power to get their way while ignoring arguments about what sort of fact is relevant to the decision. If the decision-procedure is operated in that way, then, I have argued, it ceases to be binding. It no longer binds the democrats, who, apart from being provoked by the activities of the others, might reasonably think that, since they are not bound by the decisions, there is no reason why they should always let the others have their own way. Instead of reasoning beings settling disputes peaceably, we would have the politics of confrontation: interest groups pushing their own barrows, terrorism, general increases in violence, and relationships of power rather than of authority.

There is, I have argued, no institutional way of guaranteeing that we avoid that problem, because it is at bottom a conceptual problem, and it seems fairly clear that the problem is, to some extent, already among us. To the extent that it is, people will treat political institutions skeptically and will be dubious of just how binding they are. The state will appear as an intrusion on relationships between people. This does not mean, though, that we are plunged into a Hobbesian state of nature, because the state is not the only decision-procedure available to us. Rather, it plunges us into a situation in which it is even more important to maintain democratic relationships with other members of our community. Only that way can we retain liberty and the communal relationships that are required for a full flourishing of the virtues. Democracy requires those virtues, and is itself required if they are to flourish. If the relevant relationships cannot be found at the level of the state, then we might need to concentrate on smaller-scale communities where they can be found. That might allow people to develop in ways that would solve the problem at the level of the state, at least for a while, though there can be no guarantee that it would. All that any one of us can do is to try to argue properly, to indulge in philosophical debate about public matters, to try to be tolerant, to hope that others will respond by acting in similar ways, and to hope that such public debate will pressure governments to act in such a way as to make their decision-procedures binding. That is not a recipe that ensures a happy ending, but it is the best that can be looked for.

A thesis that reflects this problem and that might, to some extent and at some levels, lie behind it is that of the autonomy of ethics: the idea that moral reasons are *sui generis*, unrelated to any others. This sort of treatment of morality makes moral reasons frivolous and undermines other things as well. It is a false thesis.

It would be surprising were the thesis true. The point of morality, at the most general level, is to enable people to live together peacefully, and other things share that point: politics, law, tradition (perhaps to a lesser extent), and, in some of its social aspects, religion. Tradition and religion can probably be brought under the umbrella of law and politics.

Law, politics (which need not be a matter merely of the state), and morality form an interrelated set. I have tried to show that there is, and must be, a political dimension to morality without which it cannot act interpersonally to allow peaceful life, the resolution of disputes, and common action. This political element shows out as the importance of toleration in morality. Politics divorced from morality, and especially from ideas of justice, is merely coercion. Law is, in part, as I have shown, a working out of those aspects of morality concerned with rights, though it can go wrong when the public procedure is wrong. What distinguishes law from simple coercive rules is its bindingness, its being rooted in morality. The natural law and the civil law, in Hobbes's expression, contain each other.

Separating morality from law and politics turns it into a purely private concern that cannot serve a social function, and it leaves law and politics as merely coercive. No institutional reform will change any of that, but only if people will argue properly about moral matters can law and politics be enlivened. Only to the extent that people will argue properly about moral matters will relationships among them be other than coercive.

Index

215